Opera and Modern Culture

Opera and Modern Culture

Wagner and Strauss

LAWRENCE KRAMER

University of California Press

BERKELEY   LOS ANGELES   LONDON

University of California Press
Berkeley and Los Angeles, California

University of California Press, Ltd.
London, England

Library of Congress Cataloging-in-Publication Data

Kramer, Lawrence, 1946–
    Opera and modern culture : Wagner and Strauss / Lawrence
Kramer.
        p.   cm.
    Includes bibliographical references (p.   ) and index.
    ISBN 0-520-24173-8 (cloth : alk. paper).
    1. Wagner, Richard, 1813–1883. Operas.   2. Strauss, Richard,
1864–1949. Operas.   3. Opera—Social aspects.   4. Sex in opera.
5. Music—Philosophy and aesthetics.   I. Title.
ML1700.K715   2004
782.1'092'243—dc22   2003025286

Manufactured in the United States of America

13   12   11   10   09   08   07   06   05   04
10   9   8   7   6   5   4   3   2   1

Earlier versions of chapters 1, 3, 5, and 7 appeared, respectively, in *Siren
Songs: Gender and Sexuality in Opera,* ed. Mary Ann Smart (Prince-
ton: Princeton University Press, 2000), 186–203; *The Work of Opera:
Genre, Nationhood, and Sexual Difference,* ed. Richard Dellamora and
Daniel Fischlin (New York: Columbia University Press, 1997), 131–60;
Cambridge Opera Journal 2 (1990): 269–95; and *Cambridge Opera
Journal* 5 (1993): 141–66. Chapter 2 is reprinted from *19th-Century
Music* 25 (2002): 190–211. This material is reprinted courtesy of the
publishers: Princeton University Press, Columbia University Press,
Cambridge University Press, and the University of California Press.
William Carlos Williams's poem "The Great Figure," reprinted in
chapter 3, is from his *Collected Poems, Volume 1: 1909–1939,* © 1938
by New Directions Publishing Corporation, and is used by permission
of New Directions Publishing Corporation.

Contents

Prologue

Thinking through Opera with Wagner and Strauss

Opera is legendary for superlative states of being, both high and low: supremacy and debasement. Just reeling off pairs of names—Don Giovanni and the Commendatore, Florestan and Leonora, Rigoletto and Gilda, Siegfried and Brünnhilde, Tristan and Isolde, Otello and Desdemona, Mimi and Rodolfo, Salome and Jochanaan—seems to tell an archetypal story. But it is far from the whole story.

The nucleus of this study was the impulse to delve into the very antithesis of both supremacy and debasement: simple normality. Looked at in historical perspective, normality had come to strike me as anything but simple and, well, other than normal, something strange to begin with and all the stranger the more one looked at it. I had a hunch that opera had an unusually resonant relation to the history of normality. And since recent scholarship on opera, a rich series of studies dating from the mid-1980s that had produced something of a golden age, often seemed to pivot on questions of normality and abnormality, rule and transgression, social compliance and resistance, the hunch seemed to have more than just instinct to back it.

By the end of the 1990s, the most exciting thought about opera seemed to be circling most often around three topics, both for their intrinsic interest and for their power to highlight the contextual relations and multimedia character of opera, matters that had come to seem just as important as opera's traditional center, music. Very broadly stated, these topics were voice, especially as an object in its own right distinct from particular voices; the phenomenon of subjectivity both as a cultural construction and as a quasi-transcendental presence; and the complex entanglements of sexuality, identity, gender, and desire.[1] But the pursuit of these topics seemed, at least to me, to be taking something else for granted, and I wanted to know what it was.

My earliest attempt to start sorting these matters out was a conference paper that eventually became chapter 1 of this book. The paper was meant as a speculative foray; it was composed in a quasi-improvisatory, quasi-operatic style. Its method was to assemble a trio of episodes in and about opera—poetry by Walt Whitman on Italian opera, a moment of *Fidelio* incorporated into a dream by a patient of Freud's, an episode from Wagner's *Götterdämmerung*—and to read them as symptomatic of an ideal type, a generic fiction that I would eventually come to think of as Opera, capital O. I would also come to think that my preference for the O was no accident, but much overdetermined: the O of exclamation, the cry, ecstasy, surprise, horror; of the open mouth; of Shakespeare's theatrical "wooden O," the theater called the Globe; and the O of the Lacanian "big Other" in its English translation.

The initiative of that first foray rippled over into the others that compose this book and also, upon reflection, gave the book its specific subject matter. The initiative could be described as an attempt to "think through Opera" in two overlapping senses: to think with some fullness about the phenomenon of Opera, and to think about matters of general worldly concern by means of Opera. The subject matter, announcing itself at the climax of chapter 1, is the version of Opera inaugurated by Richard Wagner in the middle years of the nineteenth century and brought to its logical but also its fatal conclusion by Richard Strauss in the first years of the twentieth. And here the topic of normality reveals its entrenched connections with the seemingly antithetical topics of supremacy and debasement, although the character of these connections and their full scope will unfold only piecemeal across the book as a whole.

The extreme selectivity of this subject matter is obvious, but part of my point here is that it is not merely one possibility among others, but a choice with specific historical salience, at the very least the choice that is first among equals. The great rival linguistic-national traditions are unfairly given short shrift as a result, but of course neither Italian nor French opera was unaffected by the Wagnerian juggernaut. After Wagner, the notion of "after Wagner" becomes a trope that no one interested in opera can avoid reckoning with, either in regard to new composition or to the history of the genre—before Wagner as well as after.

It's important to keep in mind in this context that Wagner and Strauss here are not being asked to carry the burden of opera in all its complex variety. They are being read as symptoms of Opera, a certain cultural fiction with an important role to play at a formative but limited moment in modern history characterized by the triangulation of normality, supremacy, and debasement. At any rate, I'm prepared to acknowledge skepticism about this symptomatic approach, and even to express some skepticism about it myself. Like the first chapter, the book is a speculative foray. It can, by those so disposed, simply be taken as a study of Wagner and Strauss per se, certainly a resonant enough topic in itself. But it is worth recalling that the first of many people to treat Wagner as a symptom of modernity was Wagner himself; that Strauss in the first decade of the twentieth century was regarded as the very incarnation of modernity in music; and that thinking in symptomatic terms is itself one of the major inventions of later nineteenth-century thought across a broad spectrum of disciplines including anthropology, sociology, and psychology.

The treatment of these topics will be guided (unobtrusively, I hope) by a small group of concepts adapted from a variety of sources, including critical and social theory and in one case even analytic philosophy. But the concepts will not act as leitmotifs throughout this book. They will rarely be invoked by name, especially once past the first chapter; I do not want to box my topic in but, on the contrary, to open it out in as many dimensions as possible. Even chapter 4, a partial exception focused on Wagner's relationship to one of these concepts, symbolic investiture, keeps the terminology as sparse as possible. The guiding concepts do most of their work from the background, taking on new forms and figurations to fit the needs of the discussion as it unfolds. I will turn to them without further ado, following a trajectory, very roughly speaking, from theory to history to Opera.

1. The philosophical concept of the best example is the basis of the book's intensive rather than extensive approach and the sponsor of its view of Opera as a symptom of a certain phase of modernity—call it middle-modernity, as seen from our late- and/or postmodern standpoint. The best example is precisely what the name suggests: the example from which one can get the best, most inclusive, most suggestive, idea of a certain category. This does not mean, however, an exhaustive example, but only one that, for historical reasons, permits the individual instance to form an index of the type, without the type necessarily having or keeping conceptual priority over the instance. Best examples are instances in which the diverse and scattered family resemblances that go to compose the type all seem to come together. The term "family resemblances" famously comes from Wittgen-

stein, who also "compared the names of classes to an old-fashioned hemp rope: it is very strong, but no one fibre runs through one hundred meters of rope. There need be no one bunch of things in common . . . to apply to a class of individuals."[2]

The philosopher Ian Hacking, whom I am quoting here, goes on to give a best example of the best example:

> Many people, asked to give an example of a bird, apparently say, "Robin." People seldom offer "ostrich" or "pelican" straight off. The robin is a best example. . . . One can make a very strong argument, in the philosophy of language, that what people understand by a word is not a definition, but a prototype [the best example] and the class of examples structurally arranged around the prototype. (23–24)

Best examples, however, have more than a merely pragmatic or analytical value. Their value is decidedly social; they are the nerve centers of a rich, sometimes tangled network of tropes and associations; they come with a history and sustain the sense of living in a historical world. The robin is a pastoral bird, situated at a genial remove from rugged seacoasts and the dusty plains of Africa for those "many people" who live in the temperate zones of Europe and America. Best examples do more than help us understand classes of things; they help produce the classes. The fact that Wagner's *Parsifal* is more likely to be cited as an example of an opera than D'Indy's *Fervaal*, or Puccini's *La Bohème* than Leoncavallo's, is basic to the construction of Opera as both an ideal type and a historical symptom.

It is the mutual constructive relationship of the best example on the one hand and history and society on the other that allowed the literary critic Erich Auerbach—to give yet another best example—to theorize the history of representation in the Western world from a close reading of two short passages, one from Homer, one from the Bible. Auerbach was writing in Istanbul, in exile from his native Germany during World War II, and his examples show it. One is the moment in *The Odyssey* when Odysseus, in disguise, is recognized by his old nurse when she sees a scar on his thigh. The other is the passage from *Genesis* in which God instructs Abraham to sacrifice the latter's son Isaac and rescinds the command only at the last moment with Isaac under the blade. The theory that Auerbach extracted from these exemplary texts looked both before and after its own moment. On one hand it was a retrospective prototype of the distinction between Hellenic and Hebraic mentality that had flourished in Germany and England during the nineteenth century. On the other it was a utopian act that, only wishfully as far as Auerbach could know, opposed the scenarios of homecoming and mercy to the Nazi domination of Europe. Like the operatic examples studied in this book, Auerbach's served both as symptoms—the indices of a multiplicity of cultural forces at work in and through them—and as unique, durable objects that, by their very status as best examples, remain open to new meanings and uses and continually exceed their own symptomatic value.[3]

2. The concept of symbolic investiture develops from the "reflexive sociology" of Pierre Bourdieu; its generalizing power has been funneled into a reading of modernity (as a "crisis of symbolic investiture") by Eric Santner.[4] Symbolic investiture is the process by which social institutions grasp the inner being of the individual in its essence, and in so doing both define and confer that essence. This is the way that persons "become what they are." Answering a "call to order" from above, the individual does not merely assume a symbolic mandate but is "filled" with it: filled up, filled out. Although often in need of later supplements to sustain its power, this process is dramatic and discontinuous, enacted in defining moments that resonate throughout the rest of the person's life and "fate." Such moments are initiations, impervious to question or critique because they operate beyond reason as the effects of what Bourdieu calls "performative magic." If, for Jacques Lacan, the human being becomes a speaking subject by unconsciously surrendering imaginary autonomy to accept dependency on a symbolic order, for Bourdieu the same human being becomes a social subject by consciously surrendering to seizure at the core of identity by the call, the name, the gift, the mandate, that marks the moment of symbolic investiture.

As Santner observes, Bourdieu emphasizes "the imperative, and, indeed, coercive nature of acts of symbolic investiture," for instance in this eloquent statement:

> "Become what you are": that is the principle behind the performative magic of all acts of institution. The essence assigned through naming and investiture is, literally, a *fatum*. . . . All social destinies, positive or negative, by consecration or stigma, are equally *fatal*—by which I mean mortal—because they enclose those whom they characterize within the limits that are assigned to them and that they are made to recognize.[5]

But this emphasis is itself coercive, however powerfully it informs Bourdieu's impassioned critique of the moral implications of social order per se. Symbolic investiture, I would suggest, can come in moments of rapture as well as terror, enfranchisement as well as confinement, even if each of these terms always harbors traces (if not more) of its opposite. The human subject is not necessarily just a rag doll in the hands of social power, and the power that the subject gains from symbolic investiture, and the uses to which it is put, are too rich and varied to be written off as mere ideological mystification across the board. One function of Opera is precisely to represent being forcibly seized by a symbolic mandate as a forceful seizing of it. The locus of that force is operatic voice, which typically grows richer and more expressive the more it embraces its fate, even if the fate is dire: a locus classicus of the Nietzschean concept of *amor fati*. If modernity really is marked by a crisis of symbolic investiture, Opera offers itself as one of the antidotes.

Typically, too, and whatever its outcome or ideological weight in the given instance, the symbolic investiture of the subject is accompanied and reflected by a parallel process. This is the elevation of an object—in the sense of that which confronts or addresses the subject, be it a material object or another person—to a higher symbolic value than reason could ever allow. This "sublime object" conducts the power of investiture like an electric current. The object is raised to the level of sublimity proportionate to the passionate depth of the subject. And once seized by this object the subject typically seizes it back and will not willingly let it go, whatever the cost. Opera knows all about this. Isolde will give up neither the living Tristan nor the music he sang with her once, even though he lies dead at her feet. Salome will have the head of Jochanaan and kiss its mouth: she says so and she will and she does. Of course, the elevation of the object doesn't always happen just this way, or at such a pitch of extremity. These are just best examples.[6]

3. The concept of the norm, like the thing, is all too familiar; it needs no definition. It does, however, need a recognition of its historical particularity. Michel Foucault was perhaps the first to point this out. Far from being a neutral tool or technique, available in more or less any social order, the norm is a regulatory device that emerged from the European Enlightenment and achieved its still-current primacy by the early nineteenth century.[7] This regime of the norm is not neutral, either. It does far more than quietly serve the disciplinary needs of complex modern societies. Rather, the regime of the norm carries with it a whole worldview, a social cosmology derived from the basic procedure of referring human conduct and identity to a central ideal type. Around that ideal, as if arrayed in concentric rings, swirls a vast number of approximations, variants, deviations, and perversions. The social order as a whole thus comes to resemble the "radial" system created conceptually by the best example, "a prototype and the class of examples structurally arranged around the prototype."

But there is an important difference, at least of degree. The norm compels where the best example attracts; it demands compliance where the best example invites emulation; it exerts force where the best example applies pressure. (Exceptions noted; deconstruction acknowledged.) Bourdieu notwithstanding, it is the regime of the norm, not the scenario of symbolic investiture, whose character is fundamentally imperative. The norm is the coercive form of the best example.

This coerciveness seems simple at first, but it is not as simple as it looks. The surface mandate of the regime of the norm is, of course, *Be normal!* The deeper mandate is *Don't be!* Don't be, so that the concentric rings of deviation and difference, the ever-widening circuits, the ring cycles, of nonconformance, can be set up; be otherwise, so that a world can be set up, ragtag but an ordered plenitude. For Foucault, that world was famously organized by a combination of institutionalized surveillance (record keeping, observation, tabulation, categorization) and a Leporello-like cataloging of sexual indiscretions. Opera's relationship to the norm is initially defined by the need to satisfy the contradictory mandates of compliance and noncompliance, assimilation and distinction. With the help of music, that universal solvent, Opera fulfills this need at the level of modeling and fantasy. In so doing it also generates the category of the operatic as a trope for similar behavior in other artistic areas and in styles of social life and sexual love.

4. Opera (big O) arises at the point of concurrence of two historical trends: the gradual replacement of aristocratic by bourgeois life as the paradigm of subjectivity and social presentation, and the rise of the regime of the norm as the paramount regulatory mechanism of middle-class modernity. Opera emerges in tandem with these modernizing tendencies in the aftermath of the collapse of opera seria. For many people, as far as the core repertoire goes, Opera begins with Mozart and Da Ponte. This acceptation might be said to begin at least as early as 1843, with Kierkegaard's reading (in *Either/Or*) of *Don Giovanni* as the supreme work of opera, past or future, the absolutely best example of the form.

The emergence of Opera on this timeline is also the emergence of new forms and dramas of symbolic investiture, as *Don Giovanni* itself suggests. Giovanni's final encounter with the Commendatore's statue, or more exactly with the statue's commanding voice, marks a moment of crisis in the history of modernity. Giovanni is called by the voice of instituted authority and defies it, precisely insofar as it is instituted authority, with a force (almost) equal to that of its call. His action defines the core condition of the modern subject, the possession, the exquisitely self-aware and often ferocious possession, of a reserve of subjectivity that no authority can touch.

At the same time, what Kierkegaard identifies as Giovanni's distinctive mode of desire, the absolute desire for each unique women in the moment of encountering her, exemplifies the alternative by which the subject is driven to invest an object—someone or something—with a significance it cannot plausibly possess.

In Opera, the medium of this investment is voice, which Kierkegaard apropos of *Don Giovanni* hears especially in the frenzied vitality of the champagne aria.[8] Opera invests voice itself with transcendental value, no longer in relation to gods and monarchs, even where these still appear, but in earthbound conditions of extremity or abnormality. These conditions, however, are intimately intertwined with the conditions of everyday life that they seem to surpass or transgress. Hence the middle-class element that is also detectible in *Don Giovanni* in the persons of Zerlina and Masetto, who, though nominally peasants engaged in an older form of class conflict, actually embody values of domesticity and companionate marriage more typical of the emerging bourgeoisie. It is they, after all, who after the infernal abduction of Don Giovanni plan to go home for dinner.

Opera, it might be said, tries to retrieve the transcendental value of the abnorm in proximity to the norm, and to do so—but this never happens, which is where the interest lies—without a remainder. These remainders are far more than awkward leftovers, as theorists from Adorno to Derrida to Žižek have emphasized in different ways. They redistribute cultural energies and fling open hermeneutic windows. They are also, as I suggested in *Musical Meaning*, a primary component of musical experience, particularly in relation to multimedia formations such as constitute the basis of opera.[9]

With the foregoing concepts as its horizon, this book will try to intertwine the topics so prominent in recent opera scholarship with the details of social and cultural history. That intertwining is the taken-for-granted element I referred to earlier. Opera, it might be said, gives voice to—evokes, invokes, vocalizes—the impressions of both a sexualized transcendence and a transcendentalized sexuality. Both impressions carry familiar tropes about the power and meaning of voice to a higher power, which, in a sense, is just what operatic voice does to the vernacular forms of both speaking and singing. The sophisticated studies that have proliferated in the recent past have tended both to study and to utilize as means of study one or another of the operatic forms of these tropes. But perhaps without sufficiently pondering them as tropes: that is, as the rhetoric of a genre whose historical mandate is precisely to uphold the links between voice, sexuality, and transcendence while at the same time forgetting the cultural and historical work performed by doing so. In saying this I don't mean to substitute one magic key or conceptual panacea for another and call it history, or to play at being more historical than other scholars, who are plainly historical through and through, even when their discourse, like opera, veils the fact. I simply want to expand the range of reference into an area that seems to me especially rewarding. I want to enhance the field of mediations between worldly circumstances and the other- or netherwordly, supreme and debased, conditions of Opera—capital O.

This book takes Wagner and Strauss as best examples of Opera on the basis, initially, of Wagner's unparalleled historical impact, embodied by the institution of the "after Wagner" trope as well as by the cultic, Delphi-like location of Wagnerian Opera at Bayreuth. (The waiting list for a ticket is currently seven years long.) In Wagner, Opera's engagement with the "radial" system of the norm and its abnorms becomes transformative. It decisively assumes the specific, historically resonant form of representing the polar extremes of supremacy and debasement. It does so in part because the terms of this polarity become invested with high degrees of libidinal energy and ideological desire in the context of the radial system, with its relentless push-pull force toward both the prototype and—ultimately—a grand antitype. So powerful is this incarnation of the inner logic of norm and abnorm alike that Wagner becomes both central and radically extrinsic to the institution of Opera, both its primary model and its primary antagonist, its authentic self, beyond emulation, and its monstrous Other.

Wagner may thus shed light on Opera even when its other central incarnations are little mentioned. This formation can be said to have crystallized in the program for the *Lohengrin* Prelude, with its entrusting of a redemptive historical narrative to a band of the elect. Written a few years after the opera, the program tasks the Prelude with fixing—and raising—the stakes of the contest staged between the superhumanity of Lohengrin and the subhumanity of Ortrud. Hence I turn in chapter 2 to a slice of cultural history centered on the Prelude, which might stand as a prelude to Wagnerian Opera per se.

The Ring cycle takes the next step—or leap, given the long span separating the romantic incest and Promethian defiance of *Die Walküre* (1854–56) from the brutal blundering, the tragic farce, of *Götterdämmerung* (1869–74). Here both the alliance and the antagonism of norm and abnorm go to extremes unheard of previously. How and why is the topic of chapter 3. One key paraphrase of my argument, or part of it, would be that the chief measure of this process, the progressive debasement of Siegfried first noted by

Nietzsche, is a primary theme of the opera in which it culminates. In a sense *Götterdämmerung* is about the failure of the attempt to shift the burden of debasement from the hero to his nemesis, Hagen, the secret pariah, the half-Nibelung who comes too close for comfort to suggesting a half-Jew. The result of this failure is that the burden must be reassumed by the supreme figure himself. Siegfried must be sacrificed both morally and physically. True supremacy can be transferred back to him only by the moral and imaginative action, the investment of the debased hero as a sublime object, by a figure whom he himself has debased, Brünnhilde.

The logic behind these exchanges is in important ways the logic of modernity. For many years Wagner formed a major nerve center of that logic, which was not only embodied by what Wagnerian Opera does, but also developed in part through what was done with Wagnerian Opera. Chapter 4 tries to sample this phenomenon beyond the confines of the opera house by showing how Wagner himself became a cultural symptom during the twentieth century. No longer merely an artist, however "great," Wagner metamorphosed into a symbolic persona subjected to complex interchanges of supremacy and debasement. As reflected in later invocations of him by writers and especially by composers, he emerges as the inescapable embodiment of the fate of Opera in modern culture.

Strauss's "modernist" operas of the first decade of the twentieth century come into the picture because they carry Wagner's broaching and expansion of the norm/abnorm question to an extreme further yet, an outer limit arguably not matched even by later works in the same spirit such as Berg's *Lulu*. Salome and Elektra are the symptoms of a cultural tendency that the operas devoted to them seek to play out to the point of exhaustion. Chapters 5 through 7 trace this effort. It is no accident that Strauss himself never again put such monstrous women on the opera stage. His next opera, *Der Rosenkavalier*, reinscribes the problem in terms suggestive of the bourgeois pathos of the nineteenth-century novel. Murderous sexuality and sexualized murder are replaced by the decision of the Marschallin, mindful that her youth is waning, to surrender her younger lover to a rival of his (or, in vocal terms, her) own age. That this sacrifice takes place in a wholly secularized world, remote from any hint of the transcendental longings that drive Wagner's characters, offers a soft consummation to an antitranscendental critique notably embedded in *Salome* and *Elektra*. These are operas that remove the idealizing rationale for transgression and reduce longing itself to its material, bodily, erotic basis: still seductively in *Salome*, but with deliberate repulsiveness in *Elektra*.

In these operas, which are deeply concerned with detritus, leftovers, throwaway parts, Strauss identifies himself as the Wagnerian remainder. The trajectory of this book thus traces a kind of chiasmus, a dialectical twist in the career of Opera. In Wagner a quest to represent supremacy leads inexorably to a theater of debasement. In Strauss a theater of debasement is formulated in the service of an anxious and unrealized quest to represent supremacy (the absent Agamemnon, the kiss of the living mouth of Jochanaan). Strauss's *Salome* and *Elektra* seek their own supremacy by debasing the Wagnerian prototype that they also, in the same gesture, the same breath, exalt.

The character of that prototype can be clarified further (with a rueful nod at a best example otherwise omitted here) by comparing the end of *Aida* with that of *Tristan und Isolde*. The narrative of *Aida* is essentially a variant of the *Romeo and Juliet* plot: two lovers transgress social boundaries with the result that their love flourishes briefly and magnificently to end in a consummation-in-death. The key innovation here is that Romeo and Juliet map onto Othello and Desdemona: their death punishes a racial transgression that lurks, unnamed, behind the transgression of national identity. Nonetheless, the difficulties of the opera are purely worldly, and the conclusion appears under the aegis of the assumption that if circumstances had been different the lovers' union could have ended in fulfillment. This assumption is made visible by the division of the stage, with Amneris placed in the temple on top and the lovers in the catacomb beneath her—under her aegis. The vocal map of this scene makes precisely the same point. Aida and Radames first sing in dialogue, then in overlapping phrases, then in unison; as they do the latter, Amneris joins in with contrapuntal interjections, all but the last of them monotones. These little vocal splinters, traipsing across the more continuous line shared by Radames and Aida, simultaneously mark Amneris's exclusion from the lovers' unison intimacy and her role as the embodiment of an arbitrary force that fatally sullies the lovers' union from outside, and in particular from above, the locus of tyrannical authority. Amneris's voice is a pure contingency that falls on the scene like a stain and won't rub out.

Tristan, which has a superficially similar plot, assumes, on the contrary, that circumstances can never, in principle, be different enough. In all circumstances, fulfillment is impossible. That does not mean, however, that it cannot be achieved: but it must be achieved only as the positive form of its negation, that is, *as* an impossible fulfillment. Hence the ending of *Tristan* is, and that of *Aida* is not, a *Liebestod*, a lovedeath (so called; Wagner's term is *Verklärung*, transfiguration). The only transcendental element attaching to Aida's and Radames's union in death comes from the blending of their voices. Isolde, whose transfiguration blinds and deafens her to everything except transcendence, has no voice to blend with, and that absence is the condition of possibility of the transcendence she proclaims.

Act 3 of *Tristan* is a broken duet. It is structured around the lovers' failure to sing together, and in doing so to overcome the interruption that had broken their love duet in act 2 at the very point of its consummation. As is well known, Isolde's transfiguration is a recapitulation of that earlier duet, but a recapitulation that is itself broken, only in a different way. The broken duet of act 2 is resumed and completed by only one party, in a third act in which the two lovers' voices touch once, briefly, but never overlap, in which each sings only in the absence of the other. Absence is the key: Isolde calls from offstage and Tristan exclaims that he "hears the light," but the two meet only in time to utter each other's name before Tristan dies. No matter: an Isolde who sings well enough can make good on Wagner's claim, on her behalf, that to be thus broken is to be fulfilled—is, indeed, the very meaning of fulfillment. The mediating element is the first long period of the opera's Prelude, which returns for the lovers' last meeting as a long dying fall. The famous deceptive cadence that crowns the passage lingers and grows ethereal, its languishing dissonance greatly drawn out before subsiding; what remains is a dark, immobile mass of sound from which the last strands of melodic motion slowly unravel. This music is all but explicit in signifying the infinity of desire in excess over all finite resources. In sum, *Tristan* denies—affirmatively—precisely the union of voices that *Aida* grants. Or rather, to speak more sternly, *Tristan* grants that union imperfectly in act 2 and, so to speak, revokes it perfectly in act 3.

Wagner's operas are similarly preoccupied with the problem of symbolic investiture, which they represent as compelling while also emphasizing its arbitrary character. Foremost among the instruments of this investiture is the ring, of course, together with its collateral instruments of magic and symbols of power. But there are also the potion in *Tristan*, Lohengrin's name game, Walther's prize song, Senta's portrait of the Dutchman, and Parsifal's swan and spear. It might even be said that leitmotific technique is the musical distillate of this combination of efficacy and imposition in the sphere of symbolic investiture. And the sheer arbitrariness of the "sublime objects" in Wagner also points to their radical insufficiency, the principle that symbolic investiture can never be complete no matter how well it succeeds. (We will see how this incompletion is built prototypically into the seminal/

liminal *Lohengrin* Prelude.) Here again one finds the prototypical form of more worldly sublime objects or names in other Operas—and in particular in the two excessive works by Strauss from which a reaction toward nostalgia and classicism may have seemed the only option. *Salome* extends symbolic investiture to its abnormal outer limit ("Give me the head of Jochanaan"). *Elektra* goes a step further (into modernist dissonance as well) by stripping away the lyrical gloss that Salome still installs at that limit.

Treated as best examples, these works by Wagner and Strauss enable a discourse that can be diffused across the whole generic sphere of Opera, as the framing chapters hope to suggest. This is not to say that these works are the cause or origin of Opera's generic absorption in the abnorm and symbolic investiture, or that the discourse on the topic could not have been produced from other examples. But it is to say that part of the historical impact of these works derives from their exposure of the generic character of Opera, a thematic representation of the genre within the work.

Some further cross-comparison may be helpful on this point. Let me propose an emblematic sequence stretching (with another rueful nod) from Verdi through Wagner to Puccini. The first item is from *Rigoletto*, Gilda's aria "Caro nome." As the text and title indicate, symbolic investiture here takes the form of a naming ritual. But there is, as there is everywhere in this opera, a twist. The investiture is true, but the name is false: "Gualtier Maldé," the somewhat preposterous pseudonym of the libertine duke whom Gilda's father, Rigoletto, serves as court jester. Melodically, the aria follows a clear course that is also the path on which Gilda becomes what she is. The opening phrases are broken, hocketlike, into single notes separated by rests, but as Gilda sings on, she smoothes out the melody and elaborates it in increasingly rapturous forms, adding ever more widely spanning fioritura anchored by ever higher top notes. She thus seizes in its essence the ecstasy that reveals, endows her with, the sexuality and worldliness withheld from her by her father (who, as her dialogue with him earlier in the scene attests, also denies her a genuine name). Thanks to the workings of her voice, the effect of investiture is independent of the name that impels it: a name invoked to frame the aria, but never sung during the aria proper. Gilda has found her symbolic mandate by treating it Operatically. And as events will prove, she will not surrender it at any cost, including her life, and no matter how cruelly the truth is revealed.

The situation is not all that different in act 1 of *Die Walküre*, which culminates in a mutual act of investiture, this time by true naming, but with an almost careless indifference to the incest taboo. What counts is the investiture, and its conducting of voice to a plane of ecstasy; the cost doesn't count at all. The process begins when Siegmund proposes a metaphor: in the union of Love and the Spring (Liebe und Lenz) "The sister as bride is freed by her brother" (Die bräutliche Schwester befreite der Bruder). What ensues is a slow, ritualistic, even foreplay-like scene of mutual recognition in which the metaphor becomes literal—and true. The turning point comes when Sieglinde names Siegmund according to her desire and thus endows him with the name that is his: "Siegmund: so nenn ich dich!" "Siegmund heiss ich und Siegmund bin ich!" (Siegmund: so I name you!—Siegmund I'm called and Siegmund I am!). And then, a moment later, as the music reaches a frenzied pitch: "Sieglinde bin ich, die dich ersehnt, / die eigene Schwester" (Sieglinde I am, who longed for you, / your own sister). To which Siegmund replies: "Braut und Schwester bist du dem Bruder" (Bride and sister you are to your brother), thus transforming his earlier metaphor into an act of performative magic.

From here (to complete the sequence more swiftly) it is only a short step to the blissful impossibility or beyond of naming in act 2 of *Tristan und Isolde*. This is a counternaming that enacts the complete absorption of the self into the other as sublime object: "no more Tristan," "no more Isolde." The statements are literally false, but their falsehood doesn't matter except in the lovers' indifference to it. And finally there is the similar, though far more down-to-earth indifference that appears in the false-but-true naming of Mimi in *Bohème:* "My name is Lucia, but they call me Mimi," and Mimi she is. It is worth noting in passing the resonance here of "Lucia" and the extinguishing of candlelight that impels the act of naming, plus the ironic movement from darkness to light that spans the opera as a whole. Light equals death; names given in darkness equal life.

All of these acts of symbolic investiture distance themselves from the norm in the name—literally the name—of a higher value. We can gain some perspective on why by considering the paradox that haunts normativity as a social structure and relating it to the idiom of supremacy and debasement in Wagner and Strauss. In the first instance, the norm is putatively controlling but lacks character, even vitality; individuation, as Foucault observes, consists in "descending" from the norm. The result, as I suggest in *Classical Music and Postmodern Knowledge*,[10] is that normative subjectivity must continually seek to borrow color and life from the abnorm (the latter always a plural term) without succumbing to identity with it (never a wholly successful project). Opera both conducts and masks this project by carrying it out under the auspices of music. The result assumes its most telling form under the topographical skewing of the supremacy-debasement system (a system, as the *Elektra* chapter will emphasize, that is cultural as well as operatic). The supreme is a hypertrophied form of the norm itself, an *über-norm* whose supremacy seems to overcome the characterlessness of, so to speak, the normal norm. In the presence (or felt absence) of supremacy, deviation bunches at a far extreme and polarizes itself against the supreme (Siegfried or Agamemnon) as debasement (Hagen or Elektra) while contaminating any mediating figures left behind in the process (Gutrune or Chrysothemis).

Yet because the supreme is an abnormal norm, its relationship to the debased is not only one of purgation and antagonism but also one of secret kinship and dependency. Hence the appearance of characters who embody both supremacy and debasement and seem capable of shifting from one position to the other at the blink of an eye or the swallow of a potion: Siegfried and Elektra. Hence, too, characters who seem to find their moment of greatest supremacy at the point of their deepest debasement: Brünnhilde and Salome.

The identities and desires of these characters move in a constant winding motion embodied in the twists and turns of the voices that embody them. The labyrinth through which those voices resound is what I am calling Opera. Opera can neither be safely recuperated for normality (whether by aesthetic appreciation or its apparent opposite, cultural critique) nor safely identified with the extravagant disregard of boundaries (whether on sexual, psychosexual, or metaphysical grounds). Recuperation to the norm confuses defensive modes of closure and control, often dug up at the last minute, with the intrinsic character of the energies subjected to closure and control. Recuperation to outlaw self-invention, the twin and rival of normality, confuses the deferral of closure and control by higher-order forms of reason and authority with simple immunity from them.

Nevertheless, there are no positions but these; there is no third term, no stable synthesis. Opera can be understood only by, and as, a continuous negotiation of the spaces between the contested positions of normality and extravagance in the fields of identity and desire. But it must be added immediately that this is not a statement of the need to mediate two positions that just happen to be in contention. Rather, the historical truth of Opera— meaning, in this book, the Opera of the core repertoire, a relatively small group of favorite works composed between the late eighteenth and early twentieth centuries; not all operas, by no means all, are Opera—the historical truth of Opera is that it must above all be understood by, and as, a negotiation between just these positions.

This negotiation, moreover, does not necessarily occupy operas in their entirety. It may concentrate unevenly in acts, scenes, or episodes: Opera (big O) is not so much a type of opera as it is a historically bounded type of social performance embedded in a limited but highly invested body of operas. The "lesson" of Opera, the lesson we go to learn and learn again, is that transcendence requires the abnorm and vice versa, the one for power, the other for justification. Recognizing the authority of the norm thus does little to inhibit its violation. Recognizing the norm as artifice does little to inhibit its power. Seeking to make sense of these paradoxes is the best way to make sense of Opera while also acknowledging its equally important nonsense, which is anything but nonsense.

Before we embark, some brief remarks on method may be advisable. The style of the first chapter implicitly raises the question of how the performative element in interpretation affects its claims to cognitive value. This question is meant to hover implicitly over the book as a whole, most of which conforms to the more usual standards of critical prose. The hovering is meant to help challenge any impulse to divorce cognition from interpretive performance, and vice versa. The question recurs explicitly in both chapter 3 and the epilogue, where its special relationship to Opera also comes into view.

Nonetheless, given the tight weave this book seeks to create between music, modern culture, and Opera, it is inevitable that for some readers the old questions of subjectivity and appropriation in interpretation—particularly of music, with its characteristically ambiguous relationship to all acts of interpretation—will rear their ugly heads. I have by now dealt extensively with these issues in other venues, and it will be necessary to take the liberty of referring concerned readers elsewhere for the arguments favoring the view that objections on such grounds are mistakes, and big ones. Suffice it for now to quote a segment from one of those other texts, not as an argument, but as a sample of the view that the arguments behind it uphold:

> There is no proof in musical hermeneutics. But then, there is no proof in any hermeneutics: no certainty to connotation, irony, implication, symbol, and the like. Meanings beyond the lexical only appear when their appearance is presupposed. The trick is to align the interpreter's art of presupposition with the work of culture, which above all is the practice of presupposition as an art. Interpretation consists neither of discovering prior meanings nor inventing new ones nor even teasing out latent meanings from a stable field of possibilities, although it may do a little of each. Instead it catalyzes meaning between different perspectives, different his-

tories, different subjectivities. Proposing a meaning is the initiating gesture of an interpretation, not its result. The meaning proposed is actualized only by being dispersed through the discursive, figurative, expressive, and pragmatic activity of interpretation itself. The result is a bounded but open-ended process that affirms rather than negates the possibility of alternative meanings.[11]

That activity is not only the way we live in culture, but also the way that culture lives in us. Emily Dickinson once compared it to "Ballet knowledge," but then, the dance not quite sufficing as a metaphor, reached for a higher compliment:

> [Although none] know I know the Art
> I mention—easy—Here—
> Nor any Placard boast me—
> It's full as Opera—[12]

1 Opera

Two or Three Things I Know about Her

HOUSE LIGHTS DOWN

Two or Three Things I Know about Her is a movie released in 1966 by Jean-Luc Godard. It consists of a series of images, interviews, and vignettes that sketch the life of a bourgeois housewife who is also a part-time prostitute. The woman does not, of course, "just happen" to be a prostitute. Like many others, she is working to support a habit—in this case precisely the habit of being a bourgeois housewife. The desire she withdraws from her sexual performances is reinvested in the material pleasures of ownership and consumption.

In form, Godard's movie is innovative. Its discontinuous, nonlinear, anti-mimetic technique, placed in the service of demystifying the facades of normal, or normative, life, can be said to prefigure the advent of deconstruction, which occurred just a year later, in 1967, with the publication of Jacques Derrida's *Of Grammatology*. In content, however, the movie is positively nostalgic, despite an abundance of ostentatious hard edges. It can be seen as a variation on an old theme from nineteenth-century opera. Variants of the underlying logic proliferate across the spectrum of nineteenth-century narratives: the price of being a proper self is susceptibility to an improper love that the self must destroy or—often *and*—be destroyed by. *La Traviata* had long since shown the intimate connections between prostitution and bourgeois yearnings—the yearnings of being bourgeois, the yearning to be a bourgeois. It had given those connections palpable, not to say palpitating, substance in its seductive music. And Godard notwithstanding, those connections are still being mystified as the stuff of true love and romance. It's scarcely a coincidence, speaking of movies, that the opera to which Richard Gere takes Julia Roberts in *Pretty Woman* (1990)—same story, happy ending, but the music makes the prostitute-heroine played by Roberts cry—is *La Traviata.*

With operas less explicit than this one, the same connections may underwrite the impression of profundity. Isn't it possible to understand *Götterdämmerung,* for example, as an archetypal bourgeois tragedy? One of the secrets of the potion that alters Siegfried's desires, and in so doing reveals their true content, is that by forgetting Brünnhilde Siegfried can retire from active duty as a mythic hero. He can settle·down as a pillar of polite society with an attractive wife and a couple of good after-dinner stories about a dragon and some magic fire. But in order for that to happen there must first be a mutual commodity exchange: Gunther must pimp Gutrune to Siegfried, and Siegfried pimp Brünnhilde to Gunther. If only the saturnine Hagen hadn't had other ideas . . .

The chain of associations from Godard to *Götterdämmerung* can be taken to suggest that opera has an exceptionally equivocal relationship to sexually mediated normality, or, more accurately, to the identification of social normality with a certain psychosexual disposition. Since the nineteenth century, such normality has generally hinged on the centrality of one version or another of bourgeois identity, from which other modes of identity may be understood to deviate by degrees. I take this fact, however, to be more exemplary than definitive; my overarching concern is not with the content of normality but with normality itself as a social and psychological function. In saying that this is also one of opera's primary concerns, I may risk seeming to reinvent the clichés that declare opera to be a uniquely extravagant, incredible, or artificial art form. At the same time I may seem to ally myself with recent revaluations that take operatic extravagance as a medium of freewheeling opposition to social and sexual norms.[1] Both the clichés and the revaluations, however, assume the prior existence of a stable, effective, unquestioned normality, the referent of both enforcement and defiance. It is precisely in *not* making that assumption that my own effort begins.

Following Michel Foucault, I regard the device of the norm and the associated concepts of the normal and abnormal not as elements intrinsic to all social organization, but as historical formations specific to modernity.[2] My suggestion is that opera, at least since the nineteenth century, has been actively involved in the production of normality and abnormality as mechanisms of social regulation, especially in the arenas of sex roles, the vicissitudes of desire, and the classification of human types. Opera's distinction is that it openly, perhaps even compulsively, seeks to do with these categories what most other cultural and social practices seek unsuccessfully to avoid doing. Exploiting the power of music to mold itself to any and every occasion, Opera destructures the field of values and desires structured by the regime of the norm. It discloses itself as alienating, questioning, or redefining both normality and abnormality in the very act of helping to produce them by various combinations of enforcement and defiance. The result tends to be that the combinations themselves, revealed or rendered as volatile, tortuous, and electric, grand love-hate romances in their own right, upstage the values whose demands set them in motion.

My aim in this chapter is to offer some reflections on this process which will contribute to an understanding of its specificities, both historical and theoretical. These reflections will be discontinuous, nonlinear, and antimimetic—just like Godard's movie, but without the subtext of nostalgia. First, however, I will have to reflect a little on the possibilities of such reflection itself, both in general and in relation to other recent efforts to reconceptualize opera. That done, I will return to opera proper—or improper, oblique to the proper in every sense of the term—and try to convey two or three things I know about her. Three things, actually, each of which emerges from a different scene in which opera is construed. The scenes depend, successively, on images, interviews, and vignettes from the world of nineteenth-century normality and abnormality. In the first, Walt Whitman listens; in the second, Sigmund Freud reads; in the third, Hagen sings a song.

But first the curtain raiser.

PRELUDE

To begin with I would like to float a simple, even naive, idea, then submit it to a series of refinements. The object is to get a generic fix on the notion of opera from, roughly, Mozart to Puccini, with emphasis on the term "notion." What I'm interested in here is the ideal type suggested and often represented by a majority of the core repertoire pieces within the range suggested, including the Wagner and Strauss pieces on which this book centers as "best examples" of the type. The result is not a statement about an empirical phenomenon, but about a cultural fiction, which in this case I have proposed to call Opera—capital O, like the big Other—and to understand as a symptom of modernity.

Which is a symptom of what, exactly? Jürgen Habermas in a famous essay calls modernity the incomplete project of Enlightenment.[3] Elaborating on an idea of Max Weber's, Habermas proposes that Enlightenment reason chiseled a once-unified worldview into several competing platforms. The three spheres of knowledge ("science," *Wissenschaft*), morality, and aesthetics disengaged from each other and became autonomous. If that is more or less right—and it seems plausible enough—Opera can be understood as one of the consequences.

Opera's mode of knowledge is typically allegory, that is, the mode of open difference between form and meaning. Wotan is overtly more and other than a Norse god, Salome overtly more and other than a Judean teenager. Opera emphasizes the gap internal to allegory by embedding dramatic action and words in an all-embracing but nonspecific support system, namely music, the semiotic openness of which both articulates the gap and fills or even overfills it. In this sense Opera is the antitype of the European novel that flourished during the same era.

This allegorical openness is the medium for the "true" action of Opera, which is staged between the other two terms of Habermas's triad. To oversimplify, but not as much as it may seem, opera constructs itself out of a divided allegiance to morality and the aesthetic, giving judicial and rational priority to the first and subjective priority to the second. This does not necessarily involve a conflict: Opera does not confine itself to embodying the typical modern condition of the head and heart at odds. The construction is a dynamic one, one of mutual interference in the service of mutual support. "Modernity," says Habermas, "revolts against the normalizing functions of tradition; modernity lives on the experience of rebelling against everything normative" (5). (The Foucauldian idea that the normative as such is itself an invention of modernity does not controvert this point; it restates the point from a reverse perspective, no matter that Habermas branded Foucault a conservative antirationalist.)

But Opera proposes a modernity without revolt. Opera embraces morally the norms it spurns affectively. It embraces those norms morally *in order* to spurn them affectively. Opera reinforces the moral norm with the strength of renunciation or denial that the norm imposes. Opera reinforces deviation from the moral norm by the degree of transgressive pleasure, including guilt and libidinal excess, that repudiation of the norm affords. The result is a "spiral of power and pleasure" like the one Foucault described for nineteenth-century sexuality: "Pleasure spread to the power that harried it; power anchored the pleasure it uncovered."[4] Controlling and classifying sex became sexual acts; evading classification and control exercised sex as power. Key to the operation of these Foucauldian spirals is their not being acknowledged by their participants, whether as a result of pretense or real disavowal. They are the perpetual subtext of regulatory exchanges between "parents and children, adults and adolescents, educator and students, doctors and patients, the psychiatrist with his hysteric and his perverts" (45). But Opera's is a spiral rendered available for enjoyment and instruction, almost rendered consumable, not one reserved for the exclusive observation posts of the disciplines.

One might say emblematically that, in the arena of divided allegiance, Mozart's *Don Giovanni* is the first Opera. And among the first instances of post-Opera—again speaking emblematically—are works such as Britten's *Peter Grimes* and *Billy Budd*, which refuse the division of allegiance and explicitly criticize the fetishizing of the norm.

But this Habermasian model remains too simple, even with a Foucauldian overlay. One way to refine it, but not one to Habermas's liking, is to call on Derrida, another thinker whom Habermas regards as a conservative antagonistic to the idea of reason that he, Habermas, is trying to salvage.

A simple Derridean critique of Habermas's view would point out that the myth of modernity as a dissociated field of knowledge, morality, and aesthetics, though certainly powerful, has too much confidence in the autonomy of its components, which on Habermas's reading actually preserve (within their specialized and professionalized boundaries) the integrity supposedly lost by the metaphysical-religious unity whose breakup produced them. This preservation can indeed be said to occur, but only in splinters. Each term in the system leaves fragmentary remainders in the others; each is always already invested by claims, images, rhetorics, and dispositions to communicative action typical of the others. A reading of opera, to be genuinely responsive to the phenomenon of Opera, should be situated within the field of this Derridean *différance*, a field that is simultaneously historical, rhetorical, and theoretical. So, to suggest a provisional protocol for such a reading, which the rest of the volume will develop, I will turn to some classic statements by Derrida and link them to Opera through the critical initiatives, originally provoked by questions of gender and sexuality, that in the decade of the 1990s substantially reconfigured the study of opera across the board.

Derrida, to be sure, may be a problematic resource. For some, he has already dated, and dated badly, in ways, for example, that Habermas has not. To some degree the concepts under review are more artifacts than current tools. I will return to this point in a little while. But this business of dating is more complex than it appears. As Derrida says of what he calls overturning (see below), "It is not a question . . . of a page that one day simply will be turned, in order to go on to other things. . . . The time for overturning is never a dead letter."[5]

In *Positions*, the earliest of several books collecting the interview transcripts by which he loves to reduce speech, literally, to writing, Derrida outlines what he calls "a double gesture" through which deconstruction must pass and continually repass. An extended quotation will be necessary here:

> On the one hand, we must traverse a phase of *overturning*. To do justice to this necessity is to recognize that in a classical philosophical opposition we are not dealing with the peaceful coexistence of a *vis-à-vis*, but rather with a violent hierarchy. . . . To deconstruct the opposition, first of all, is to overturn the hierarchy at a given moment. To overlook this phase of overturning is to forget the conflictual and subordinating structure of opposition. Therefore one might proceed too quickly to a *neutralization* that *in practice* would leave the previous field untouched. . . . We know what have always been the *practical* (particularly *political*) effects of immediately jumping *beyond* oppositions, and of protests in the simple form of *neither* this *nor* that. . . . On the other hand, to remain in this phase is still to operate . . . from within the deconstructed system. . . . We must also mark the interval between inversion, which brings low what was high, and the irruptive emergence of a new "concept," a concept that can no longer be, and never could be, included in the previous regime. (41–42)

Derrida notoriously offers a surplus of names for "the irruptive emergence of a new 'concept,'" but the one he favors in *Positions* is "dissemination," which he characterizes as "an irreducible and *generative* multiplicity" of meanings (45).

I will shortly suggest that the course of recent efforts to reconceptualize opera has corresponded fairly closely to Derrida's double gesture, but without fully realizing the disseminal character of the second phase. The reason for this new gap or interval (it is in no sense a failure) is that the disseminal phase does not constitute a unified field—as, on its own terms, it ought not to do. A closer reading of Derrida's text suggests that his disseminal phase incorporates a double gesture of its own, a second double gesture that recapitulates the original movement from overturning to dissemination.

On the one hand, Derrida outlines what we might call a phase of mixture, in which an opposition breaks down when it encounters a concept it cannot assimilate. The result is to scramble and conjoin the terms that the opposition is meant to keep separate. Mixture is marked by the appearance of "undecidables": terms that "inhabit" an opposition without belonging to it and "*without ever* constituting a third term" by which the opposition could be resolved dialectically (43). The best known of these undecidables is *différance:* the movement through which the elements of "language, or any code, any system of referral in general" enter into the interrelationships of difference and deferral by which, and by which alone, they become meaningful. The movement of *différance* is wayward, unsimple, constantly "enmeshed in [a] work that pulls it through a chain of other 'concepts,' other 'words,' other textual configurations" (40). Yet it is not purely contingent because the production of difference and deferral is unremitting. Any classical opposition is inhabited by something that "indicates that each of [its putatively self-standing] terms must appear as the *différance* of the other, as [itself] the other different and deferred."[6]

Opera, as it happens, furnishes a fine example in the classical form of its conjuncture of words and music. As Avital Ronell observes, "In the demand that their encounter make sense, opera figures the irreducible difference between words and music. Language, for its part, is left a little emptied by the encounter, for it discovers that it can never hear itself unless music plays the other of itself. . . . [But] music finds in language that it has been critically denied access to saying what it means."[7]

On the other hand, Derrida envisions a phase in which the terms dislocated by mixture enter into a pure conceptual mobility, an unbounded generativity from which previously unsuspected meanings proliferate. At a certain point (Derrida simply invokes a floating "then"), "the operator of generality named *dissemination* insert[s] itself into the open chain" of undecidables. In contrast to the phase of mixture, which is said to produce resistance and disorganization within a conceptual field, the more radical phase of dissemination "*explode[s] the semantic horizon.*" Dissemination is even glossed as, in effect, the *différance* of *différance* itself: it is "seminal *différance*" (*Positions*, 44–45).

Opera criticism after 1990 can be said to have "overturned" the reigning assumption that opera is a form of drama in which the dramatist is the composer (Joseph Kerman's phrase)[8] in favor of understanding it as a preeminently multimedia and, so to speak, multimediated (culturally saturated) form. The way was led by feminist critiques of operatic representation based on critical concern with the same problem that preoccupied opera itself in the 1890s: the problem of "woman," or, more exactly, the construction of "woman" as, precisely, a problem. In a classic instance of overturning, Catherine Clément's *Opera, or the Undoing of Woman* treated opera as a form grounded, not in the transcendence of shoddy librettos by beautiful music, but in the use of beautiful music to glamorize feminine suffering and death. Susan McClary's *Feminine Endings* grounded opera's frequent representation of madwomen in the need to control a fascinating but threatening feminine excess.[9] These initiatives were quickly followed by studies in mixture (already implicit in McClary's text) along the now-familiar lines of power and resistance, compliance and transgression. The "phase" of such mixture is ideally that of a principled ambivalence that cannot, and should not, be overcome. It is an ambivalence that must be *practiced*. The practice of it in opera studies has given rise not only to accounts of gender, sexuality and sexual orientation, and the body, but also of theatricality, subjectivity, the supersensual and numinous, and more.[10] The initial concern with, broadly speaking, questions of desire and identity has continued, but it has also diversified and inspired diversity.

In sum, there was, there has been and continues to be, a shift in priority from opera as music to opera as musical theater. Music, to be sure, remains the sine qua non: if the music fails, the opera fails, whereas an opera can survive bad staging, bad acting, a bad libretto, and even bad singing on the strength of its music. But opera as a conglomerate form and a barometer of cultural styles in subjectivity has become the center of attention. Opera is no longer art, exactly; it is a heterogeneous patchwork of media contributions, no one of which has automatic priority in shaping either aesthetic value or cultural meaning.

What is still missing from this heady mixture is the force of dissemination, the force that makes Opera something intractably strange, something unfolded through music but never fully rationalized or normalized by it. To some degree, the very acts of focus on gender, sexuality, noumenal subjectivity, and so on that have opened up the study of opera to new, increasingly sophisticated modes of understanding have tended to edge the unruly operatic patchwork toward the more monolithic status of the *Gesamtkunstwerk*, even without anyone wanting or intending that outcome. There is really no way to avoid this, but there is also no need to rest content with it. The disseminal force, which is to say the multifaceted, thick-description–seeking, intertextually dense activity of opera, the experience of opera, and writing about opera, can also be made available. It can be let loose.

Which is also, surprising as it may seem, to let history loose. The concept of dissemination belongs to a short-lived era of high theory that has been superseded largely because of its insufficient attentiveness to history. Part of the intent of recent opera scholarship has certainly been to restore the historical (that is, the worldly and contingent) import so often blunted by too exclusive a focus on strictly musical questions. Yet that intent has itself been somewhat blunted, as just noted, by the idealizing tendencies of its own discourse—something for which dissemination is a well-known pharmacy item.

Dissemination, I would suggest, can help us comprehend opera historically because there is a sense in which the disseminal *is* the historical, the very phenomenon it is commonly denounced for opposing. Dissemination is the mode of operation of historical contingency at the level of meaning. Mixed media applications depend on its potentialities—the open field of combinatory possibility, up to and including sheer chance. Opera, as mixed in its media as an art form can be, and as historically saturated, is dissemination as (musical) theater.

Opera plays out this paradox all the time. Its plots and styles are often blatantly historical—Opera is the bodice-ripper genre of high art—but its historical, mythographic, costume-drama features are presented as the agencies of transcendental tropes: opera produces history as metaphysics, metaphysics as the conjunction of voice and body with historical fictions. Many recent studies have tended to perpetuate this mystique in the act of analyzing it, whether their transcendental terms of choice have been gender, voice, body, or the noumenal. My effort here is not to oppose this trend. The world that made these tropes, and that these tropes make, is my world too, and I welcome the widening range of subject matter gained by exploring it. But I do want to contextualize, and therefore detranscendentalize, the trend's initiatives by working always within earshot of the sociohistorical formations within which the physical and metaphysical tropes make sense. With Opera, that brings us back to the regime of the norm, and especially to the correlated extremes of supremacy and debasement.

The regime of the norm might be said to enable the forms of excess or transcendence against which it seeks to protect the good subject, but on whose energies it must draw in order to make that subject plausibly animate: good to have as well as good to be. One might speculate that the social function of opera within this historical envelope is to allow the good subject to adopt figures of excess—characters overlapping with the singers who impersonate them—as ego ideals, imaginary persons who translate common, nontransgessive actions into something tacitly higher, grander, and more pleasurable, guides or imagoes that reward precisely the ego that does *not* emulate them, except figuratively. This explains the intensity of identification that radiates through the world of opera—or rather of Opera—and the magnification of person that will appear in each of the essays in this book. Opera reassures those who love it that it loves them back, or more exactly loves their secret selves. Opera reassures the good subject that its ordinary life is secretly sublime.

Another name for this sublimity is dissemination, the whirligig of meaning in motion behind the facade of the good subject and the guiding spirit of the three acts to follow starring Whitman, Freud, and Wagner. The curtain is ready to go up.

FIRST SCENE: WALT WHITMAN LISTENS

Whitman's favorite music was serious Italian opera, and he cheerfully admits that his taste for it is perversely erotic. When he lists his favorite scenes in "Proud Music of the Storm," nearly all of them turn out to involve despairing love and impending death. His response typically combines a voyeuristic fascination with erotically charged details and a masochistic identification with someone in anguish:

> I see poor crazed Lucia's eyes' unnatural gleam,
> Her hair down her back falls loose and dishevel'd.
>
> I see where Ernani walking the bridal garden,
> Amid the scent of night-roses, radiant, holding his bride by the hand,
> Hears the infernal call, the death pledge of the horn.
>
> (ll. 78–82)[11]

At their peak, these erotic responses fuse into an orgasmic sense of being filled, physically penetrated, by the operatic voice from which "passionate heart-chants [and] sorrowful appeals" (l. 43) stream forth. This is from *Song of Myself:*

> I hear the violoncello ('tis the young man's heart's complaint),
> I hear the key'd cornet, it glides quickly in through my ears,
> It shakes mad-sweet pangs through my belly and breast.
>
> I hear the chorus, it is a grand opera,
> Ah this indeed is music—this suits me.
>
> A tenor large and fresh as the creation fills me,
> The orbic flex of his mouth is pouring and filling me full.
>
> (ll. 596–602)

Opera thus seems to be the medium in which Whitman's sexuality achieves its greatest clarity and intensity. It is not that opera reflects his sexuality, or feeds his sexuality, but rather that it *becomes* his sexuality. In particular, Whitman's way of listening to mournful bel canto song gives him access to certain kinds of pleasure that he otherwise feels compelled to deny to his textual body.[12]

In the passage about the tenor from *Song of Myself,* the pleasure is homosexual, in particular a pleasure suggestive of anal penetration; note the chain of associations leading from the young man's heart's complaint, through the cornet singled out by its phallic key, to the gliding-in that shakes transgressive pangs through belly and breast. The identification between the ear, traditionally the most spiritual of orifices, and the anus, traditionally the most corporeal, fulfills erotically a claim that Whitman has made rhetorically earlier in the poem: "I keep as delicate around the bowels as around the head and heart" [520]. When the tenor appears, his voice supplies the loving same-sex body, large and fresh, by which the listener is filled. It is even possible that a particular tenor role is the latent origin of this sequence. The identification of the young man's heart's complaint with the sound of a cello suggests the conjunction of a solo cello with Edgardo's dying lament in the final scene of *Lucia di Lammermoor*. The scene is one that focuses intense sympathy on the suffering young man through an on-stage group of male onlookers, and in this respect it may form what for Whitman is the Ur-scene, or primal scene, of operatic pleasure.

The role of the cornet in mediating between this scene and the orbic mouth of the primal tenor (large as creation) is intriguing enough to warrant some speculation. The cornet assumes a virile character through its popularity as a military band instrument, despite its "soprano" voice—which, in relation to Edgardo's cello, may almost have a visionary-transgressive value here resembling that of Lucia's flute. At the same time, the cornet's size and shape are such that, of all brass instruments, it brings the player's mouth, the "keys" (valves), and the bell into closest proximity. Its voice is thus literally closer than any other to the player's, which, correspondingly, comes closer than any other to singing through its "key'd" instrument.

Where the singer in Whitman is a woman, the pleasure she offers in parallel with the tenor's is a lachrymose sentimentality that draws the poet into a posture of abjection. The focus of this sentimentality is motherhood; for Whitman, the diva is always maternal, even if she is singing *Lucia*.

Consider, for example, "The Singer in the Prison," an embarrassing poem by latter-day standards but by the same token a revealing one. Here Whitman commemorates a concert he may have attended at Sing Sing, where a famous diva, flanked by "a little child on either hand," supposedly reduced an audience of hardened convicts to "deep, half-stifled sobs, the sound of bad men bow'd and moved to weeping, / And youth's convulsive breathings, memories of home, / The mother's voice in lullaby, the sister's care, the happy childhood" (44–46). As they often do in nineteenth-century texts, the spasmodic sobs and tears form the basis of a publicly sanctioned mode of hysteria.[13] Their presence allows a convulsive eroticism to appear as edifying moral grief, the ultimate reference for which is the childhood innocence preserved (only) in the image of the mother. (Consistent with the masochistic pleasure it incites, that image is sometimes slightly detached or cold.[14] The diva in Sing Sing is a "large calm lady" who "vanish[es] with her children in the dusk" immediately after her performance.) What Whitman adds to this cult of the *mater dolorosa* is the location of its eroticism in the operatic sound of the mourning maternal voice "Pouring in floods of melody in tones so pensive sweet and strong the like whereof was never heard" (3). The voice in this role counts as what Jacques Lacan calls the object a: the seeming object of a desire that exists only insofar as no object can ever satisfy it.[15]

The operatic passage from *Song of Myself* supplies the (phantasmatic) origin of the scenario in "The Singer in the Prison" when a soprano takes the place of the tenor. Combined with or dissolving into the orchestra, the female voice gives pleasure by wrenching Whitman away from his usual sense of identity and throwing him figuratively from planetary to oceanic space with casual and cruel omnipotence. The music is less something he hears than something he swallows; he feels it in his throat like a sob or a gasp or the classic *globus hystericus,* as lacerating and smothering as it is ecstatic:

> I hear the train'd soprano (what work with hers is this?)
> The orchestra whirls me wider than Uranus flies,
> It wrenches such ardors from me I did not know I possess'd them,
> It sails me, I dab with bare feet, they are lick'd by the indolent waves,
> I am cut by bitter and angry hail, I lose my breath,
> Steep'd amid honey'd morphine, my windpipe throttled in fakes of death.
>
> (ll. 603–8)

The "honey'd morphine" suggests the satiation of the infant "steeped" in the mother's breast that soothes away all bitter and angry wounds. The "indolent waves" licking the poet's bare feet present the same suggestion from a reverse perspective. (Mother Music tends you from head to foot, bathing and nourishing; like the singer in the prison, she goes with her children everywhere.) But music as honey'd (mellifluous?) heal-all is also music as sweetened poison. It must register as poisonous because by reducing Whitman to a helpless, preverbal state, it doubly suspends his subjectivity. It gags him both as a speaking subject and as a poetic voice. Traces of this gagging carry over, together with traces of bliss, into the verses that describe both. The images of steeping and throttling press back on the rhyming exhalations of "breath" and "death" that enfold them; the sighing vowel sounds of "steep'd amid honey'd morphine" adjoin the plosive-glottal bolus of "pipe throttled."[16]

Although Whitman is genuinely absorbed in (and by) the maternal image, his receptivity to male "tremulousness" is even more acute. This is how "Proud Music of the Storm" evokes a beloved scene from Donizetti's *La Favorita:*

From Spanish chestnut trees' dense shade,
By old and heavy convent walls a wailing song,
Song of lost love, the torch of youth and life quench'd in despair,
Song of the dying swan, Fernando's heart is breaking.

(ll. 86–89)

This vignette is striking for the undisguised purity by which it transcribes erotic pain as erotic pleasure, a pleasure conveyed viscerally in the hypnotic rhythms grouped around the word "song." Even more striking is the surge of syntactic distortion; the coherence of the passage as a statement collapses under the pressure of its urgency as a rhythmic event. Instead of producing the "normal" effect of poetic speech, the illusion that a referential transparency has fused seamlessly with a rhythmic impulse, this passage appears less as reference than as substance, a material manifestation of the poet's pleasure. It becomes a dab of honey'd morphine.

For Slavoj Žižek, this kind of passage constitutes what he calls a "phallic anamorphosis."[17] In other words, it is a structural deformity—a blot, stain, or nub—that "sticks out" of the work in which it appears. Except for the quibble on "sticks out," the phallic character of the blot has nothing to do with male anatomy. Žižek uses the term *phallus* in a strict Lacanian sense to refer to "a signifier without a signified." The effect of this opaque signifier is one of simultaneous discovery and concealment. The lack of the signified endows the text with mysterious depths of meaning—the very depths, so to speak, in which the signified has been lost. The opacity of the signifier marks the site of this loss and blocks all attempts to plumb the depths with certainty. As if on a perverse treasure map, the signifier is the spot that marks an X.

Lacan calls this "master signifier" the phallus by analogy to the Oedipal prohibition that both awakens and punishes primary desires. Whitman, however, is not a strict Lacanian. In producing the phallic anamorphosis, he also reunites the phallic function to an idealized image of the virile body, in particular the tenor's body. In the passage on *La Favorita*, this reunion becomes evident in the traditional phallic image of the torch, which, though quenched for the fictitious Fernando, is reignited in the tenor's torch song. All the verses need to do is sing along. Instead of seeking to plumb the depths of the mystery produced by the blot, Whitman simply enjoys the blot as substance, as fluidic pulsation, by linking it to a homoerotic fantasy. In another poem, "The Dead Tenor," he even more explicitly juxtaposes the tenor voice as pulsating erotic substance, "So firm—so liquid-soft— . . . that tremulous, manly timbre!" with the same voice as the signifier of an indecipherable "lesson" that constitutes "[the] trial and test of all."

For Whitman, this combination advances the social experiment of American democracy by identifying cultural work, not with the repression or sublimation of sexuality, but with its channeling, the creation of a national circulatory system for the fluid dynamics of desire. As a sexual politics, this program requires the affirmation of both heterosexual love and the cult of maternity. Cultural supremacy, however, belongs to a specific form of homosexuality, the masochistic reception of the tenor voice.

The channeling of this sexuality is realized most complexly in the passage quoted earlier from *Song of Myself*:

> A tenor large and fresh as creation fills me,
> The orbic flex of his mouth is pouring and filling me full.
> (ll. 601–2)

Another anamorphosis here: these lines compel special attention because on the surface they make so little sense. The tenor is not a piece of fountain statuary spouting water from the mouth. Nonetheless, it is the music pouring from the tenor's mouth that fills the poet full, and that corresponds to the earlier phallic gliding of the key'd cornet. At one level, the equation of the music with a kind of penetrating fluid is probably literal. Whitman was a believer in animal magnetism, and what he is recording here is probably the sensation of having his body charged (literally "thrilled") by an influx of electrical fluid.[18] Emitted from the tenor's mouth, the fluid passes as from a mesmerist to his subject, completing the charismatic circle of magnetic treatment. This process was often represented as having a phallic character. What allows it to act phallically for Whitman, however, is once again the overlay of a penile fantasy on the phallic nub. The imagistic blend of orbic flexing with pouring and filling endows the music with the "firm— . . . liquid-soft" character that grounds Whitman's homosexual desire. At its height, the operatic experience becomes an encounter in which two men, without touching each other except in the magnetic medium, come together in their "pensive" sadness and—come together.

SECOND SCENE: SIGMUND FREUD READS

Shortly before the end of the nineteenth century, one of Freud's patients, described in *The Interpretation of Dreams* as "a young man with strong homosexual leanings, which were . . . inhibited in real life," dreamed the following dream:

> He was attending a performance of *Fidelio*, and was sitting in the stalls at
> the opera beside L., a man who was congenial to him and with whom he

would have liked to make friends. Suddenly he flew through the air right across the stalls, put his hand in his mouth and pulled out two of his teeth.[19]

The young man added shamefacedly that "the state of sensual excitement provoked by his [frustrated] desire" for a similar "friend" had once led him to masturbate twice in rapid succession. We can surmise that he acted twice in order to stage the masturbation as mutual, once on behalf of his own body, once on behalf of the absent body of his "friend." The young man, it turns out, had never made love to anyone, male or female, and "pictured sexual intercourse on the model of . . . masturbation." Freud, who can take a sexual hint, located the dream's transcription of this double masturbation in the pulling out of two teeth. He adds that the same action also gives a double visual form to a German slang expression for masturbation, *sich einen ausreissen,* "to pull one out."

But why set this scene at the opera? And why at *Fidelio* in particular? Freud's answer depends on noticing a small textual adventure. The finale of the opera contains a joyous phrase, "Wer ein holdes Weib errungen" (He who has won a lovely wife), lifted from Schiller's "Ode to Joy"; the same phrase thus also occurs in the finale of Beethoven's Ninth Symphony. What makes this important is that the young man described his feeling of flight as one of being "thrown" *(geworfen)* in the air, and that the key phrase in the symphony is immediately preceded there by another one:

Wem der grosse Wurf gelungen,
Eines Freundes Freund zu sein

[He who has won the great throw
To be the friend of a friend]

On this reading, the dream identifies the young man's masturbatory scene as the "great throw" of homosexual love. Freud adds that this image of the throw is ambivalent. On the one hand, the throw represents rejection, the feeling of being "thrown out," and repeats in symbolic form the dreamer's compensatory act of double masturbation in the friend's absence. On the other hand, the throw fantasizes a blissful fulfillment of the dreamer's homosexual desire. We might even add that it fulfills his specific wish for a mutual masturbatory consummation—to pull *two* out, eines *Freundes Freund* zu sein.

Freud's construction of this chain of associations exemplifies the kind of reasoning that often infuriates empirically minded readers. The chain is not constructed by linking each well-grounded association to the next, but by filling in the gaps between the best-grounded associations. Evidential value is invested more in the associative pattern as a whole than in any of its components. This is hardly the place to present a rationale for this practice. Suffice it to say that the primary resources for filling associative gaps are language habits and practices, which are understood to inform all speech acts continuously. At issue in this case is the influence of a text so familiar in the milieu of Freud and his patient that Freud's expository paragraph does not bother to identify it; that everyone has it by heart goes without saying. I do not find this much of a stretch. From a latter-day perspective, however, one might also suggest that the resemblance between Schiller's phrase and the central dream image is indicative of the discursive positioning of homosexual desire in culture. Such desire, one might say, is always a gamble; and in the passage from the homosocial in Schiller to the homosexual in Freud's patient, the throw of the dice becomes something more violent, a throw of the body. This troping on the throw, implicit in the meaning of *Wurf,* also points to the pervasive theme of violence in the dream, which always positions the dreamer as victim.

At this point Freud stops, but if we want to know something about opera we have to go further. When the young man displaces material from the Ninth Symphony into *Fidelio,* he sexualizes the social relationship of male friendship. The logic of the dream suggests a pair of complementary motives for this process.

First, the opera provides a compelling parallel to the dream's image of a bliss that becomes mutual by dividing into two identical parts. Florestan and Leonora find such a bliss in the duet "O Namenlose Freude!" which is in every sense the climax of *Fidelio.* The peculiar quality of a self-twinning pleasure is figured not only in the intertwining and echoing of Leonora's and Florestan's voices, but also in their very articulation of the key phrase: "O namen- namenlose Freude!" Even more important in this context, however, is the duet's *visual* doubling. The fact is so obvious that no one makes anything of it, but the duet is a drag scene: although what we *hear* is Florestan and Leonora, what we *see* is Florestan and the cross-dressed Fidelio, a man and a youth. In the "nameless joy" of this couple, Freud's dreamer may well have found an image of his own "unspeakable" desire.

That image, moreover—and here the second motive emerges—is an altogether idealized one, the very nucleus of a redeemed community as the opera presents it. In "real life" the young man found his desires shameful, but there is no trace of shame in his dream. With his great throw, he visualizes the literal uplifting, the sublimation, of his desires onto the edifying plane of Beethoven's music, and especially onto the superidealistic plane of the

Ninth Symphony. The displacement from the Ninth to *Fidelio* is a way of affirming that operatic sexual crossovers carry their own idealism, and that male friendship can freely be sexualized without losing its ideal character.

But the dream also contradicts this affirmation in a startling way. The dreamer appears in the act of masturbation when he puts his hand in his mouth and pulls out two teeth; but he also appears, proleptically, as the actual substance that "takes flight" from the "great throw" of the masturbatory climax. In other words, the dream identifies the young man with his own semen. What's more, it propels him, in that form, "right across the stalls," which is to say that it propels him right toward the adjacent orchestra pit and stage. It is literally *toward the opera*, and away from his friend in the stalls, that the dreamer-as-semen is traveling. Only by marking the opera with this sign and substance of his desire can he hope to gratify that desire. Only, it seems, by thus defiling and adhering to the opera can he render himself visible to his friend as an object of mutual desire, as Florestan is to Fidelio, and vice versa.

This aspect of the dream is obviously an index of the young man's desperation, and as such it demands an empathetic response. It may, however, also picture a recognition of something distinctive to opera. It is worth noting that although both Freud's interpretation and mine make reference to specific scenes in *Fidelio*, the dream does not. The young man as semen-subject is actually thrown toward the *locus of opera as such*, regardless of what appears there at a given moment. This perplexing gesture makes the most sense if we interpret the semen, not primarily as the bodily fluid produced by a particular sexual act, but as a representative of the adhesive quality of sexual desire in general—of what Whitman called "the fluid and attaching character" and Freud, of course, called libido. In a more recent formulation, Lacan characterizes the libido as an imaginary bodily organ he calls the *lamella* or *l'hommelette*.[20] The latter term means both "omelet" and "little feminine man"; Lacan offers it as a witty play on Plato's myth that human beings were originally egg-shaped androgynes who were only later divided into the two sexes. Lacan, knowing how to make a good French omelet, also knows how to capture the floating, insistent, sometimes queasy character that desire assumes when imagined or intuited apart from its objects. He simply breaks some eggs: "Let us imagine it, a large crepe moving about like the amoeba, ultra-flat for passing under doors, omniscient in being led by pure instinct, immortal in being scissiparous. Here is something you would not like to feel creeping over your face, silently while you are asleep, in order to seal it up."[21] Isn't it possible that what is thrown toward the opera in the dream of Freud's young man is not something proper to the dreamer's

body but the adhesive substance of l'hommelette? And since the throw targets no specific scene, but only the operatic conjuncture of music and drama,
orchestra pit and stage, wouldn't it be possible to see in the throw a recognition that opera is always already the site of l'hommelette, always already
covered at every point of its surface with the substance of desire?

Perhaps when Ernst Kurth described the harmonies of Tristan und Isolde
as forming "a light, thin, and extraordinarily sensitive film,"[22] he recognized
unawares not only the erotic substance Wagner produced by breaking a
twinned subjectivity into a musical hommelette, but also the libidinal substance of opera in general. The singularity of this substance in Tristan is simply that the harmonies make it more humid, so that it gets in the listener's
face more than usual.

THIRD SCENE: HAGEN SINGS A SONG

No one ever has a good word to say for Hagen. Most dramatic villains elicit
at least a twinge of human sympathy; not this one. Hagen is more like Iago
than like Shylock, both of whom he resembles in important ways. He is so
awful that when he treats Alberich with contempt we even feel sorry for
the old wretch with his plaintive refrain of "Hagen, my son." Besides, Hagen wrecks havoc not only dramatically but also musically, smearing blots
and croaks across the texture of Götterdämmerung with his snarling basso
profundo. He even has the chutzpah to interfere with the sublimity of the
final conflagration by shouting "Hands off the ring!" (Zurück vom Ring!).

One has to admire Wagner's ingenuity with Hagen: this monster is hateful for what he does, not what he is, but there is no way to keep the two
apart. And what is Hagen but the archetypal half-caste degenerate of nineteenth-century racialist anti-Semitism? Not a Jew in any literal sense, he is
the object of cultural phobia that Jews are imagined to embody: the Other
who is not quite other enough, the Sigismund by which every son of Siegmund is shadowed.[23] Hagen is the half-assimilated pariah whose very existence bespeaks a contamination of once-pure bloodlines. He is the parasite who feeds on the virtues of a nobler but more vulnerable breed whose
weaknesses he draws out with his superior, amoral cunning. You can tell,
once again, by the baseness of his voice.

But perhaps the very virulence of this portrait should prompt us to give
Hagen his due: "Stand up for bastards!" to call on Shakespeare again. After all, Hagen is the only character in Götterdämmerung who is absolutely
true to himself, if to no one else. His integrity, however malign, may be more
palatable than Gunther's tortured ressentiment, Gutrune's abject wheedling,

and even Siegfried's tedious vanity. Only Brünnhilde's rage rivals Hagen's mania in purity—but Hagen is not engaged in self-betrayal as Brünnhilde is, and besides, the rage and the mania both have the same outcome: the spear in Siegfried's back.

The core of Hagen's purity is his absolute lack of sexuality. Alberich may have renounced love, but Hagen alone lacks desire—lacks it, indeed, with no sense of lacking anything. His intent to possess the ring is not even fetish-istic; it is more like an empty placeholder, a purely formal function of his purely abstract integrity—just something, as he tells Alberich, that he has sworn to himself. Hagen's dark voice marks the void left behind where desire has been abolished.

It is no wonder, then, that when Hagen wants to round up some wedding guests he does so in the form of a call to arms. On learning that Siegfried, in Gunther's form, has come home after abducting Brünnhilde from her rock, and that she and Gunther are near, Hagen takes the stage by himself. Perched on a high rock of his own, he summons the Gibichung vassals with striking vehemence:

> Hoiho! Hoihohoho!
> Ihr Gibichsmannen, machet euch auf!
> Wehe! Wehe! Waffen! Waffen!
> Waffen durchs Land! Gute Waffen!
> Starke Waffen! Scharf zum Streit.
> Not is da! Not! Wehe! Wehe!
> Hoiho! Hoihohoho!

> [Hoiho! Hoihohoho!
> You Gibich vassals, rouse yourselves!
> Woe! Woe! Weapons! Weapons!
> Weapons throughout the land! Good weapons!
> Strong weapons, sharp for the strife!
> Danger is coming! Danger! Woe! Woe!
> Hoiho! Hoihohoho!]

This call deserves some reflection. It constitutes the one moment in the opera when Hagen "lets himself go" expressively, and baleful as it is, it is compelling, too. With the fate of the others in his grasp, Hagen sings a song. The "Hoiho! Hoihohoho!" with which he frames his call has a saturnine jauntiness to it, a sunless exuberance that, just for a moment, can become infectious. It is certainly infectious for the orchestra, which responds by over-laying the grinding bass geared to Hagen's voice with brassy outbursts and turbulent flourishes. In the swirling music of this scene, Hagen already enjoys possession of the ring of power, though he doesn't know it.

Hagen's song is yet another phallic anamorphosis, another blot that produces deep truths by seeming to distort their appearance. Why give stage time to the trivial act of calling the vassals? And why should Hagen himself stage the call as such a charade? He otherwise conducts his villainy with exquisite economy; the ham-handed joke of his wedding call is superfluous. We might say that his lack of desire hobbles him here by acting something like autism. Hagen can name desire but not comprehend it, so his invitation to a wedding flips over into a war whoop. Belligerence is something he does comprehend, or at least knows how to mimic. But the music of this scene bespeaks grotesque power, not blustering automatism. We are meant to remember the power when Hagen later uses his plangent "Hoiho" motive to prefigure the announcement of Siegfried's death. What the music of this scene says is that Hagen is telling the truth when he cries out that danger is coming. It *is* coming—and coming in the form of Gunther's bride.

Hagen's erotic autism, then, acts in this scene not as a lack but as a positive force or presence. As such, and strictly following the logic of the blot that both demands and resists interpretation, the autism points beyond Hagen himself to the other characters. They, after all, not he, are the ones who swirl in currents of lust, envy, delusion, jealousy, and rage. Hagen is simply *their* phallus, a kind of golem pieced together from the rejected pieces of *their* desires.

Chief among these pieces is Siegfried's desire for Brünnhilde, which is supposedly cloaked by Hagen's magic potion. In slightly anachronistic terms: when Siegfried accepts this drink from his new hosts, he acquires a repressed desire; he becomes a Freudian neurotic. This formula is the outcome of a symbolic one, according to which Hagen's potion (like its counterpart in *Tristan und Isolde*) only does what its victim wants; the "symbol" becomes most revealing when it is understood with the greatest literalness. On these terms, what Siegfried wants is to shift his desire for Brünnhilde onto a more conventional mate. This change of heart has nothing to do with the mimetic plausibility it so obviously defies; instead it represents the position that Siegfried must occupy to enter the social order of the Gibichungs, an order constituted by kinship alliance, the homosocial bonds of blood brotherhood, and "normal" heterosexuality, the pivot on which all else turns. Hagen's potion in effect accelerates the process by which desire becomes socialized; the heavy-handedness of the symbolism exposes the machinery of normalization, the coerciveness of what Lacan would call the symbolic order. (Siegfried, victim of a Dickensian childhood, enters that order belatedly; hence the hurry.)

Like Hagen's "autism," Siegfried's lack of desire for Brünnhilde is not just a negativity, but a destructive force. The object of hostility is, of course, the former object of desire, whose presence at the desire's point of origin almost has the power to reawaken it. Siegfried's rejection of this reawakening fuels the cruelty of his actions. When Siegfried-as-Gunther reenters the ring of magic fire that once mirrored his desire and protected it from the world, Brünnhilde asks him who he is. His voice falters as he replies; the voice he assumes, deeper than his own *(dann redet er mit verstellter—tieferer— Stimme an)*—the voice in which he hears Gunther but in which we can hear Hagen—quavers a moment *(mit etwas bebender Stimme beginnend)*. Just for that moment, Siegfried's surly Gunther-music catches in his throat. The words that would reawaken desire are on the tip of his tongue. No matter: it is too late for old flames.

The sheer strangeness of the love between Siegfried and Brünnhilde helps make sense of this outcome. At the end of *Siegfried,* the couple achieve a sexual consummation that the music tells us is unparalleled. But no sooner has Siegfried loved Brünnhilde than both agree (in the Prologue to *Götter-dämmerung*) that he has to leave her. His love for her constitutes a heroic ideal; it is meant to guide his conduct as an image, not to constrain him by domestic or sexual demands. Although Siegfried's relationship to Brünn-hilde is consummated by a sexual act, it is not a sexual relationship. Only Gutrune offers him that. Torn between these women, Siegfried suffers from a particularly subtle and perplexed form of the infamous nineteenth-century division of all women into either objects of love or objects of desire. In seizing Brünnhilde for Gunther, he is trying to choose desire over love. But he can do that only if he violates the bond of love with the maximum of brutality. That is why the abduction scene assumes a ritualistic, quasi-sacrificial form, crowned by a piercing scream from Brünnhilde and her collapse "like something shattered" *(Sie schreit heftig auf . . . sie wie zer-brochen in seinen Armen niedersinkt)*. And that is why the music of the scene is so full of gloating malevolence; the ponderous fanfares of heavy brass, pretending to judicial gravity, are Hagen's serenade. The violent two-note figure that punctuates the end of the scene even bears comparison to Hagen's "Hoiho." Deep-voiced and false-faced, Siegfried is Hagen's mouthpiece here. Yet Hagen, through this mouthpiece, once again speaks the truth. Siegfried's abuse of Brünnhilde is the positive, aggressive form of his disavowed desire for her. In that form it will feed his garden-variety desire for Gutrune, to whom he will boast about his exploit when he gets home. It's a kind of foreplay.[24]

Poor Siegfried: he can't hold on to the phallus because his penis keeps getting in the way. Even after his marriage, he is tempted by the charms of the Rhinemaidens, like Alberich before him. Except in the dragon and fire business, he is really a very ordinary fellow. His charisma can be restored only through his death—only, indeed, through his corpse: by the unknown power that raises his dead fist to keep the ring from Hagen's grasp, by the mourning community brought into being through the orchestra's funeral music, and above all by Brünnhilde with her heart and voice set on immolation. By comparison, Siegfried's own self-restoration in his dying moments is a smallish thing. Yet it is not a contemptible thing. In its own way, as Siegfried once again chooses love over desire, heroic truth over social fabrication, and as the orchestra wraps him in a shroud of lyricism, his death is a kind of minor *Liebestod*.

CURTAIN

In the readings offered here, these constructions of Opera by Whitman, Freud's patient, and something in Wagner—it is not quite Wagner himself— all tend to support the same conclusion. Let me approach a first formulation by recalling Godard. In exposing the relation of prostitution to bourgeois luxury, *Two or Three Things I Know about Her* employs a classic technique of unmasking by which the abnormal is shown to be the hidden truth of the normal. Opera, in contrast, suspends the difference between the normal and abnormal, so that the two terms can neither supply each other's truth nor fail to do so.

In order to make this point more rigorously, I will frame it twice more, first deconstructively, then psychoanalytically. First, then, Opera suspends the difference between the normal and the abnormal by presenting each of these terms as always already enmeshed in the movement of *différance*, always already the trace of a presence "that dislocates itself, displaces itself, refers itself [elsewhere]" en route to the semantic "explosion" of dissemination (24). Opera, indeed, opens up something that Derrida regards as impossible, a veritable "kingdom of *différance*" (22). For Derrida, *différance* is "definitively exempt from every process of presentation by means of which we would call upon it to show itself in person" (20). It never becomes perceptible in itself, but only in textual traces. Opera seems bent on revoking this limitation. Its *différance* appears materially, seductively, in and as the bodily interplay between singing voice, instrumental envelope, and receptive ear.

Second, Opera suspends the difference between the normal and the abnormal by suspending the "deeper" differences supposed to ground this proximate one: the differences between policing and transgressing, edifi cation and debasement, the symbolic and the imaginary, eros and the death drive. One consequence, already implicit throughout this chapter, is that Opera constitutively undermines its own aesthetic pretensions. Opera is always in danger of being exposed as a purveyor of what Freud called the "forepleasure" that screens fantasy;[25] Opera as high art continually risks being reduced to an alibi for the practical art of psychosexual equivocation.

In response, we might look for evidence to support the alibi; some alibis, after all, are true. But we might also choose to believe our ears. We might recognize Opera as part of a historical project that required the *ingredients* of aesthetic pretension and forepleasure, alibi and equivocation, regardless of how they fit together in any given case. Among recent critical theorists, Philippe Lacoue-Labarthe has emphasized the persistence of a quasi-sacramental operatic aesthetic from the Florentines through Wagner and beyond, while Žižek and Avital Ronell have emphasized the parallel persistence of irreducible difference, both within operatic subjectivity and in the "broken contract" between music and language.[26] These disparate insights are bound together by their common concern with the process of "binding" itself. Opera, on this reading, would register both an urgent and historically specific need for such binding, as if, in the age of Opera, human subjectivity had somehow come undone. The most familiar name for that coming undone, a name that also applies to widening circles of experience during the age of Opera, is modernity. Could it be, then, that Opera is part of a broad cultural effort that first crystallizes in the early-modern period and has only recently, if at all, begun to wane? Could Opera be part of an effort to deal with a human subjectivity understood—I would say *formulated*, designed to be understood—as a tendency to wander, a potential aberrance or ab-normality, that becomes intelligible only by means of the techniques meant to regulate it?

2 Contesting Wagner

The Lohengrin *Prelude and Anti–anti-Semitism*

The pinnacle of fame for a piece of music is often marked by its composer's attainment of anonymity: fame to a higher power, the social construction of the universal. How many couples who walk down the aisle to the wedding march from Wagner's *Lohengrin* have any idea who its composer was, or suspect that the marriage originally celebrated by this music was, let's say, less than successful? How many who follow tradition and finish the ceremony with the wedding march from Mendelssohn's incidental music to *A Midsummer Night's Dream* have any inkling that they're pairing the arch–anti-Semite of Western music with his one named musical nemesis in the infamous article "Judaism in Music"? In a work of fiction such turns of fate would be ironic, but there is no real irony here, even in the culmination of fame in transcendental obscurity, because history has no author: there is no ironist. What there is instead is an instance of the ordinary workings of cultural signification, which is not always user-friendly. Appropriations like that of the wedding marches are mechanical, not allusive, mere cogs in the citation machine of culture in which phrases, signifiers, tropes, images, and gestures are endlessly recycled and redeployed with little or no reference to their "original" contexts. This process has usually been interpreted in antihumanistic terms to suggest that even the most deliberate allusions smack of the mechanical. Even fictional irony is more than a little fictitious. But it is equally plausible to make the counterclaim that even the most relentless mechanism can become allusive, and hence be resurgently humanized, much as abstract computer-generated forms tend, once set in motion, to become lifelike.

Take the case of *Lohengrin* in particular—a case that has been haunting me of late.[1] The relevant music here is less the wedding march (which will, however, come up again) than the Prelude, a piece that has been programmatically recycled by an unusually distinguished list of figures, including Liszt, Baudelaire, W. E. B. Du Bois, and Charlie Chaplin, not to mention Wagner himself, who does not occupy the "original" place in this series. To focus the issue, begin at the end, with Chaplin, whose 1940 film *The Great Dictator* uses the *Lohengrin* Prelude as the underscore to what quickly became its two most famous sequences: a silent solo dance number for Chaplin as Adenoid Hynkel, the film's travesty Hitler, and an impassioned anti-Nazi speech by Hynkel's double, a Jewish barber also played by Chaplin, who at this point slips out of character to become Chaplin himself. To a moviegoer unfamiliar with Wagner, the soundtrack would still have sounded familiar because Wagner's musical rhetoric, in the higher fame of anonymity, had already become part and parcel of the classical Hollywood narrative film. But Chaplin is obviously engaging with Wagner's music and its legacy on intimate and critical terms; he is tinkering with the mechanism of citation to notify Wagner's ghost that this music has been turned against the Hynkel-like values it was meant to serve and, better yet, that Chaplin will retrospectively have prevented Wagner from perverting his own music to serve those values, which the music itself innately opposes.

In what follows, I suggest that Chaplin is only finishing what Franz Liszt started: a series of appropriations of the *Lohengrin* Prelude that are inconsistent with the cultural and political values of the opera and its composer—ecumenical messages that, for Liszt and Chaplin, are also specifically anti–anti-Semitic. These figurative messages enormously complicate both the vexed question of anti-Semitism in Wagner's music and the wider, if less ethically pressing, question of the role that "original" contexts play in the determination of musical meaning. By turning the citation machine into a smart device, an artificial intelligence, it is often possible to contest or override "original" meanings without in the least effacing them. This is not to say that preferred meanings are retrospectively installed in violation of the music's integral character, but to make precisely this kind of claim appear dubious and simplistic. No particular meaning or set of meanings emerges as authoritative from this process; what does so emerge is a proliferating series of dialectical or dialogical relationships between the sonorous and semantic dimensions of the music. It may quickly appear, though, that even this seemingly complex formula is too simple.

1

Too simple, certainly, to deal with Liszt, whose intervention with the *Lohengrin* Prelude is both implicit and marginal. To my knowledge, it has never been noticed, and was probably never meant to be. It consists of just a few sentences from the program that Liszt constructed for the Prelude shortly after giving the opera's first performance, which took place at the end of August 1850. The program formed part of an article about the opera that was first published in October of that year and republished in book form, with an earlier article of Liszt's on *Tannhäuser*, in 1851. The sentences look innocuous enough:

> This introduction encompasses and reveals the mystic element always present and always hidden in the piece [i.e., the opera], the divine secret, the supernatural force, the supreme law of the characters' destiny and of the chain of events we are about to contemplate. To teach us the unrepresentable [*inénarrable*, literally "un-narratable"] power of this secret, Wagner first shows us the ineffable beauty of the sanctuary, inhabited by a God who avenges the oppressed [*venge les opprimés*] and asks nothing but love and faith from His worshipers [*ses fidèles*]. He [Wagner] initiates us into the Holy Grail: he causes to shimmer before our eyes the temple of incorruptible woods, with fragrant walls, doors of gold [etc.].[2]

The crux of this passage is the conclusion of the second sentence, which stands out from its larger context because of its seeming irrelevance, even its contradictoriness. The whole opera, Liszt says, is governed by a mystical secret, something so unrepresentable that Wagner's Prelude avoids giving it direct expression, instead focusing on the sanctuary that houses it.[3] Despite this ineffability, Liszt strangely appends a pair of stipulations about divine justice and grace. He then ignores these entirely, going on to give a detailed physical description of the sanctuary itself, the revelation of which will eventually be correlated to the musical unfolding of the Prelude. The conceptual content of the stipulations clearly lies outside the expressive scope of the Prelude as Liszt constructs it.

What are these clauses doing here? And why ask? They can certainly be read as the boilerplate of a sentimental religiosity, and/or loosely linked to the plot of the opera, but if one pauses to think about them they raise some nagging questions. Why, in what seems a purely celebratory context, do they strike a tone of admonition, warning that God above all avenges those oppressed and warding off external tests for membership in the community of the faithful in favor of purely internal criteria? With respect to the exposition that follows, nothing would be lost by not asking these questions. But if we do ask them, it becomes possible to understand Liszt's stipulations as his effort to put a personal imprint on an opera to which he was ardently devoted and in which he took, with considerable justification, a proprietary interest. (Not only had he dared to stage it while its composer was a wanted criminal in Germany, he had rehearsed it an unheard-of forty-one times. He knew it better than Wagner did.) It becomes possible, too, to see this imprint as a reaction against Wagner's anti-Semitism, which, as it happens, would begin its rise to notoriety just one week after the premiere of *Lohengrin*.

Pursuing these notions, of course, risks making too much of a trifle—the interpreter, to recall H. G. Wells's jibe at Henry James, as Leviathan fetching a pea—but in this case the littleness may be deceptive. It is possible to take Liszt's stipulations, not as simple statements, but as speech acts situated among many others to be found in the Liszt-Wagner correspondence of the early 1850s, and culminating in Wagner's own version of a program for the *Lohengrin* Prelude, written in 1853, which contains stipulations of its own. Within these textual borders, Liszt and Wagner played out an unspoken struggle over where to position *Lohengrin* with regard to Wagner's cultural politics, especially in their uglier aspect.

Tracking this contest requires us to go deep into the sphere of illocution, the performative, implication, intimation, a place where nothing is certain, not only to us but also to the original contestants. Yet this uncertainty is not a barrier against interpretive intervention but rather a call for it; no discourse is immunized against a generalized performativity, and it is certainly possible to suggest with greater or lesser degrees of confidence what may plausibly have been involved in a series of richly contextualized speech acts.

But the story needs to be told with a certain indirection in order to put all the relevant information in place. The minute particulars are interesting in themselves, but their significance, and even their type of significance, will emerge fairly late in the game. Following the story, I should add, also involves reading some of Wagner's anti-Semitic texts more closely than usual. Noxious though they are, both their style and their argument can be revealing.

2

In the spring of 1849 Wagner sent the manuscript of *Lohengrin* to Liszt, who received it warmly, but with a note of caution: "The admirable score of *Lohengrin* has interested me profoundly; nevertheless I fear at the performance the *superideal* color you have maintained throughout."[4] The experience of performing the opera turned Liszt's warmth to fervor, and on exactly the superideal grounds that had earlier given him pause:

> Your *Lohengrin* is a sublime work from one end to the other. The tears rose from my heart in more than one place. The whole opera being one indivisible wonder, I cannot stop to point out any particular passage, combination, or effect. A pious ecclesiastic once underlined word for word the

whole *Imitatio Christi;* in the same way I might underline your *Lohen-grin* note for note. In that case, however, I should like to begin at the end; that is, at the duet between Elsa and Lohengrin in the third act, which to my thinking is the acme of the beautiful and true in art. (2 September 1850; CWL 87)

This passage contains the germs of the two ideas, the mystical sublimity of the opera and its formal continuity, that Liszt's later essay would develop. But the passage is unusual. Most of the Liszt-Wagner correspondence about *Lohengrin* focuses on practical matters: first on whether Liszt was willing and able to stage the opera, then on how it could be staged effectively. On three occasions, however, the correspondence moved onto trickier territory that brought *Lohengrin* into proximity with Wagner's infamous anti-Semitic screed "Judaism in Music" (Das Judenthum in der Musik), which appeared under a pseudonym in the *Neue Zeitschrift für Musik* on 3 and 6 September 1850.

The first of these is probably just a coincidence, but one with a symbolic potential that may have been activated in retrospect. Liszt began working on his *Lohengrin* essay within two weeks of the publication of Wagner's Judaism article. He writes Wagner on 25 September to inform him about the essay-in-progress and to request that Wagner supervise a German translation from Liszt's original French. It is impossible to say whether "Judaism in Music" played any part in Liszt's decision to write about *Lohengrin*. The 25th of September, after all, is also just three weeks after the premiere of the opera, and we do not know exactly when Liszt read "Judaism in Music" and when he surmised Wagner's authorship, though he had certainly done both by the spring of the following year. Still, Liszt knew both Wagner's aesthetics and his literary style very well by this point. It is hard to believe that he would have remained oblivious or indifferent to the nearly simultaneous appearance of the article and the opera—"his" opera—once he had done the reading and made the surmise. As we will see, he came to regard anti-Semitism and superideal creativity as indicative of the warring principles of Wagner's character. At this early moment, however, what comes across most clearly is the importance Liszt set on his essay. He clearly wanted to stake a claim as the principal interpreter of *Lohengrin*:

In a week or so I shall send you a *very long* article of mine about *Lohen-grin*. If personal reasons of your own do not prevent it, it will appear in Paris in the course of October. You are sufficiently acquainted with the habits of the Paris press to know how reluctantly it admits the entire and absolute eulogium of a foreign composer, especially while he is still living. In spite of this, I shall try to overcome this great obstacle, for I make it a point of honor to publish my opinion of your work; and if you were fairly satisfied with my article, you might perhaps give me a pleasure that would not cost you more than a day or two of tedium. This would be to make a translation, revised, corrected, augmented, and authenticated, which [could be published] signed with my name. . . . You will see that the style is carefully French, and it would therefore be very important not to destroy the nuances of sentiment and thought in their passage to another language. (25 September 1850; CWL 110–11)

Although his tone is courtly to the point of deference, Liszt is quietly insisting that his account of the opera be honored down to the last nuance. In the event, the translation would take considerably more than a few days to make, revise, correct, augment, and authenticate.

Its impending publication was the prompt for a well-known exchange of letters in April 1851, the exchange that led Wagner to declare that his anti-Semitism was as necessary to him as gall to the blood. Liszt must understand that the bile of "Judaism in Music" is paradoxically necessary for both Wagner's health and his racial purity—the image of blood is telling. Liszt elicits this declaration, and much more, by asking, like Elsa, a forbidden question. And he does so precisely in the environment both of *Lohengrin* and of the German version of his article about it, a copy of which he sends to Wagner for proofreading along with his letter.

Liszt begins on a note of apology: he has been in too much trouble and distress to write. But he quickly turns to what really interests Wagner, namely, Wagner. He reports that a performance of *Lohengrin* in Weimar has had to be postponed, but that the opera will nonetheless be given twice during the current season. He mentions his article, asks Wagner to read proof *quickly*, and discusses publication plans for the French version. More business follows: a long paragraph on money matters—Wagner was constantly badgering Liszt for money—and a word of assurance about a new supporter, Franz Müller. The letter can be picked up at this point, just before Liszt's bombshell of a non sequitur:

Müller's letter I sent yesterday. . . . He will doubtless soon write to you, and you will find him a trustworthy, prudent friend, who genuinely esteems you.

Can you tell me, under the seal of the most absolute secrecy, whether the famous article on the Jews in music in Brendel's paper is by you?

The Princess has remained in Eilsen, still confined to her bed. . . . You may imagine how deeply her long illness has grieved me.

Write soon, and do not forget to correct the proofs . . . at once.

Your, F. Liszt

P.S.—The "Lohengrin" article must be signed thus: "From the French of
F. Liszt." Request the printer's reader kindly not to omit this and to call
the editor's special attention to it.

(9 April 1851; CWL 142)

Why did Liszt throw in the question about "Judaism in Music," seemingly
apropos of nothing? Wagner wondered, too, and his response, which needs
to be examined in detail, suggests a credible answer. For the moment, we
can simply note that Liszt seems unusually anxious about his *Lohengrin*
essay and that his anxiety goes beyond seeing the essay handled quickly to
making sure that it appears over his signature, a topic also alluded to in his
first letter to Wagner about it. We can note, too, the pointed contrast between Liszt's insistence on signing his own name and Wagner's use of an
obvious pseudonym for "Judaism."[5]

Wagner's reply begins with effusive thanks and praise, then picks up the
gauntlet. I will quote the relevant portions of his letter piecemeal, with comments interspersed:

> You ask me about the "Judaism." You must know that the article is by
> me. Why do you ask? (18 April 1851; CWL 145)

The force of Wagner's question is to suggest that Liszt's should not be
taken literally; its real object is something other than the authorship of "Judaism," which Liszt must surely know. The lengthy discussion that follows
proves the point by being, strictly speaking, superfluous. The literal question has been asked and answered, but Wagner continues in order to answer
the real question, which he correctly surmises to be important.

His first impulse is to hear Liszt asking *why* rather than *whether:*

> Not from fear, but only to avoid that the Jews should drag this question
> into bare personality, I appear in a pseudonymous capacity. I felt a long-
> suppressed hatred for this Jewry, and this hatred is as necessary to my
> nature as gall is to the blood. An opportunity arose when their damnable
> scribbling annoyed me most, and so I broke forth at last. It seems to have
> made a tremendous impression, and that pleases me, for I really only
> wanted to frighten them in this manner; that they will remain the mas-
> ters is as certain as that not our princes, but the bankers and the Philistines,
> are nowadays our masters.

Three separate self-justifications are woven into this passage, each implicitly meant to ward off a condemning judgment that might be lurking behind Liszt's mildly worded question. First (to paraphrase): why did I hide
behind a pseudonym like a coward or a sneak? It was a point of honor: the

topic is too important to be written off as mere personal griping. Second: why did I write this at all? I couldn't do otherwise; my health and character (which you, Liszt, value so highly) depend on the cathartic release of my hatred. Third: why did I write so savagely? I was just trying to throw a scare into these people. Don't take the savagery too seriously: I may have made a tremendous impression, but nothing will come of it. The Jews are in control; I'm just a harmless gadfly.

The last of these points is particularly important because it renews the language of "Judaism in Music" itself. By the 1840s, the traditional association of Jews with money had evolved into an identification of Judaism with the heartless domination of modern capital, the outcome of which was a universal alienation from true humanity and organic society. With some help from Karl Marx himself, anti-Semitism grafted itself onto a critique of "political economy" that had no need for it. Marx's essay of 1843 "On the Jewish Question," a work often compared to Wagner's "Judaism," had formulated the new trope memorably:

> What is the worldly cult of the Jew? *Hucksterism.* What is worldly god? *Money.* . . . Money is the jealous God of Israel, beside which no other god may exist. Money abases all the gods of mankind and changes them into commodities. Money is the universal and self-sufficient *value* of all things. It has, therefore, deprived the whole world, both the human world and nature, of their own proper value.[6]

Wagner sets up his own argument in similar terms. He uses the trope of Jewish capital to ground his claim that the mark of Jewish influence in art is aesthetic debasement:

> Quite imperceptibly the "Creditor of Kings" [*Gläubiger der Königen*] has become the King of Creeds [*Könige der Gläubigen*], and we really cannot take this monarch's pleading for emancipation as otherwise than uncommonly naive, seeing that it is rather *we* who are shifted into the necessity of fighting for emancipation from the Jews. According to the present constitution of this world, the Jew in truth is already more than emancipated: he rules, and will rule, so long as money remains the power before which we and all our doings and dealings [*Thun und Trieben*] lose their force.[7]

Wagner's letter says as much to Liszt, who is expected to tolerate the idea, if not assent to it, because as an artist and man of the world he opposes the rule of the Philistines. Wagner's chiasmatic rhetoric, the wordplay at the beginning of the passage and the larger reversal of the oppressed and the oppressor, is also noteworthy; its significance will emerge later on.

Wagner continues with an analysis of his relationship to Meyerbeer, his nameless nemesis in the Judaism article. The guiding thread in this passage is the need for difference, which is cast in terms of a crisis of self-recognition. Wagner all but says that he must polarize himself as man and artist against this Other who threatens to become his double:

> Towards Meyerbeer my position is a peculiar one. I do not hate him but he disgusts me beyond measure. This eternally amiable and pleasant man reminds me of the most turbid, not to say most vicious, period of my life, when he pretended to be my protector; that was a period of connections and back stairs when we are made fools of by our protectors, whom in our inmost heart we do not like. . . . As an artist I cannot exist before myself and my friends, I cannot think or feel, without realizing and confessing my absolute antagonism to Meyerbeer, and to this I am driven with genuine desperation when I meet with the erroneous opinion even among my friends that I have anything in common with Meyerbeer. Before none of my friends can I appear in clear and definite form, with all that I desire and feel, unless I separate myself entirely from the nebulous outline in which many see me. (CWL 145–46)

This passage includes a tacit rebuke to Liszt, who had remarked in his *Lohengrin* essay that Meyerbeer anticipated Wagner—who of course has far surpassed him—in the use of recurrent melody to capture the full psychology of character.[8] But for Wagner any comparison with Meyerbeer threatens to erode the boundaries of his identity. The threat is both internal (Meyerbeer is disgusting, he must be expelled) and external (he puts the figure of Wagner under a cloud). At this point, however, the specifically Jewish dimension of that threat has faded from view. The real accomplishment of this passage has been to shift the discussion onto the high ground of artistic integrity and away from "Judaism in Music" altogether.

Nonetheless, Wagner turns back to the Jewish question because he realizes that Liszt's question, the real one, has still not been answered. That question is not a *why* but a *whither*. Liszt is about to anoint Wagner as the great musical genius of the age, the redeemer and transfigurer of opera. What he needs to know is what kind of commitment he is making. Does love for Wagner's music demand agreement with his politics? Is swallowing the bile of "Judaism in Music" required to enjoy the manna of *Lohengrin?* Wagner is more than happy to be generous on this point:

> What you will think of this—that—just imagine—I do not as yet know exactly. I know who you are and perfectly feel what you are, and yet it must appear to me as if in this point you could not as yet be entirely your own self. But enough of this. There are earthly things on which we may

occasionally be of different opinion without ever parting from each other in divine things. If you don't approve of something here, shut your eyes to it. (CWL 146–47)

So of course it is possible to be a Wagner-lover without being a Jew-hater, even if Wagner says this with a certain veiled regret: Liszt would be truer to himself if he grasped the truth and necessity of the anti-Semitic credo. But good friends can agree to disagree, and besides, art, the heavenly thing, comes first. The Jewish question is a worldly matter, and Wagner, "perfectly" knowing and feeling what Liszt is, can trust his friend's worldly wisdom. He guesses correctly that Liszt, though no anti-Semite himself, will be willing to tolerate anti-Semitism in those close to him. (Besides Wagner himself, the list of intimates would include the Princess Wittgenstein, Hans von Bülow, and of course Cosima Liszt, the future Frau Wagner.) Wagner can thus afford to close with an imperative—"shut your eyes to it"—that reads equally well as a plea for indulgence and a grant of permission.

3

Matters might well have ended there had Wagner been willing to restrain himself. He wasn't. The exchange about "Judaism in Music" marks a turning point in his correspondence with Liszt. Prior to it, Wagner's letters contain not a single word about the Jews. Subsequent to it, nasty anti-Semitic remarks can pop up at any time. They amount altogether to no more than a small handful, but they carry gall. For the most part, Liszt follows Wagner's bidding and studiously shuts his eyes to them, though his silence might also be taken to imply disapproval. In April 1853, however, he made an exception.

Writing from Zurich on 20 March, Wagner urges Liszt to make good on a promised visit:

My impatience *to see you* grows into a most violent passion. . . . On May 22nd I shall be forty. Then I shall have myself rebaptized; would you not like to be my godfather? I wish *we two* could start straight from here to go into the wide world. I wish you, too, would leave these German Philistines and Jews. Have you anything else around you? Add the Jesuits, and then you have all. "Philistines, Jews, and Jesuits," that is it; no human beings. (CWL 272)

This toxic brew of deep personal feeling, overheated dreams of comradeship, and raging bigotry was apparently more than Liszt could stomach in silence. His reply is remarkably generous, especially given Wagner's fantasy of rescuing him from the society of subhuman beings. The passage requires quotation in full:

> Your letters are sad; your life is still sadder. You want to go out into the wide world to live, to enjoy, to luxuriate. I should only be too glad if you could, but do you not feel that the sting and the wound you have in your own heart will leave you nowhere and can never be cured? Your greatness is your misery; both are inseparably connected, and must pain and torture you until you kneel down and let both be merged in *faith*.
>
> "Let yourself be converted to faith anew; it is happiness"; this is the only thing that is true and eternal. I cannot preach to you, nor explain it to you; but I will pray to God that He may powerfully illuminate your heart through His faith and His love. You may scoff at this feeling as bitterly as you like. I cannot fail to see and desire in it the only salvation. Through Christ alone, through resigned suffering in God, salvation and rescue come to us. (8 April 1851; CWL 273)

Liszt does important work here with his speaking silences. By ignoring his own role as sidekick in Wagner's wanderer fantasy, and declining even to decline rescue from the Jews and Philistines, Liszt brushes off both proposals. But he does so mainly to clear the air. For perhaps the first and only time in their correspondence, he will speak from his own deepest feelings. Wagner's precious gall is stinging and wounding Wagner himself. His only cure is to rid himself of it by an inward turn to faith, as opposed to the pseudoritual of a new baptism—another topic Liszt politely ignores. What Wagner thinks of as the cure is actually the disease.

The principles Liszt invokes in these remarks closely parallel the stipulations in his program for the *Lohengrin* Prelude. The link to the stipulation of love and faith is obvious. Wagner can find rescue only through the faith of a heart that has been illuminated by God's own love and faith. The change of heart would relieve him of the festering hatred expressed most forcibly in his anti-Semitism. The link to the stipulation of justice is less direct, but no less firm. The statement in the program can be taken as both a comfort to the oppressed, whom God avenges, and a warning to the oppressor, on whom the vengeance falls. But there may be more. Liszt's most likely Biblical source suggests a reading that meshes closely with the advice he offers in his letter:

> If it be possible, as much as lieth in you, live peaceably with all men. Dearly beloved, avenge not yourselves, but rather give place unto wrath: for it is written, Vengeance is mine; I will repay, saith the Lord. (Romans 12:18–19)

As Liszt knew well, Wagner banked heavily on the anti-Semitic bromide that the Jews are the true rulers from whom "we" need emancipation. From Wagner's standpoint, *he* is the oppressed. In light of this feeling, the clause in the program can be read to carry the same message as the advice in the letter. Knowing that Wagner needs to feel oppressed as a spur to his art (his greatness and misery are inseparable), Liszt concentrates on the outcome of the feeling rather than its cause. Don't yield to hatred, he says, however oppressed you feel; resign your wrath to God and suffer resignedly in Him.

Of course, the program was not addressed to Wagner but to the public, and there is nothing in its stipulations that explicitly addresses the Jewish question. But the stipulations are, if not philo-Semitic, at least anti–anti-Semitic. They are so because they are ecumenical, the maxims of a mystical Christianity that offers salvation to any illuminated human heart. Their presence in the program may have been meant as a quiet reassurance to audiences that the opera, like its champion, Liszt, does not subscribe to the message of "Judaism in Music." More certainly, their presence is a small mark of Liszt's identification with the opera, a little hermeneutic hook that binds *Lohengrin* fast to the "ideal mysticity" that Liszt had found in it from the beginning. Or shift the figure: the stipulations are like a brushstroke by which one painter at once restores and alters a canvass by another. Liszt's *Lohengrin* is not really Wagner's. It is not really a tragedy, because its music constantly reembodies the divine order that its human characters fail to uphold. It is not subject to the charge of spiritual elitism courted by the image of the Grail brotherhood because its music anticipates and refutes the charge: the Prelude itself initiates any listener, even German Philistines and Jews, into the Grail. The composer of Liszt's *Lohengrin* is less the historical Wagner than the wishful figure constructed in Liszt's letter of advice.

Both men seemed inclined to shut their eyes to this split, but the historical Wagner, understandably enough, still wanted the last word. Within a month of receiving Liszt's letter, he began writing his own program for the *Lohengrin* Prelude, which he would soon conduct in Zurich. His work was guided, however, as much by Liszt's program as by his own music. He says as much in an impromptu letter of thanks that also credits Liszt's faith in *Lohengrin* with rescuing him from depressive self-doubt (9 May 1853; CWL 282–83); the beginning of his letter on "Judaism in Music" had expressed similar feelings. On the surface, the result is an exemplary meeting of minds between artists and friends. In many respects Wagner's program is closely modeled on Liszt's. Both involve the gradual appearance and more rapid dissipation of a divine vision accompanied by what Baudelaire, noting the similarity in 1861, called "the sensation of spiritual and physical bliss."[9] Both use the same idiom of sensuous, heavily scented religiosity. But Wagner has recontextualized the visionary narrative so that it takes place in a world more harmonious with "Judaism in Music" than with Liszt's stipulations, which, needless to say, do not make the cut.

The nucleus of Wagner's revision seems to have formed in his reply to Liszt's letter of advice. Where Liszt offers divine love, Wagner puts the quest for a human love that has vanished from the world: "The state of lovelessness is the state of suffering for the human race; the fullness of this suffering surrounds us now, and tortures your friend with a thousand burning wounds" (13 April 1853; CWL 278). But the wounds are cured by the spear that made them: the key to a love-filled future is precisely the painful recognition of lovelessness as the error of the present. Wagner makes no connection here between the crisis of lovelessness and the rule of capital that, in "Judaism in Music" and elsewhere, he equates with oppression by the Jews. But that is precisely what he does do at the very beginning of his program for *Lohengrin*:

> Out of a world of scorn and squabbling *[des Hasses und des Haders]* love seemed to have vanished: in no community of men did it still clearly show itself the lawgiver. Out of the barren care for profit and property *[der öden Sorge für Gewinn und Besitz]*, the sole organizer of worldly traffic *[Weltverkehres]*, the deathless love-longing of the human heart finally yearned again after the requital of a need that, the more ardently and irrepressibly it mounted under the pressure of reality, the less it was satisfied in this reality. (179)

It is important to tread lightly here. The condemnation of a world in which money replaces love can certainly be taken at face value. But for the Wagner of "Judaism in Music," as for the Marx of "The Jewish Question," money means modern capital, and the role of the Jews in its triumph over love goes without saying.

Wagner, at any rate, had said it plainly enough in his essay, which tells us that the assimilated Jew in particular is barren in his relations to an organic society: "He stands in relation only with those who need his money. . . . If he has any sort of relationship to [our] society, it must be to that offshoot that is utterly cut off from its true, healthy root; but this relationship is entirely loveless, and this lovelessness must become ever more obvious to him" (74, 75). Such resonances do not mean that Wagner's program, let alone the *Lohengrin* Prelude itself, can be boiled down to a crypto–anti-Semitic subtext. What they do mean is that the program is framed, and frames the Prelude, in terms consistent with the anti-Semitic worldview to which Wagner also clung.

4

Wagner's revisions do not stop with these few sentences. They ripple over into both the narrative form of the program and the modulations of its style, each of which carries on the shift in worldview initiated by the opposition of love and money.

The narrative form is Wagner's trademark movement from debasement to transfiguration, fallenness to redemption: already old news when the exasperated Max Nordau bemoaned it in his best-selling polemic of 1895, *Degeneration*.[10] The terms of debasement correspond to the "thousand burning wounds" of alienated modern existence, which the premodern settings of the operas universalize and mythify. Wagner's diagnosis of modernity depends on a large fund of equivalences that the operas can both leave openended and evoke without making definite commitments to any particular item. Some of the chief interchangeable terms are lovelessness, rootlessness, capital, the loss of the purely human, the failure of European civilization, and, of course, Judaism. In his program for the *Lohengrin* Prelude, Wagner installed a historicized redemption narrative precisely where Liszt had omitted one. Liszt describes the visionary revelation of a perennially existing shrine, the mystical guarantee of love and justice from a God whose presence in history is constant. Wagner describes a unique historical event, the delivery of the Grail to "highly favored *[hochbeglückte]* men." This event conceals the divine presence from all but a few and structures history itself as a lack. History unfolds outside the Grail temple in a world where the "pure" are consecrated to "fight for eternal Love." But the structuring event itself is purely fictitious. Wagner describes the Grail as a symbol that was invented to compensate for the world's lovelessness by setting the origin and end of love outside the world. The true structuring event was not the descent of the Grail but the invention of the Grail myth. Where Liszt's *Lohengrin* Prelude embodies Christian faith, Wagner's provides a Christian symbolization for a historical crisis that is purely human.

That crisis belongs to the nineteenth century and can at least be brought into parallel with the nineteenth-century crisis described in "Judaism in Music." The impression of contemporary urgency is built into the narrative structure (as opposed to the narrative type) of the program itself.

Another comparison may be helpful here. For the overtures to his other two Romantic operas, *Der fliegende Holländer* and *Tannhäuser*, Wagner wrote programs consisting of simple present-tense narratives: without a context, without an identifiable narrator, and with little or no reference to the music except as part of the narrated action. The implication (which Wagner spells out in the *Lohengrin* program) is that the music and the visual images suggested by the narratives form the halves of an intelligible but unrealizable whole. Any realization would have to wait for the combination of synchronous soundtrack and the moving image, perhaps especially in animated film: Wagner was anticipating *Fantasia*.

The *Lohengrin* program is very different. It uses a present-tense Grail narrative that makes no reference to the music, but it does so only after embedding the narrative in a double frame. First comes the crisis narrative of lovelessness, written in the past tense but with reference to no specific historical moment, only to a world obsessed by greed that turns out to be continuous with the present. The historical crisis thus registers simultaneously in the legendary time of the Grail and the historical time from which Wagner is narrating. As the account of the crisis indicates, progress toward resolution requires the invention of a symbolically potent narrative, which in turn requires the intervention of an authoritative narrator. This requirement leads to the second frame, a transitional passage in which Wagner appears in person as Lohengrin's tone-poet and then, shifting from past tense to present, claims the powers of representation *(Darstellung)* and dramatic presentation *(Vorstellungskraft)* and announces the Grail narrative.[11] His musical imagination has allowed him to write as an eyewitness: a surrogate Grail knight. The ensuing narrative is thus doubly anointed as the antidote to a world debased by too much money and too little love, with all that may imply. Just as important, though, is the shift from Liszt's mode of narrative time, which excludes historical crisis and radical debasement, to Wagner's, which first installs these things and then draws both expressive and ideological urgency from the encounter with them.

The Grail narrative also heats up the program's already fervid prose style to a degree that, while no rarity for Wagner, may also share some of its feverishness with his anti-Semitism. The spark for this connection remains the love-money topic, but the connection itself, like its narrative counterpart, is not topical but structural. It also touches on dimensions of Wagner's anti-Semitism that go beyond the inciting topic, which, as John Deathridge notes in relation to "Judaism in Music," is "only a prelude . . . to a jungle of biological metaphor and jingoistic palaver . . . that vilifies Jews on a personal level and burdens them collectively with the 'curse' of Ahasuerus and the prospect of 'redemption' through self-willed 'destruction' [*Untergang*]."[12]

5

To follow this lead requires a detour through critical theory. Slavoj Žižek has recently developed several models of the psychological-ideological basis of racial and ethnic hatred. Two of these in particular, and more particularly the gap between them, should prove helpful here.

The first model identifies the hated figure as a "spectral object" devised to give positive form to an ideological void. If modern society cannot have both "capitalist competition *and* pre-modern solidarity," the desire to have both, anyway, sustains itself by inventing a "specific object" that "gives body to, externalizes, the cause of the non-satisfaction of this desire."[13] In anti-Semitism, which Žižek takes as the paradigmatic case, the figure of the Jew is simply "a filler holding the place of some structural impossibility." Once this figure is installed, all right-thinking people have a duty to abase it. (Hating it becomes as necessary to them as gall is to the blood.) The duty to be inhumane, however, is in conflict with fully internalized moral standards, and it therefore supports itself with the allure of an "obscene" supplement: a publicly unacknowledged pleasure in a common transgressiveness, something typically manifested in excesses of cruelty or verbal abuse.[14]

The second model identifies the hated figure as one who has stolen, or threatens to steal, a pleasure that belongs uniquely to "our" group and therefore guarantees the group's identity and solidarity. Both difference and distance are put at risk. Once in the Other's possession, "our Thing" (the substance of our enjoyment) turns ugly: "What really bothers us about the 'other' is the peculiar way he organizes his enjoyment, precisely the surplus, the 'excess' that pertains to this way: the smell of 'their' food, 'their' noisy songs and dances, 'their' strange manners. . . . The basic paradox is that our Thing is conceived as something inaccessible to the other and at the same time threatened by him." A related paradox is that "our" enjoyment tends to organize itself precisely, not to say obsessively, with reference to the surplus enjoyment of the Other.[15]

Pleasure plays the key role in both these models, but the role is different in each. In the first model we find our pleasure where it doesn't belong; in the second we can't find our pleasure where it does belong. How do the two fit together? The obvious answer, and the one I want to explore here, is that the two are reciprocals: the pleasure cruelly lost in the second model is recovered in the cruelties of the first.

This idea clarifies the relationship in "Judaism in Music" between the "jungle" of metaphor and palaver and the notorious vilification of Jewish bodies ("disagreeably foreign"), speech ("unbearably jumbled blabber"), and song ("gurgle, yodel, and cackle").[16] What is not obvious, given the toxicity of Wagner's message, is that this relationship is as much literary as it is polemical. "Judaism" licenses its verbal excess by incorporating a pair of literary genres in which such excess is the norm.

License itself is the key to the first of these, the Rabelaisian satire that revels shamelessly in the spectacle of debased bodies. The spirit (made familiar by Mikhail Bakhtin) derives from the traditional pre-Lenten carnival, with its exuberant inversion of both physical and social standards of propriety.[17] Wagner's "carnivalesque" writing is pungent but intermittent, reaching its peak in his lengthy denunciation of Jewish speech ("What first strikes our ear as thoroughly outlandish and disagreeable is a hissing, squealing, buzzing, and snuffling vocalization of Jewish speech-style")[18] and lending its force to the climactic metaphor of music infected by Judaism as a decaying corpse ("then the flesh of this body altogether dissolves into a swarming aggregation of worms").[19]

Compared with Rabelais's or Swift's, Wagner's bodily jibes are nasty but modest, a trait explained by the second, and prevailing, genre of his text, Juvenalian or "bitter" satire. Satire has traditionally been divided into two branches based on the Roman models of Horace and Juvenal: one genial and urbane, the other full of "savage indignation" (saeva indignatio). Juvenalian satire combines unlimited ridicule and contempt with a high rhetorical style and an attitude of moral strenuousness. Wagner virtually announces the genre early in his text, when he acknowledges the moral taboo against open expression of anti-Semitism and calls for its violation in the name of honesty and rationality. The prescription is a textbook case of Juvenalian moral logic, and its execution is faithful enough to make further illustration unnecessary.

"Judaism in Music" thus transgressively regains the stolen pleasure of "our Thing" in the forms of scandalousness and grandiosity, the vehicle for which is the excess of its literary language. The two forms also overlap at the point of a further transgression, the shift from strict satire, which targets the generic figure of "the Jew," to lampoon, which targets specific individuals: Mendelssohn, Heine, and especially the unnamed Meyerbeer. The net effect is supposed to give Wagner's prose as such, regardless of its momentary content, the power to sustain ideological desire. As Julia Kristeva suggested of the anti-Semitic writing of Louis Ferdinand Céline, the prose acts out a "delirium" produced by the lack at its core, and in so doing "procure[s] for the subject both *jouissance* and stability which, without the adhesive of delirium, would disintegrate rapidly" and take the subject with them.[20] Something like this effect even seems to be required by the text itself. Wagner's sorest grievance against the Jews is that they cannot express anything "purely human" because they are incapable of speaking idiomatically in the European languages. His own supposed display of linguistic virtuosity would thus fill precisely the lack embodied by "the Jew." But since the gap is impossible to fill, his language can sustain the illusion of filling it only in one way: by constantly growing more delirious.

The Grail narrative of the *Lohengrin* program goes about the same thing a little differently. The Grail's relation to ideological desire is positive rather than negative, but it is no less a spectral object than the hated Other. It, too, holds the place of a structural impossibility. Because it embodies the satisfaction of a desire that can never be satisfied, the Grail is in essence a lost object. Its revelation belongs to a mythical past and its recovery to a constantly postponed future. For this reason, it cannot be represented directly. (*Parsifal* is still a long way off.) Wagner's narrative describes only the perceptual experience that accompanies the vision of the Grail, while also suggesting that the vision paradoxically disappears in the very process of its appearance. To sustain ideological desire, the Grail, too, needs to induce a delirium. Wagner tries to supply one by calling on all the expressive mannerisms of his prose—the hyperbole, the wordplay, the phonetic and grammatical "music"—to concentrate in a single brief utterance and rise to a delirious new level. This is one reason he does not refer to his music, in significant contrast to Liszt, whose program is a close paraphrase of the music's expressive content joined to its formal design. (Liszt's program, in short, is musicological, Wagner's purely poetic.) The Grail as presence or prophecy could be grasped fully only through the ideal conjunction of the music and the narrative's imagery, but that conjunction, too, is a structural impossibility in 1850. In its place Wagner offers the excess generated by his prose, its halo of extraverbal rhythms and sonorities.

In place of a labored analysis of these patterns, suffice it to say that their chief resources are high levels of alliteration, assonance, grammatical parallelism, and periodic sentence construction. Rhyme and half-rhyme, and even patches of metrical prose, also contribute. For illustration I cite two passages in both German and an approximate translation meant to suggest the feel of the original. The first marks the moment when the vision crosses the threshold of the sublime:

> Wie die Erscheinung immer deutlicher sich kundgiebt und immer ersichtlicher dem Erdenthale zuschwebt, ergießen sich berauschend süße Düfte aus ihrem Schoße: entzückende Dünste wallen aus ihr wie goldenes Gewölk hernieder, und nehmen die Sinne des Erstaunten bis in die innigste Tiefe des bebenden Herzens mit wunderbar heiliger Regung

gefangen. Bald zuckt wonniger Schmerz, bald schauernd selige Lust in der Brust des Schauenden auf . . . (180)

[As the vision ever more clearly appears and ever more visibly floats toward the earthly vale, forth pour intoxicating sweet scents from its center: scintillant mists surge outward from it like golden gauze, and seize the senses of the astonished one until caught in the innermost depths of the quivering heart by miraculous holy impulse. Soon presses blessed desire, soon gathers blissful smart in the heart of the gazer . . .]

The second is both the conclusion of an enormous periodic sentence and the peak moment of the visionary experience:

da schwinden dem Schauenden die Sinne; er sinkt nieder in anbetender Vernichtung.

[then vanish the viewer's senses; he sinks down in devout extinction.]

What the translation can't capture is the way the annihilating "nicht" of "Vernichtung" terminates—in both senses—the assonantial series that runs suggestively from "schwinden" (vanish) through "Sinne" (senses) to "sinkt" (sinks). The delirium winds down from this point as the vision ebbs.

To pull the threads together: although no one is obliged to read anything anti-Semitic into Wagner's program for the *Lohengrin* Prelude, the program nonetheless has a strong community of interest with the topical, narrative, and rhetorical underpinnings of its composer's anti-Semitic credo and the worldview that supports it. The continuity may run underground, but for that very reason it runs deep.

In spite of which, the most striking thing about Wagner's programmatic efforts is that they failed in the face of the music. His invocations of historical crisis and ideological desire went largely unheeded, even though his program was (and is) ritually quoted, as if it were the authoritative statement it claims to be and not a belated effort to appropriate a piece that Wagner had never heard and felt he had lost touch with. (His "chief object" in the Zurich concerts, he told Liszt, was "to hear something from *Lohengrin*, and especially the orchestral prelude, which interested me uncommonly" [30 May 1853; CWL 286].) The terms on which the music was heard tended to be Liszt's, not Wagner's: initiation into a timeless reality, not a glimpse of redemption from a fallen time; a dream vision, not an allegory in sound. The effect of the Prelude was not to edify, but to entrance, even hypnotize, its listeners.

Baudelaire was perhaps the first to say so, in part on the authority of Liszt, whose program he quotes extensively, and links to his own with a quotation from his sonnet "Correspondances." The quotation tropes on both Liszt's image of the Grail temple and the music's suggestions of distant origins and sensuous immediacy:

> La Nature est un temple où de vivants piliers
> Laissent parfois sortir de confuses paroles. . . .
>
> Comme de longs échos qui de loin se confondent
> Dans une ténébreuse et profonde unité,
> Vaste comme la nuit et comme la clarté,
> Les parfums, les couleurs, et les sons se répondent.
>
> (ll. 1–2, 5–8)
>
> [Nature is a temple where living pillars
> Sometimes let forth indiscernible words. . . .
>
> Like sustained echoes that mingle from afar
> In a unity shadowy and profound,
> Vast as the night and as the light,
> Fragrances, colors, and sounds correspond.]

For Baudelaire, the Prelude conveys "an ecstasy *consisting in voluptuousness and knowledge,* and soaring above and very far away from the natural world."[21] In 1888 Nietzsche made similar observations from—famously— a hostile standpoint. Blaming "[Wagner's] choices of tempo and tonal color . . . [and] the lingering, soothing, mysterious, hysterical quality of his 'endless melody,'" he complains (not without grudging admiration) that "the *Lohengrin* Prelude furnished the first example, only too insidious, only too successful, of hypnotism by means of music."[22] Jumping forward to 1930, we can find Thomas Mann arbitrating the implicit dispute: "When Baudelaire, in naive artistic rapture, and quite without moral prejudice, speaks of the 'ecstasy of voluptuousness and knowledge' which the *Lohengrin* Prelude put him in, and raves of the 'opium intoxication,' of the 'desire that circulates in high places,' he shows much more courage and intellectual freedom than Nietzsche with his suspicious caution."[23]

With Du Bois, the dissolution of Wagner's ideological desire begins to become its reversal. The analysis of racial injustice conducted by *The Souls of Black Folk* culminates in an extended parable, "Of the Coming of John." Perhaps not surprisingly, given the intensity of American Wagnermania at the time, the narrative is organized around two performances of the *Lohengrin* Prelude, one real, one imaginary. In the first, John Jones, recently graduated from one of the South's black colleges, hears the Prelude at the Metropolitan Opera before being expelled for accidentally touching the arm of the white woman next to him. The music gives him imaginary entry to the world of human possibilities to which his real entry is forbidden. More than that, it embodies his *right* of entry, which it reveals to him as if for the first time:

> The infinite beauty of the wail lingered and swept through every muscle of his frame and put it all a-tune. . . . A deep longing swelled in his heart to rise with that clear music out of the dirt and the dust of that low life that held him prisoned and befouled. . . . Who had called him to be the slave and butt of all? And . . . what right had he to call when a world like this lay open before men?[24]

What the music conveys is not the impossibility of an ideological desire, but the necessity of freeing desire from ideology, "impossible" though that is in John Jones's America.

The impossibility surfaces at the end of the story, which plays out the sexual undercurrents "touched" at the opera. A white namesake tries to rape John's sister, a lynching offense were the races reversed. But there will be a lynching, anyway, because John, intervening, kills his sister's attacker. As he resigns himself to the fury of a mounted mob, presumably Klan-led, he hears the music of the *Lohengrin* Prelude again, which wraps him in a kind of transcendental envelope against the violence. He meets his fate after humming the theme of the bridal chorus; a quotation of its opening words is slightly altered so as to invoke the traditional figure of hierogamy, the sacred marriage that reconciles human desire and cosmic harmony. It is a very Wagnerian ending, though hardly one on which Wagner would have smiled.

He would have smiled even less on Chaplin, who reintroduces the *Lohengrin* Prelude to the sleeping dragon of Wagner's anti-Semitism. The Wagnerian *pas du seul* in *The Great Dictator* begins a few moments after Hynkel has been reminded by his sinister, Goebbels-like lieutenant of their plan to "kill off the Jews" on the way to world domination. ("We'll never have peace," he replies, "until we have a pure Aryan race.") Left alone in his office, Hynkel is drawn to his globe of the world, actually a large balloon, as the music of the Prelude seeps onto the soundtrack. He begins to toy with the globe, claims it as "my world!" with a cartoon villain's laugh, and embarks on an extended pantomime, the first half of which is particularly telling. The Prelude has started from the beginning, where its most ethereal sonorities are concentrated. While they hover over the scene, Chaplin's movements as Hynkel become progressively more debased along a familiar map of the body. He handles, twirls, and tosses the globe in the air;

he drop-kicks it overhead with his heel and toe; and, having kept it aloft by butting it with his head, he switches to butting it with his rear end as he lies on his desk. Each change in movement involves a body part with lower status and a corresponding increase in improper pleasure. The pantomime thus begins with a systematic travesty of the Nazi "worldview," or more accurately of the very idea of a Nazi worldview, based on visual renderings of three verbal clichés of domination: having the world in one's hands, feeling the heel of the oppressor, and being told to kiss someone's ass. The link between the third image and the head-butting that precedes it suggests an equation of top and bottom, upper and lower body. Another scatological idea is, of course, also in the air: Hynkel, to put it politely, is shown to be a butt-head. And, in fact, the last shot in the scene, once the balloon has burst, is of Chaplin/Hynkel's behind.[25]

The music hovers ambivalently above this performance, rendered absurd by the truth of its connection to the scene while at the same time it renders the scene itself more absurd—a point underlined repeatedly by the lack of synchrony between the music and the pantomime. The result is extremely complicated. Hynkel's performance at once shows off his malicious pleasure, satirizes it, invites the audience to share it in the guise of comedy, and uses the music to distance it or escape from it even as the music's implication in it is constantly reaffirmed. The Wagner-Hitler tie, mediated by the anti-Semitism that introduces the pantomime, both becomes ridiculous and stubbornly lingers as a danger—one realized visually in the peculiar gracefulness that never deserts Chaplin's movements. The same ambiguity radiates from the vicissitudes of the globe itself, floating with slow-motion grace while evoking a handful of its era's filmic clichés: the logos of Universal Pictures and RKO, the introductions to newsreels, the sing-along summons to follow the bouncing ball.

The conclusion of the film repairs the breach made in the music—a loud, dissonant twang—when the ball/bubble bursts. The climax of the barber's anti-Nazi broadcast is an apostrophe to Hannah, his refugee beloved, asking if she can hear him and enjoining her to look up while the Prelude returns on the soundtrack. The broadcast seems to be out of her earshot, but she does look up, and she does hear something. We watch her listen as she first lies, then stands, amid fertile fields—the alien corn. Asked whether she has heard the barber, she brushes the question aside with an injunction of her own: "Listen!" At this point we realize that what she has been hearing is the music of the Prelude mysteriously descending from the heavens: in filmic terms, extradiegetic music inexplicably crossing over to the diegesis.

Hannah, like Du Bois's John, is uplifted by hearing what it should not be possible to hear. The music begins in midphrase shortly before the point of its interruption in the pantomime and continues beyond that point while its sonority begins to grow richer and fuller. The more the music persists, the more intent the camera grows on the image of Hannah, tracing a broad arc from a long close-up of her face and shoulders against the fields and sky, to long shots of her full figure posed against the same background, to another extended close-up, tighter this time, of her face against the clouds as the music finally draws a radiant smile from her. The imagery becomes the visual realization of the Prelude as prophecy and election—a big dollop of kitsch, to be sure, but highly effective in its own historical moment.

The epiphany in the film replicates the one described in Wagner's program, but it does so for anti-Wagnerian purposes: the Grail knight has been replaced by a Jewish exile, and a woman to boot. This conclusion also symbolically reverses that of *Lohengrin* itself. Hannah, a living Elsa, takes heart from her distant beloved, from whose speech act the music of the Prelude materializes to end the film as it does the opera, but on a note of promise, not regret. (The barber-beloved may himself be the un-Lohengrin: an anti-authoritarian figure, a Jewish Figaro, whose name we never learn.) With these reversals, these attempts at a redemptive irony, the film reaches the endpoint of the decontextualizng process started by Liszt. It becomes a flat refusal to hand Wagner's music over to his ideology—which, however, results not in the disappearance of that ideology but in its renewed insistence. The ideological context is not allowed to rule; the film puts it at a second remove by taking the music itself as the revelation that, programmatically speaking, the music merely represents. But there is still no way to take the music fully "out of context," and the film doesn't try. On the contrary: Chaplin makes explicit the Jewish question lurking in Wagner's program and claims that the music holds the answer.

Ironically, what this answer involves is exactly what Wagner (and Marx) were seeking through anti-Semitism: a fullness of being free of the stresses of modernity, a freedom embodied here in the "timeless" imagery of woman and the earth and in the slowly accumulating fullness of the Prelude's orchestral sonority. Hence the peculiarity that, in the kitschiness of its imagery, the closing scene is all too close to the popular aesthetic of its antagonist, the Third Reich. Nonetheless, the kitsch becomes a medium for transforming the music into an icon of ecumenical, utopian tolerance— an icon that, shunted by Wagner through the implicit negation of Jewishness, culminates in Chaplin by taking Jewishness as the substance of its iconicity.

6

It is now time to ask, as one must ask, what the music itself contributed to its apparent insistence on being heard—intermittently, for roughly a century—as a means of liberation from the very ideology it was retrospectively intended by its composer to enforce. This reception history is exemplary for showing how problematic the concepts of "the music itself," "reception," and even "history" may be, but before interrogating the question let me suggest a few possible answers.

Liszt's answer, implied by his programmatic paraphrase, begins with the supposition that the Prelude combines formal clarity and sensuous fullness to an unusual, indeed unique, degree. The blending of these traits becomes manifest in a musical process whose seamless continuity becomes the vehicle for the "ideal mysticity" symbolized by the Grail.[26] The result is not at all badly described by Baudelaire's "ecstasy consisting of voluptuousness and knowledge." The knowledge rests on the perception of something cyclical or wavelike. The Prelude consists of four quasi-strophic episodes framed by what Liszt calls "a wide, still sheet of melody" in violin harmonics backed by flute and oboe. The strophes differ in detail, but they all begin in the same way and all spin out the same melodic period in flowing counterpoint. The voluptuousness rests on the incremental filling of sonorous space. The first strophe is for violins alone, four solo, the rest divided in four parts; subsequent strophes add instrumental choirs one by one (upper winds joining the violins, now in four parts; horns, bassoons, and lower strings, the violins now in the usual two parts; heavy brass and percussion). The music thus unfolds through, or rather as, an increase in the richness of its texture and an extension of its registral span from high to low, heaven to earth. The climax of this process comes in the fourth strophe, which is exceptional in several respects. A big crescendo, short and sudden, ushers in the only loud passage in the Prelude, after which the strophe splits in two, its tranquil second half slowly fading away into the frame passage. (Still lush, the texture at this point thins and simplifies as the violins emblematically retrace a long descent through three full octaves.) Knowledge and voluptuousness combine as the transparency of the former frees the listener to become absorbed in the richness of the latter. The voluptuousness of texture both enunciates and obliterates the knowledge of form, and the reciprocity between the two produces the famous effect of quasi-hypnotic trance for which the music was famous.

As the long-distance quarrel of Nietzsche and Mann suggests, this state of trance was a locus of social as well as aesthetic contention. For Max Nordau, such manifestations of "mysticism" were symptoms of degeneracy, the marks of a crisis of modern attention that threatened the future of civilization. The typical blend of sensuous, erotic, and religious feeling with loss of conscious will was a toxic brew. As Ian Hacking has observed, trance phenomena exerted considerable fascination during the nineteenth century from just beyond the borders of science, where they were maintained as "marvels," mysteries "too full of meaning, of hints, of feeling" to be rationalized: "marvels are meanings out of control."[27] In a sense, then, Nordau was right: the interest in trancelike states represented a social practice at odds with the controlled, focused, self-scrutinizing forms of subjectivity that seemed to be required on all sides. Entrancement was an in-house rebellion against the norms of what Mary Douglas terms enterprise cultures.[28] It cultivated an ecstatic second self impervious, if only briefly, to both the claims of responsibility and the "forensic" consistency of memory.

For Catherine Clément, anyone who listens to music is familiar with this experience. But her remarks apply better to specific pieces such as the *Lohengrin* Prelude, which she might just as well be describing:

> However *pianissimo* a piece of music may begin, it compels one to leave without moving from the spot where one is, and to come back to oneself where one already knows one will not find oneself. Once this moment has passed, one has crossed over the disharmony with reality, and one has found, with music, fundamental harmony.[29]

Liszt's description of the Prelude's musical process traces a similar pattern of affirmative self-alienation. Yet the "fundamental harmony" he finds with this music is also fundamentally at odds with the redemptive crisis narrative installed by Wagner's program. The music entrances, not with the promise of a future redemption, but with the step-by-step revelation of an ever-present plane of transcendence to which anyone who listens can have access. As "the first example . . . of hypnotism by means of music," the Prelude travels beyond the bounds of Wagnerian allegory into the more open space of desire and fantasy on which Liszt, Baudelaire, Du Bois, and Chaplin all seize.

Harmony in a more literal sense may also have been conducive to the Prelude's trance effect, though only Liszt might have said so, and he didn't. The harmony at the beginning of each strophe is unambiguous but also unemphatic, more something intimated than something declared. More decisive harmonic formulas appear later in each strophe, particularly near the end of each; the formulas grow progressively stronger through the third strophe. Each of these quasi-cadential formulas, though, dissipates abruptly into something dim and indefinite, which forms the transition to the succeeding strophe (example 1). The strophes, in other words, each seem to be evolving an end-oriented narrativity, only to conjure it away in favor of cyclical recurrence. The true "end" is the return to a condition of open-endedness that intensifies with each turn of the wheel.

With the fourth strophe, this process reaches its self-consuming climax. Strophes 1 through 3 have traced a harmonic circle, beginning respectively on the tonic, dominant, and tonic. The fourth strophe breaks the circle and surges onto the subdominant, thus perhaps invoking an ecclesiastical trope but also ensuring that the cyclical process of the Prelude reaches its peak in a harmonic place apart, a transcendental elsewhere that, as Liszt says, can occupy only a "unique instant" before it fades. (The dislocation affects the texture, too: for a moment or two the strings disappear, marking the peak of the climax as the antithesis as well as the culmination of the first strophe.) The textural disintegration that follows sustains and extends the loss of harmonic bearings, sustains and extends the trance, until the closing re-transition to the framing passage—the threshold of the larger cycle within the strophic cycles are embedded.

The work "itself" can thus be said to enact its own incompatibility with the worldview underlying Wagner's program. Both its textural and harmonic processes tend to validate Liszt's "ideal mysticity" more than they do Wagner's narrative of crisis and redemption.

This incompatibility may even be enacted in the opera, which makes scant use of the Prelude's music, as Liszt was the first to observe. As Michael Tanner remarks, until the frame music turns up to introduce Elsa's dream narrative, the relevance of the Prelude to the action onstage is entirely unclear.[30] Music from the Prelude, in fact, recurs primarily to declare the incompatibility of worlds—to supply a place apart for Elsa's dream in act 1 and Lohengrin's narrative in act 3, and to end the opera after Lohengrin's departure, when the cyclical fadeout assumes a new and more desolate significance. The recurrences never even approach the epiphanic fullness reached in the Prelude; they get no further than the first strophe, part of which accompanies Lohengrin's narrative when the opera is nearly over. Unlike its unrepresented counterpart in the Prelude, the world of the opera is incapable of receiving a divine gift, the compensatory return of Gottfried notwithstanding. Whenever it reappears, the music of the Prelude declares that it belongs elsewhere, wherever "here" may be.

From Wagner's perspective, the proper inference is that the Prelude belongs to the utopian future, to a world where a Lohengrin could be welcomed

EXAMPLE 1. Wagner, excerpts from the Prelude to *Lohengrin*.

a¹. First strophe, beginning.

b¹. Second strophe, beginning.

c¹. Third strophe, beginning.

on the required terms. But those terms reconnect the music to the coercive rule of ideological desire. The opera's villains may have a point about its hero: the world he cannot save is one that refuses blind trust in his charismatic authority. For Wagner, the Prelude's incommensurability with that world shows us that the desire for blind trust—desire to give it, desire to have it—cannot be satisfied; and the rare moments at which the Prelude's music recurs provide the suture that binds that ideological desire, together

a². First strophe, near conclusion.

b². Second strophe, near conclusion.

c². Third strophe, near conclusion.

with the associated crisis narrative, to the "Romantic," "fairytale" opera. Regarded ideologically, the Prelude entrances the listener to blind trust in the guise—which is not wholly a guise—of visionary rapture. But the same entrancement also makes it easier to ignore Wagner's ideological project altogether and, in a Lisztian mode, to hear in the opera a perennial division between the fallible mortal world and the eternal world on which it can always repose love and faith.[31]

7

As promised, all this throws new light on what it means to ask what the work "itself" contributed to its own reception. The assumption behind this question, as I want to ask it, is not that there is some prepotent form or embodied intention in the work that causes or encourages later reception and provides the standard by which to evaluate it. On the contrary: that is what history shows never happens, even in the simplest senses. The assumption, rather, is that the acts of reception cumulatively construct the work in retrospect, so that, in a sense, it exists only in retrospective forms, even when, as in the case of Liszt and Wagner on *Lohengrin,* the retrospection virtually precedes the work "itself." The subsequent vicissitudes of the Prelude through Baudelaire, Du Bois, and Chaplin are entirely unexceptional.[32] What the work does is supply certain grounds on which the retrospective construction can rest. These can be evoked through description, and to understand the work "as such" means to understand, that is, to have a reading of, the multifaceted interaction between the work as constructed and the acts that construct it, always on the understanding that the construction is never quite finished and certainly never immutable.

The issue can be clarified by reference to Ludwig Wittgenstein's consideration of "seeing-as," that is, of perceiving something as one thing rather than as another, or as something other than its nominal self. Wittgenstein was interested, not in explaining this phenomenon, but in characterizing it, taking it at face value, *as* a phenomenon. Some of his examples involve music:

> Children play this game. They say of a chest, e.g., that it's now a house; and it is thereupon interpreted altogether as a house. . . . And someone who knew how to play this way, and in a particular situation with a special expression exclaimed, "Now it's a house!"—he would be giving expression to the lighting-up of an aspect *[Aufleuchten des Aspekts].* . . . But the expression in voice and gesture is the same as if the object had changed and had ended up by *becoming* this or that. I have a theme repeated to me, each time played in a slower tempo. Finally I say *"Now* it's right" or *"Now* at last it's a march" or *"Now* at last it's a dance."—In *this* tone the lighting-up of an aspect expresses itself.[33]

What I want to suggest about what is too loosely called "reception" is that certain ways of listening or performing prove capable of "lighting up" aspects of music so that it is the same as if the music were an object that had changed. The change installs a variety of interpretive possibilities into this virtual object, which may develop connections with the object's other perceptible features. This process, moreover, is not just one of many possibilities that can befall a piece of music. Listening or performing always comes with an "-as"; without the lighting up of an aspect, music is just inert sound. It is impossible here to do more than allude to the many cultural-historical mediations to which this process is subject; suffice it for now to acknowledge its necessity and force.

Take, for instance, an aspect of the *Lohengrin* Prelude. Wagner's program identifies the epiphany evoked by the music with the gradual annihilation of the Grail knight's senses, a possible aesthetic correlative to the social purification of which the program is an allegory. The "breakthrough" moment of sanctification clearly corresponds to the climax in the fourth strophe. One thing (among others) that this correspondence may "light up" is the pair of loud cymbal crashes, linked by tympani rolls, that sound out at the culminating point. These crashes now seem meant, like speech acts, to make the listener wince, and in so doing to partake of the sensory blackout. The metallic clang, both violent and brief, also embodies the paradox borne by the climax as a whole as a revelation that all but vanishes in the act of appearing. (A softer stroke of the cymbals even initiates the disintegration that follows the climax.) That paradox situates the Prelude in the world of crisis and cultural debasement; the pathos of brevity testifies to the impossibility of the bliss that the massed orchestral forces "deliriously" seek to realize.

But the passage need not be heard this way at all. Du Bois hears it only as a swell of "mightier harmonies" linking the ethereal opening and close, the gossamer lightness of which is the correlative of their capacity to linger in the mind and memory. Liszt notes only the "glistening" brass, not the percussion, and constructs a paradox in which the "blinding" effect creates a higher insight, "as if . . . the holy edifice had blazed before our blinded gaze in all its luminous and radiant magnificence." Even on Wagner's terms the lit-up aspect is unstable. With a little reflective distance on the listener's part—which the music admittedly tends (or once tended) to inhibit—the cymbal crashes may fall out of the sphere of ideological desire and impossibility and onto the stage of grand opera illusionism, suggesting a vision at once entirely "present" and convincing and obviously trumpery. The cymbals, their percussive force supposedly an index and icon of the light of sense going out, cut across the homogenous sound world so far sustained by the Prelude and reverberate toward something conspicuously less "pure." Thanks to their longstanding associations with "Turkish music," culminating in the finale of Beethoven's Ninth Symphony, the cymbals are even a bit exotic, eastern, maybe even a little Jewish. At least the spirit of the hated Meyerbeer is not far off.

8

The history of the *Lohengrin* Prelude unsettles not only the issue of reception but also the metronomic pattern of debunking and defense, either/or
and both/and, through which the question of anti-Semitism in Wagner's
music, and the politics of the Other in art generally, have tended to be framed.
The Prelude's reception thus has implications for the thornier cases of more
complicated works such as the *Ring* and *Parsifal*. Context, in this case, failed
to hold text in place from the start, and Wagner's own efforts to stop the
drift had little effect. Wagner may have meant or bent the music to deliver
an implicitly anti-Semitic message, but if he did, a distinguished group of
his most attentive listeners returned the message to sender and issued a contrary one in its place.

Discussion of Judaism in Wagner's music has usually focused on whether
it is possible to "prove" that certain of the operas harbor anti-Semitic messages or characterizations. Those who think not can say with Dieter Borchmeyer that "in all Wagner's innumerable commentaries on his own work,
there is not a single statement which would entitle us to interpret any of
the characters in the music dramas or any of the details of their plots in anti-
Semitic terms, or even to interpret them as allusions to Jews."[34] Wagner was
in fact careful to avoid explicit anti-Semitism in his operas, most likely because he considered the topic too "parochial" for the universalizing scheme
proper to the artwork. Anti-Semitism in this context ranks with vegetari-
anism, also a subject about which Wagner was passionate. But it is hard to
see what "proof" would consist of here. If it had been Wagner instead of
Adorno who said that all his villains were Jewish stereotypes, no proof would
be needed; if it had been Hans Sachs to Beckmesser rather than Wagner to
von Bülow who said that there was something too Jewish about one of the
latter's compositions, no proof would be needed.[35] Short of such smoking
guns, the presence or absence of anti-Semitism in Wagner's operas is no
more "provable" than any interpretation.

Which is to say, it is not provable at all, and the fact doesn't matter. For
the whole issue here is wrongly framed. Wagner's operas cannot be isolated
like specimens on a microscopic slide. Once a sufficient number of interpretations have made a certain connection, say to anti-Semitism, once those
interpretations have been made and heeded, repeated and disputed, once the
process of understanding has multiplied links between the operas, their composer's ideology, and the anti-Semitic discourse of his era, the operas become inextricable from the question of anti-Semitism. They change their
appearance, as an aspect is "lit up" in Wittgenstein; and since, as works of

representation, they are structures of appearance, when they change their appearance they change their being. That is all the "proof" that is possible and all that is needed; "proof" is intelligible only in the sense of trial and test, not of verification.

This does not, of course, mean in Wagner's case that the operas turn into bald anti-Semitic screeds or that in order to like them we have to entertain shoddy notions like the composer "transcending" himself on the wings of genius. What it does mean is that, with Wagner's music, anti-Semitism must eventually be remembered even if it is not perceived. The burden of memory is both ethical, a point that should need no elaboration, and structural, the point I have been trying to elaborate. The social, cultural, and political values of widely disseminated artworks are often contested at levels far removed from the explicit locutionary surface of their own discourse and the discourse about them. One result of the effort to understand such works, something that may as well happen inadvertently as by design, is to bring those illocutionary levels into the foreground.

The case of the *Lohengrin* Prelude is paradigmatic. Let me summarize. Everything we know about the opera suggests that it has no anti-Semitic subtext; it is perfectly oblivious to the "Jewish question." Wagner himself, however, repeatedly reinterpreted this opera, and seems to suggest that he needed to do so more than with his others; the gap of time separating the opera's composition and Wagner's first hearing of it in 1861, and its role as a transitional work between Romantic opera and music drama, seems to have alienated him from it in the sense of defamiliarizing it. When he writes to Liszt to say that the latter was right, it was Wagner's best thing to date, he sounds genuinely surprised. Part of his own attempt to reappropriate the opera involves constructing the program for the work that encapsulates it, the Prelude. And when Wagner did that in 1853, he made the program consistent with the anti-Semitic worldview he had assumed and enunciated in 1850 in "Judaism in Music." Assumed: the overt program pivots on the emancipation of the world from the rule of capital. Enunciated: the program articulates in redemptory form the underlying structure of anti-Semitic and other pariah-generating ideologies.

The relationship of this reading to the Prelude itself, however, is vexed. To generate the reading at all, Wagner revises Liszt's program, which is the source of his own, to prune the little patch, the twin stipulations, possibly meant to immunize the work against anti-Semitic readings. In the process Wagner changes the temporal character of the Prelude and its world, replacing Liszt's steady-state world governed by sacred time to a world of de- and regeneration governed by a millenarian or apocalyptic time. But although Wagner's program is routinely quoted, on the assumption—false in this case—that it has the authority—questionable in any case—of an original intention, the "reception" of the work has tended to refuse Wagner's reading of it. At least in certain milestone instances, the Prelude has been returned to Lisztian sacred time and understood as oblivious of or even an antidote to social injustice in general and anti-Semitism in particular. Only in Chaplin's film does this become explicit, but once the film's initiative has been recognized and taken seriously, it has a ripple effect that reaches both back to Wagner and Liszt and forward to ourselves and perhaps beyond. New aspects light up; the *Lohengrin* Prelude becomes the music of the future.

3   The Waters of Prometheus

Nationalism and Sexuality in Wagner's Ring

UNHOLY GERMAN ART

None of which is to say that what's broken in Wagner can be fixed. Wagner bedevils everyone, or he should. He's certainly bedeviled opera, not only by his anti-Semitism, but also by the more comprehensive "delirium" of which anti-Semitism is the most toxic symptom and embodiment.

Take nationalism and sexuality: these very topical concerns of the present and recent past are also the historical terms of the infamous "case of Wagner," *Der Fall Wagner,* as Nietzsche called it: the instance, medical problem, and criminal investigation of that "neurosis" (Nietzsche's term) whose "magnificently equivocal, suspect and compelling" work (Thomas Mann's phrase) makes you love what is hateful and forget what must above all be remembered, and that *keeps on doing this* no matter how shrewdly you resist it.[1]

What is left to say at this late date about the case of Wagner—about the wizard, charlatan, and minotaur (Nietzsche, again) whose music all too compellingly, all too seductively, mobilizes deeply entrenched dynamics of sexual identity and desire to promote a reprehensible end: the grandiose, sentimental, anti-Semitic nationalism that would in time inexorably become the Third Reich and the Holocaust? Even as those atrocities increasingly fade from living into textual memory, changes in the way we think about music make it harder and harder to disengage Wagner's aesthetics from his politics. The argument that music as great as his transcends the dross of history is scarcely presentable in its bald form anymore, especially on this topic, so such statements of it as appear tend to be ever more subtilized. Is Edward Said, for example, boxing the moral compass or indulging in wishful thinking when he bravely claims that the close of *Die Meistersinger,* with its elevation of "holy German art" as a politico-cultural sacrament, is a false patch on the truth of the larger whole:

As for Wagner's neurotic closure . . . we can take that as the merest crude attempt to grab once and for all what has already been proved to be a possession far in excess of, therefore transgressing, the clutches of one owner, be that owner an individual, a town, or a nation. [Pierre] Boulez is quite right to say that Wagner's "music by its very existence refuses to bear any ideological message it is intended to convey." *Die Meistersinger* cannot really be reduced to the nationalist ideology its final strophes stress. It has set forth too much in the way of contrapuntal action, character, invention.[2]

The burnished tunes and gorgeous orchestration of this opera, the nobility of Hans Sachs's renunciation of Eva, the ravishing beauty of the Prize Song—anyone moved by these musical wonders wants Said to be right. But what about the arguments of Marc Weiner and Barry Millington that the burnished glow of this music is broadly applied with the dirty rags of anti-Semitism? What about Arthur Groos's contention that the processional scenes of the third act conjure up a trope of medieval Nuremberg as a once and future nationalist utopia, a kind of *Wagner Welt* theme park?[3] And what about the way the nobly lyrical tunes and splendid "contrapuntal action" of the overture form a sonoric image of this utopian space, within which the listener is decisively situated for more than four bewitching hours? Can the music really refine this dross in its expressive magic fire? Or does the dross render it inescapably a music of national and "racial" supremacy— the music Nietzsche heard in the overture and described as "something arbitrary, barbaric, and solemn . . . something German in the worst and best sense of the word"?[4]

Said's impulse to contradict Wagner about the ideology of the latter's own music is genuinely tempting. When, for example, we learn that Wagner said of the third act of *Siegfried,* "That is Gobineau music . . . that is race," the claim that he is spouting nonsense seems close to self-evident.[5] What could Joseph-Arthur de Gobineau's racist theories of pure blood, which admittedly weigh heavily on *Parsifal,* have to do with the splendid love duet between Siegfried and Brünnhilde that brings *Siegfried* to an orgasmic close and gives the *Ring* cycle its consummate interlude of happiness? But perhaps, having asked this question rhetorically, it would be better to ask it in earnest.

WAKEUP CALL

I invoke the love duet here because, for Nietzsche at least, it marks the historical crux of the case of Wagner, the moment after which the fires of musical art cease to refine the dross of sexual and national brutality. Nietzsche is not quite explicit on this point, but his description in *The Case of Wagner* of what he takes to be Wagner's betrayal of both himself and his listeners in the *Ring* leaves little doubt of it. The part of the saga that leads upward to Brünnhilde's rock, to the love duet ringed by magic fire, compels both Nietzsche's admiration and his identification with Siegfried as a "free spirit." The ascending Siegfried is cherished as an exemplary immoralist, a breaker of ossified contracts, and a liberator of women (this, yes, from the arch-antifeminist philosopher, whose enthusiasm we might read in Derridean terms as an embrace of the putatively feminine abilities to evade morality and break contracts—and get away with it).[6]

This good Siegfried, in what proves to be a cardinal relationship, is at once pro-erotic and antinationalist. On the erotic side, his entry into the ring of magic fire initiates "the sacrament of free love; the rise of the golden age; the twilight of the gods for the old morality—*all ill has been abolished*" (CW 163). On the nationalist side, he embodies the spirit of the French Revolution in mythic, which is to say world-historical, terms: "Half his life, Wagner believed in the Revolution as much as ever a Frenchman believed in it. He searched for it in the runic writing of myth, he believed that in Siegfried he had found the typical revolutionary." The revolutionary Siegfried is the very antithesis of a Germanic hero, almost an incarnation of universalism versus parochialism, the spirit of French Enlightenment versus that of German *Aufklärung*. Insofar as he (like his creator) is indeed a revolutionary, Siegfried is "an incarnate protest against all 'German virtues.'"[7]

Wagner's great betrayal, Nietzsche continues, is the reactionary substitution of ideology—nationalist false consciousness—for free thought and the cognate substitution of displaced and tormented sexuality for the simplicity of free love. When Siegfried descends from Brünnhilde's rock he blunders into the modern world, the scene of social organization rather than mythic adventure, of kinship alliance rather than glorified incest. This is a world that dupes and belittles the hero who is still somehow supposed to redeem it: the Gibichung world of rich Junkers and their nubile sisters, of corrupt Germans and crafty Jews, of bourgeois marriage and adultery. Siegfried's mind, never his strong point, becomes cloudy in this world. The clarity of utopian optimism dies into the murk of Schopenhauerian pessimism with the monstrous twin birth of the political and the sexual unconscious. On the political side, writes Nietzsche, "What did I never forgive Wagner? That he *condescended* [in the sense of lowering himself, debasing his divinity] to the Germans—that he became *reichsdeutsch*" (EH 248). On the sexual side, this Teutonization takes the form of abjection and disillusionment: "So he translated the *Ring* into Schopenhauerian terms. Everything goes wrong, everything perishes, the new world is as bad as the old: the *nothing,* the Indian Circe beckons" (CW 164).

Nietzsche's construction of the good versus the bad Siegfried constitutes a classic nineteenth-century *Doppelgänger* narrative, a type that regularly personifies and opposes the socially acceptable and unacceptable forms of masculine personality. As a reading of the *Ring,* this narrative is suspect both because it fits Nietzsche's own philosophical agenda too comfortably and because it is obviously ripe for deconstruction; who would be surprised to learn that the good Siegfried is always already the bad one, that Wagner the reactionary is always already inscribed on the text of Wagner the revolutionary? But Nietzsche's reading is powerful, too, and has a great deal to offer, including some important clues to the case of Wagner, if we decline to deconstruct it prematurely. (One might say that deconstruction, like stand-up comedy and good sex, requires a keen sense of timing. The point is to deconstruct an opposition only after one has learned what it has to teach, so that its undoing can teach something, too.) Accordingly, I want to entertain for awhile the notion that the *Ring* cycle pivots on the strange transformation by which the revolutionary lover who is Siegfried in the eponymous *Siegfried* becomes the social-climbing philanderer who is Siegfried in *Götterdämmerung.* And I want to entertain, too, the broader implication that this transformation uncovers a real antithesis between nationalism and eroticism—an antithesis, moreover, with its own keen sense of timing. The erotic, in this structure, first inhibits or defers the advent of the national, then becomes appropriated to the national, and finally undoes the appropriation to undo the national.

Siegfried, then, becomes a nationalist hero only when he becomes vain, stupid, brutal, and lecherous. This is not a joke. Only in the world of *Götterdämmerung,* where political consciousness is mystified and sexual desire never recognizes its object, can the national hero come to be, and even then only on the condition that he come to grief. The national hero is born to be a martyr. Wagner probably thinks of this as a cautionary tale; Siegfried is, after all, brought down by the machinations of the saturnine Hagen, the half-caste and half-breed, the parasite whose relation to his hosts replicates the phantasmatic relation posited between Germans and Jews by the racialist anti-Semitism that Wagner embraced. Siegfried's fate foretells what will happen to Germany if the race is not kept pure.[8]

From another perspective, however, this compulsory default in the national hero is the source of his authenticity. The hero does not incarnate national identity by what he is, but by what someone else imagines him to be. The Siegfried of *Götterdämmerung* is debased on stage, but ennobled in Brünnhilde's fantasy; the bad Siegfried becomes good again when desire and misrecognition install him in the place where she lacks him, the place where he has always already betrayed and abused her. This Siegfried does not appear until after the "real" Siegfried's death. And although this final Siegfried is strangely still capable of action—his dead hand rises up to prevent Hagen from taking the ring—he has no voice except, belatedly, Brünnhilde's voice in mourning for him. He becomes present, to her and to us, only in the music that expresses Brünnhilde's love and grief for him, music always tuned to absence rather than presence, whether at the beginning of *Götterdämmerung* with its love duet marking the parting of the lovers, or at the end, with its double threnody of funeral music and immolation scene.

But do Brünnhilde's acts of mourning and fantasy really bring back the good Siegfried or merely idealize the bad one? When she conjures the hero up is she a revolutionary herself, uncontainable by the constraints of her sacrifice, self-betrayal, and abjection, or has she, too, become *reichsdeutsch*, no longer a Nietzschean-Derridean figure of truth truly evaded, but only a kind of hapless *Mädchen* in Valkyrie uniform?

These questions particularly beset me when I listen to the funeral music, although I will dwell more here on the subsequent immolation scene. My first experience of this music, more than forty years ago, remains unforgettable, and traces of it persist even in my canniest moods of resistance. I placed a scratchy monaural LP casually borrowed from the library on a cheap record player and was physically staggered by what I heard. (Nothing had taught me yet to hear these sounds in the spirit of the Third Reich and of the dread that had hovered namelessly over my childhood in questions my parents wouldn't answer, neighbors with tattoos that couldn't be explained, leaflets imprinted with old German script, left in doorways and hurriedly snatched away.) I was stunned by the music's combination of ferocity and solemnity, by its power to turn its climactic drumbeat figure into the pounding of the blood at my temples, and to turn this impact on my body into a ritual of heroic mythopoeisis. But was I really hearing a transfigurative threnody for a solar hero, a world-historical Promethean figure ultimately consumed by his own gift but soon to rise again, phoenixlike, in the song about him sung by the loving enemy who is preparing to share his funeral pyre like an Indian widow? Or was I just hearing the most sublimated possible form of the *Horst Wessel* song?

Perhaps we need to consult a fiery revolutionary to get some sort of answer. Nietzsche's good Siegfried is a late-blooming instance of Romantic Prometheanism, a figure who defies authority by ringing himself with magic fire. Perhaps we should search the runic writing of myth for him, eventually including the runes of modern myth, which is to say, of theory.

MAGIC WATER MUSIC

Prometheus, thief of fire—"[Hephaestus's] flower, the brightness of fire that devises all," says Aeschylus. In the Aeschylan version of the myth the gift of fire is what enables humanity to make the epochal transition from nature to material culture. Prometheus finds human beings "liv[ing] like swarming ants in holes in the ground, in the sunless caves of the earth"; fire, as if putting the sun in human hands, "[becomes] the teacher of each craft," culminating in metalwork.[9] In Classical terms, Prometheus the fire-bringer is a personification of Bronze Age technology. Only much later, in the Promethean texts of European Romanticism, does the emphasis shift from material to symbolic culture, from technique to value. (Another example, here, of oppositions to be deconstructed—but not prematurely, and therefore not in this context.) Only then does Prometheus become a culture hero in the full sense. Byron's Prometheus gives "precepts" that "strengthen Man with his own mind," thus grounding human identity in a putatively unalienated self-consciousness. Shelley's champion of humanity explicitly subordinates the material to the ideal; though he has taught the uses of the fire and the other elements, in his culminating act "He gave man speech, and speech created thought, / Which is the measure of the Universe." Goethe's Prometheus, somehow with impunity, his virile outrage somehow transmuting itself to creative-procreative sexual difference, sits in inspired solitude and fashions the human race in his own image "to suffer, to weep, / To enjoy and rejoice, / And pay [the Thunderer] no heed."[10]

Yet something strange happens at this turning point in the mythography of Prometheus. For some reason the fire becomes expendable. Byron does not so much as mention it, and in all the vast bulk of *Prometheus Unbound*, Shelley can manage it only the one perfunctory nod as a technological convenience. More revealingly, Goethe displaces the fire into Prometheus's "holy glowing heart," a prototypical gesture of internalization that refigures a material agency as a symbolizing power. It is as if the advent of culture in the symbolic sense coincided not with the gift of fire, but with the gift of fieriness as a character trait of the heroic rebel and lover. It is this fieriness, moreover, which establishes him as universal, primordial, and therefore as transnational: an elemental, not a historical, hero.

When the good Siegfried ascends to Brünnhilde's rock the first thing he discovers is his own Promethean fieriness. His relation to fire, like that of his archaic precursor, marks his defiance of divine authority, but he is not the figure who gives fire; he is the one who masters it. He takes it as his element and thus takes it into himself, and in so doing turns it into a symbol. The passage from technique to value is enacted through his crossing of the fiery threshold: what Brünnhilde has proposed as a practical device to keep cowards from taking sexual advantage of her, Siegfried turns into a sign of the enveloping, protecting passion that he will consummate with her.

Reflecting on this prospect, Siegfried states that he will "bathe" in the fire to win his bride:

> Ha! Wonnige Glut! Leuchtender Glanz!
> Strahlend nun offen steht mir die Straße.
> Im Feuer mich baden!
> Im Feuer zu finden die Braut!
>
> [Ah, marvelous glow! Radiance gleaming!
> Shining now the road stands open before me:
> To bathe in the fire!
> In the fire to find my bride!]

It is a curious metaphor. Curious, because it identifies fire with the water that extinguishes fire, and curious because it identifies mastery over fire with the bodily pleasure of *not* extinguishing it. The bad Siegfried will be consumed, if also redeemed, by fire, but the good Siegfried will be cleansed and refreshed by it, like some primordial Tamino whose ordeals by fire and water occur simultaneously and in the form of pleasure rather than pain. But what does it mean, this water of Prometheus?

One answer, traced in the runes of myth, can be found in Freud's *Civilization and Its Discontents*. To be sure, this is one of Freud's looniest ideas, even he admits that, but it becomes less so if you regard it as metaphor rather than history. (Influenced by the evolutionary anthropology of the late nineteenth century—of which more in chapter 7—Freud regarded many metaphors as "survivals" of superseded practices. Wagner often thought the same way.) Freud says that "primitive man" gained control over fire when one man, one day, resisted the homosexually tinged desire to put out a fire by urinating on it. Thus that man became Prometheus, the thief because not the murderer of fire, the godfather of the arts and sciences.[11] One becomes the first culture hero by renouncing the "pleasurable struggle"—Freud's phrase—to which the fire beckons with its phallic flickering.

This theory is itself a piece of mythmaking, part Promethean and part Rabelaisian. Meant to inscribe, with a certain polemical gusto, the humble bodily beginnings of high cultural forms, it is of a piece with Mikhail

Bakhtin's near-contemporary theorization of the grotesque body in both carnival and the text of Rabelais: the "open," orifice-studded body that, in its frank connection to the material world through the passage of fluids and substances, opposes the dead—and deathly—seriousness of official culture.[12] (One might say that opera, especially, is the art of the open body insofar as operatic voice so palpably courses from the body's depths into the breadth of theatrical space—and that this is particularly so with Wagner, whose vocal extremity is not a matter of roulades and high notes but of singing at high pressure so that the voice bursts as if from within the notes in streams of suffering or pleasure.)

It is tempting to underscore Freud's point by taking note of the boyish romance of firemen and their red trucks, from Walt Whitman's erotic fascination with "The march of firemen in their own costumes, the play of masculine muscle through clean-setting trowsers and waist-straps"[13] to William Carlos Williams's notation of a phallic pictograph, "The Great Figure," the luminous insignia of a water carrier piercing the nocturnal depths of the city with clangs of glee:

> Among the rain
> and lights
> I saw the figure 5
> in gold
> on a red
> firetruck
> moving
> tense
> unheeded
> to gong clangs
> siren howls
> and wheels rumbling
> through the dark city.[14]

But something is amiss with Freud's formulation. There is something he misses because as usual he errs on the side of severity; he pits debasement against supremacy, all or nothing, the stakes of a scene of castration. His version of taking mastery over fire posits a psychological relation of sublimation between bodily urge and cultural form. Partially renounced, the urge achieves partial satisfaction in the substitutive embrace of form. But what if the relation between these terms is as much tropological as it is psychological, a question not only of the body denied and symbolization affirmed, but also of the body affirmed precisely as a field of symbolization? Certainly, one way to take power over fire is not to put it out: I can endure the answering fire in my body and choke off the instinctual impulse. But another way is to *perform* the impulse rather than either restraining or releasing it: to find a liminal zone between tension and release in which the impulse can produce meanings and feelings in tandem with a fire that it does not altogether put out, at least not all at once. I can approach the fire with Promethean assurance if I make the bodily impulse exquisite, playful, rhythmic, ritualistic . . . artistic.

Yes: if I do that, if I trace my impulse cursively in the shape of the fire, I don't extinguish the fire at all. Rather, I defer its extinction, I shape and inscribe and finally perpetuate the fire in the form by which it's extinguished: fire unkindled as water. If this is a Rabelaisian gesture, most suitable to Gargantua's legendary act of pissing *Par ris* (for laughs) on a great city, thus endowing the city with its name,[15] it is a gesture that can also be invested with lyricism, pathos, tender irony, and mythopoeic force—effects all present when James Joyce has recourse to it in the "Ithaca" chapter of *Ulysses.*

Like the *Ring*, *Ulysses* centers on a woman who emblematically reaches her sexual peak on a high rock and who confers identity by purely imaginary means on the wandering hero who loves her. Here then are Leopold Bloom, a cosmopolite like the good Siegfried, accompanied by Stephen Dedalus, a sectarian like the bad one, contemplating, from the garden of the Bloom house at no. 7 Eccles Street, Dublin, the "visible luminous sign" denoting "the mystery of an invisible person" in the bedroom window of Molly Bloom, singer extraordinaire and "flower of the mountain": "At Stephen's suggestion, at Bloom's instigation both, first Stephen, then Bloom, in penumbra urinated, their sides contiguous, their organs of micturition reciprocally rendered invisible by manual circumposition, their gazes, first Bloom's, then Stephen's, elevated to the projected luminous and semi-luminous shadow."[16] Between the two men, between their gazes of unspoken desire, between the shadowy penumbras of their Promethean waters, a mute duet unfolds, something suggestive of those iridescent Baroque duets between two high voices intertwining with each other regardless of sameness or difference of sex, the contralto-soprano couple presenting an ideal both parallel with and counter to the pederastic ideal implied by the combination of the older and younger man, as if Molly Bloom's unheard operatic voice were taking both parts in its approving silence.

Admittedly, any link between Siegfried and the lyrical Rabelaisianism in the Blooms' garden exists only in theory. And no doubt Siegfried's mastery over fire has only the most vestigial relationship to his ability to hold his water—though let it be recalled that Wagner must have valued this ability as a test of acculturation: in his day there were no facilities for relieving oneself at the *Festspielhaus* in Bayreuth. ("Mercilessly denying the fact of human bodily needs," writes Beat Wys in an analysis of the architecture of Wagner's Bayreuth, "Wagner's dictatorial art cancels the public as corporeal fact. . . . The Wagnerian stage corresponds to the historicist idea of cultural formation, wherein the claim of culture withdraws to an interior 'soul' while on the outside, the unsightly material circumstances are tolerated as necessary evils.")[17] Only in theory, then: the good Siegfried, with all due qualifications entered, to some degree acts as a Freudian Prometheus when he first passes the ring of fire and emerges on Brünnhilde's rock. Having bathed in the fire, Siegfried discovers the bodily pleasures, and becomes the conduit for the musical pleasures, of controlled, ritualized impulsiveness as he slowly discovers that the nature of his relationship to Brünnhilde is mutual desire. Having bathed in the fire, he finds it reproduced as the liquid radiance of the sun in Brünnhilde's awakening words—"Heil dir, Sonne! Heil dir, Licht! / Heil dir, leuchtender Tag!"—and bathes anew in the same fire now transfigured as the purifying waters of eros: "ich selbst, wie ich bin, / spring' in den Bach: / O, daß seine Wogen mich selig verschlängen" (Hail to you, sun! / Hail to you, light! / Hail to you, radiant day! . . . I myself, as I am / will leap in the stream: / O that its waves devour me in bliss!).

This nuptial baptism by fire is both the prelude and the form of the free-spirited bliss that Nietzsche celebrates. *Contra* Wagner, the "immoralist" philosopher hears the fire-punctuated love duet as the very antithesis of Germanic "race music"; any racial or national character the music may seek (even in its composer's retrospect) is drowned in sexual fire. But is it?

This question arises with exemplary acuteness near the start of the scene, just after Brünnhilde has been awakened by Siegfried's kiss. The hero, who has had his mother much on his mind while musing over the sleeping bride, and who will soon misrecognize Brünnhilde herself as his mother, responds to the miraculous awakening with a maternal invocation that Brünnhilde at once echoes, the musical phrases of the couple overlapping and intertwining:

SIEGFRIED: O Heil der Mutter, die mich gebar,
              [Hail to the mother that bore me]

BRÜNNHILDE: O Heil der Mutter, die dich gebar,
              [Hail to the mother that bore you]

SIEGFRIED: Heil der Erde, die mich genährt!
              [Hail to the earth that nursed me!]

BRÜNNHILDE: Heil der Erde, die dich genährt!
              [Hail to the earth that nursed you!]

The music for these lapped phrases is remarkable for the way it vaults beyond the stilted machinery of the epic hail to express the "sublimest rapture" *(erhabenste Entzückung)* (example 2).[18] Each phrase begins at full cry with jagged, leaping melody, then eases a little into something smoother and more continuous. As each partner finishes an utterance, the other bursts forth to mirror that utterance. In a cycle of reciprocations, the melodic movement of each voice from intensity to repose rekindles the spark of intensity in the other voice. The cycle itself intensifies as the second pair of phrases compresses the first, complicates the mirroring effect, and adds harmonic breadth. Once complete, the cycle calls forth an ardent closing passage celebrating the mutual gaze of discovery, during which the voices shift freely between caressing counterpoint and shared melody, and finally coalesce in one of Wagner's rare perfect cadences.

The vocal interchange of the "Heil der Mutter" passage couples Siegfried and Brünnhilde in sexual desire and pleasure long before either one of them recognizes the fact. It propels them immediately from maternal to erotic love (or, if you prefer, from pre-Oedipal to Oedipal sexuality) in apparent disregard of the maternal imagery of the text. This imagery, however, is not there just to be disregarded. It also enhances the radical, "free-spirited" character of the incipient lovers' desire by recalling the transgressive desire of Sieglinde, Siegfried's incestuous mother and the alter ego for whose sake Brünnhilde defied Wotan's law. A transgressive link of this sort is basic to Nietzsche's claim that free sexuality is antithetical to the production of race music.

The only trouble is that the maternal invocation is also the very thing that *establishes* the love duet as race music. At the crudest level, the presentation of an epic genealogy that Wagner—foolishly, according to Nietzsche— thought was *echt*-Teutonic, the invocation can always be denationalized by the kind of Nietzschean hearing I have just proposed for it. But Wagner's introduction of the mother at this point has a deeper resonance. The displacement of heroic genealogy from the father's line to the mother's is not only a way of taking a position beyond and against the compacts of paternal law, but also a way of establishing Siegfried's racial purity, which is to say, his identity as a German, not a Jew. In context, the maternal invocation is just as much a test as the magic fire is.

That context is intricate, twisting through a lifelong preoccupation with the nature of maternity; I will single out just two strands. First, in reading the works of Ludwig Feuerbach while developing the libretto of the *Ring*, Wagner (as Jean-Jacques Nattiez has shown) discovered something highly congenial to him: an association between the sexual love of man and woman

EXAMPLE 2. Wagner, *Siegfried,* act 3: love duet ("Heil der Mutter").

EXAMPLE 2 *(continued)*

(continued)

EXAMPLE 2 *(continued)*

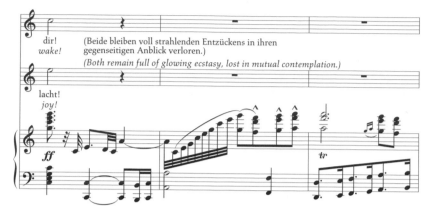

and the realization of universal human being through the annihilation of the ego, ultimately in death. This association would come to have an obvious bearing on the love duets of *Die Walküre* and *Siegfried*. The same association, however, also had a third, a "racial" element. Since the Jews (for Feuerbach) are characterized by a refusal to surrender their individuality, since "their principle—their God— . . . [is] egoism, or, more specifically, *egoism in the form of religion*," it follows that the loving, transcendental union of man and woman must coincide with the negation of all that is Jewish.[19]

Second, at about the same time that Wagner, having read Gobineau, identified the music of the love duet with "race," he was much preoccupied with the question of contaminated bloodlines. Here again, a coincidence of sexual and racial themes emerges. Racially, the problem is miscegenation: Jewish blood is impervious to it. "Let Jew or Jewess intermarry with even the most foreign of races; a Jew will always be the result."[20] (Jewish law, as Wagner may or may not have known, would half agree, in terms with some pertinence to our topic: regardless of the father, anyone born of a Jewish mother is considered a Jew.) Sexually, the source of danger in the crossing of bloodlines is (unsurprisingly) feminine: "In the mingling of races, the blood of the nobler male is corrupted by that of the less noble female: the male suffers, character is destroyed, whereas women gain so much as to take over from men."[21] It follows that the worst possible racial impurity would issue from the union of a man of noble (that is, Germanic) race and a Jewish woman.

When Siegfried spontaneously cries out "Heil der Mutter" at the sight of the newly awakened Brünnhilde, he signifies his readiness to enter into a transcendentally loving union by recognizing that he is the offspring of one. In the act of invoking his mother, he intuits her ability to sustain such a union; in intuiting her ability, he discovers and validates his own. In racial terms, what Siegfried discovers is his mother's purity: the fact that she could transmit her beloved's noble blood without taint, and the cognate fact that she could annihilate her ego, along with her beloved's, in a way that annuls egoism, and therefore Judaism, as a principle. These racial terms, of course, are not the only ones that apply here; we have already seen some of the others. But they do apply; they must be applied. By insinuating them, Wagner provides the audience (and no doubt himself) with a reminder, and a reassurance, of which Siegfried has no need. In her own love duet in *Die Walküre*, Sieglinde anoints herself, along with Siegmund, as a member of a pariah race, the Wälsungs, a clan chosen by (a) god for sufferings and greatness. But any resemblance between this race and another chosen people is purely coincidental. The Wälsungs are not Jews.

So, at any rate, Wagner would like to believe, or at least to pretend. But as Thomas Mann showed trenchantly in his short story "The Blood [*Blut:* blood, bloodline, race] of the Wälsungs" (*Wälsungenblut*), the racial ideology of nineteenth-century Germany made an identification of the Jews and the Wälsungs the most obvious thing in the world—and the most anti-German. Mann's Siegmund and Sieglinde, Jewish twins from a wealthy family, attend a performance of *Die Walküre* shortly before Sieglinde's arranged marriage to a German—a wooden, maladroit figure, a travesty of Hunding, the original Sieglinde's thuggish husband. (The basis of the marriage is predictable: his name for her money.) Once home, the twins live up to their names by making rapturous love on a Wagnerian bearskin. Ordinarily arch and petulant, they achieve an unaccustomed gravity through their incest, which they haltingly understand as a form of "revenge." Mann's irony here spares no one, certainly not Wagner, but the racial link between the two sets of twins holds firm, if only because it, too, is ironic. The pleasure of incest is the revenge of the Other. Mann's twins make explicit the racial fantasies of which Wagner's twins are partially the product. (Jews, runs the anti-Semitic bromide, care only for other Jews; they incarnate endogamy.) Wagner's twins, however, do more than stumble unwittingly across the imaginary position of the Jewish Other. Rather, in the love duet that is the primal scene of the *Ring*, they impel the listener to identify unreservedly with the subjectivity of the Other. Their love, too, is a revenge, the object of which is the very medium of its expression. They fulfill the erotic imagery of medieval Germanic *Minnesang* from a self-conscious racial position of alienation, defiance, and transgression.

The mother-test, then, or something like it, would be necessary because Siegfried, as a Wälsung, cannot avoid being racially suspect. He is even doubly suspect because his origins are tainted with the pleasures of otherness and "free love" that must in part be reenacted in the rapture on the rock. Wagner's matrilinealism is a means of resolving these racial uncertainties by disavowing them, and, like disavowals generally, it works none too well. In the very act of quelling racial anxiety, the mother-test underscores the possibility that Siegfried's status as pariah and Nietzschean immoralist risks turning the figure who will be (but is not yet) a German national hero into a *Judenbube*—or, to make the point more circumspectly, risks installing Siegfried originarily in the Jewish subject position of the nineteenth-century German symbolic order.

That position is above all the place where Siegfried cannot be: not only because it is the pariah position par excellence, beyond revocation or redemption, but also because, in terms of nineteenth-century Germany's conceptualization of the "Jewish question," it is precisely the position from which national identity is refused, declared impossible, thrown implacably into dispute. "The Jew," wrote the Young Hegelian Bruno Bauer in his *Die Judenfrage* (The Jewish Question), "can only adopt a Jewish attitude, i.e., that of a foreigner, toward the state, since he opposes his illusory nationality to actual nationality, his illusory law to actual law." "We discern in Judaism," wrote Karl Marx, "a universal *antisocial* element of the *present time*, whose historical development, zealously aided in its harmful aspect by the Jews, has now attained its culminating point."[22] "The Jew," writes Wagner more pungently than either, "strikes us first and foremost by his external appearance, which, no matter which European nationality he may belong to, has something about it that is foreign to that nationality and that we find insuperably unpleasant."[23]

Thus the free-spirited bliss that Nietzsche saw in the love duet of *Siegfried* dances, in true Nietzschean fashion, on the edge of a nationalist-racialist abyss. At the height of Wagnerian immoralism there is a pivot, a hinge, that swings the other way.

Nietzsche, pretty plainly, would have liked the *Ring* to end with the rapture on the rock. In a sense, he even made it do so in fantasy by taking as his favorite work by Wagner the instrumental poem "Siegfried Idyll," which draws largely on the music of the love duet. In this piece Wagner himself might be said to have recomposed the *Ring* without *Götterdämmerung*, to have given Siegfried and Brünnhilde (or himself and his wife Cosima, to whom the work was given as a birthday present) an idyllic alternative world immune from the catastrophe of modernity. The rapture on the rock, however, was also destined to be replayed in *Götterdämmerung* itself in debased form, by a Siegfried who adopts a debased form for the purpose: the physical form of his shady blood brother Gunther, a form assumed by magic so that Siegfried can abduct Brünnhilde in order to enact a primitive bride exchange with the other man, who will hand over his own sister in return. We will have to reckon with that. And we will have to reckon, too, with the torsion of gender in the utopian sexuality of the love duet, which, for all its free-spiritedness, is still distinctly, not to say egregiously, lopsided, giddy with the dream of heroic virility. The price of the rapture on the rock is Brünnhilde's debasement—a debasement that is perversely understood to be her normality, her natural decline from godhead to womanhood.

MUCH ADO ABOUT NOTHUNG

Why, indeed, is the bad Siegfried of *Götterdämmerung* so willing to go pimping for Gunther? Or more exactly, why does he desire to? For the magic potion that impels him, like Tristan and Isolde's, only uncovers a real desire in the guise of imposing a deluded one. Isn't it that Brünnhilde has now become the vehicle for the bad Siegfried's erotic union with Gunther, a classic vehicle of sexualized homosocial—in other words, of disavowed homosexual—love? I ask this question rhetorically because the idea it proposes has long since ceased to be surprising in itself.[24] For that reason it is important to specify that what Siegfried finds desirable in Gunther is not only the generic aura of masculinity, but in particular the virile spirit of *Heimat*, the national rootedness that he, Siegfried, may embody but cannot possess himself in his role as itinerant hero. Gunther represents social rather than mythic masculinity, secure patrilineal legitimacy rather than transgressive maternal suffering and pleasure. Gunther needs no mother-test to establish his lineage; he passes muster as the scion and symbol of normal community even though his actual mother, Grimhild, has borne a child to the loveless, greedy Nibelung, Alberich, the mythological equivalent of a Jewish banker. Siegfried, it turns out, harbors a secret burning desire to condescend to Germans.

To do that he has to enter the corrupted modern world, where free spirits are turned into Teutonic poster boys, the world that each noble (but stupid) Gunther must always share with a base (but ingenious) half brother (Hagen, Alberich's son, whose "base," basso profundo voice sticks out in *Götterdämmerung* like the Jewish nose of anti-Semitic caricature, or its cognate, the supposedly croaking Jewish voice that, according to Wagner the anti-Semite, brings the true German to instinctive immediate recoil.)[25] The modern world, in turn, reveals that the sexuality on which the free spirit staked so much is no longer either simple or unambiguous, and indeed never was, not even during the rapture on the rock. The discovery of Brünnhilde is not as heterosexual as it may seem at first—though this is not to say that its homosexuality can be reduced to the bad Siegfried's furtive, bad-faith misalliance with Gunther.

When the good Siegfried bridges the fire, he sees something quite remarkable:

> Ha! In Waffen ein Mann:
> wie mahnt mich wonnig sein Bild!
> Das hehre Haupt drückt wohl der Helm?
> Leichter würd' ihm, löst' ich den Schmuck.
> Ach! Wie schön!
> Schimmernde Wolken säumen in Wellen
> den hellen Himmelssee;
> leuchtender Sonne lachendes Bild
> strahlt durch das Wogengewölk!

> [Ha! A man in the armor!
> How delighted I am at the sight!
> Does the helmet cramp his noble head?
> It would be lightened for him if I loosened the catch.
> Ah! How lovely!
> Shimmering clouds border in waves
> the shining lake of heaven;
> the radiant sun's laughing face
> gleams through the billowing clouds!]

Brünnhilde, sleeping beauty in armor, is an image of lovable maleness before the good Siegfried's discovery of her breasts makes him cry out—comic, naive, amazed—"Das ist kein Mann!" (That's no man!). The discovery of sexual difference, and more particularly of a masculine sexuality oriented around a feminine counterpart, is what makes it possible for Wagner to represent Siegfried's union with this figure initially limned by sexual likeness.

This heterosexual turn neither falsifies its homosexual impetus nor is falsified by it; the sexual formation arises in the dynamism that mediates the two modes of desire. The concomitant indeterminacy is viable, even vivifying, in the world of *Siegfried,* but it is fatal in the world of *Götterdämmerung.* When the bad Siegfried goes back, a newly minted Perseus, to the nuptial rock, his nonrecognition of Brünnhilde's body constitutes an announcement that, *from the perspective of the modern social and symbolic order,* he has never really known her in the first place. That knowledge will not be forthcoming from this new rendezvous, either—which is why, betrayed, Brünnhilde hates Siegfried so fiercely: not that the good Siegfried was false to her, but that the bad one did not know her, and never had. (Between *Siegfried* and *Götterdämmerung*, Brünnhilde slides from misrecognition to misrecognition down a slippery Oedipal slope, from the postures of motherhood and virile youth to that of another man's bride.) Muddled in mind as well as body, Siegfried knows no one now but Gunther, the blood brother whom *we* know as the tarnished mirror image of both the hero's identities: Siegfried's "good" Gunther, the ideal friend, the fellow hero, and Hagen's "bad" Gunther, the effete aristocrat corrupted by the blandishments of the Nibelung's son, the supposed pillar of the Reich befooled by an assimilated Jew, by a Leopold Bloom with attitude. Siegfried's sexual ignorance of Brünnhilde is the medium for his sexual knowledge of Gunther.

Not that he knows this, either. Wagner's libretto swears that punch-drunk Siegfried and ravished Brünnhilde slept with the sword *Nothung* between them, in a classic case of heroic bundling. But the music, vintage Hollywood *Begleitungsmusik* before its time, says that they did something else that could not be shown. (Siegfried confirms this later, if confirmation were needed, by making double entendres about it to his fiancée, Gutrune.) The need *(Not)* signified by the sword is not only that of a proof of the unity *(Vereinung)* of blood brotherhood but that of an emblem of denial *(Verneinung)*: the need to say that what happened was nothing—nothing at all. But the music puts this nothing at naught. In the tumult of the music, Siegfried now sleeps *for the first time again* with Brünnhilde. In the hidden depths of the cave, the counterpart to the theatrical hollow in which the audience at Bayreuth sits and dreams the *Ring* (as Hagen dreams, with eyes wide open), Siegfried relives in darkness the sexual act that he consummated in light on the open heights of the rock. He transforms the woman who was the author of his mythic identity into the medium of his social identity. He acts as a sexual surrogate for Gunther so that when Gunther repeats the sexual act on the official wedding night the two men can meet in the medium of the woman's body.

In this surrogation, what was once the discovery of mutual desire between man and woman becomes a contest of wills. In other words, it becomes rape, which is something that the music also avows beyond the libretto's disavowal; glowering brass fanfares of doom and a recurrent two-note bump-and-grind figure leave the ear in little doubt. We are not, of course, supposed to like this. We are even invited to feel it from Brünnhilde's perspective, as a savage violation. Nothing in the opera, however, suggests that the ugliness of this violation is inherent in Siegfried's behavior as such. Aryan blood brothers do these things for each other; the problem here is that Gunther is cheating and lying, violating a code that itself goes unquestioned, but is unable to withstand the corrupted modernity that it is ultimately meant to redeem. In the logic of this code, the consolidation of national identity in masculine identity requires the sexualizing of the homosocial. That sexualization, in turn, requires not only the interposition but also the violation of the woman's body. Brünnhilde's rock thus becomes the symbolic birthplace of German confraternity precisely to the degree that it becomes the site sacred to, made sacred by, a woman's body on which adoration and abuse are inflicted by the same man in identical sexual acts.

Sublimate this compact a little more, wrap it in the odor of sanctity, and the result will be *Parsifal:* Wagner's veiled anticipation of Freud's thesis that social feeling has its origin in homosexual libido, and by far the thorniest problem in the whole case of Wagner. "In the art of seduction," writes Nietzsche, "*Parsifal* will always retain its rank as the *stroke of genius* in seduction.—I admire this work; I wish I had written it myself. . . . Never before has there been such a *deadly hatred* of the search for knowledge!— One has to be a cynic in order not to be seduced here; one has to be able to bite in order not to worship here" (CW 184). It should go without saying that this seductiveness has nothing to do with Kundry, who as a femme fatale is the most spectacular (and grateful) failure in all opera. Wagner's last stroke of genius was to realize that the nexus of physical suffering, sin and repentance, and sacred ritual could elevate German confraternity like a host and place it at the center of a translucent closet: translucent, not transparent, because Kundry's body is still required to unite Parsifal and Amfortas, a process that immolates her—she is the real sacrifice here, her speech and her will the burnt offerings on this pyre—but that, burning at the core of the *Bühnenweihefestspiel,* allows the translucent chamber to fill with a soft, steady glow.

REDACTION FOR THE REDEEMER

Nothing in the *Ring* is as vindictive as this. Brünnhilde, however abject she must become to fulfill the contrary logics of free- and national-spiritedness, is never deprived of voice as Kundry is, and, though cruelly deprived of agency by both father and lover, she recovers it in a literal blaze of glory at the close. The importance of this recovery lies less in its welcome resistance to the kind of bottomless, self-sanctifying abjection on offer in *Parsifal*— something of the sort can even be found in *Parsifal* itself—than in its formulation of the logic, the inner dynamic, of that resistance.

The dynamic begins in the love duet of *Siegfried,* where Brünnhilde's regrettable maidenly vulnerability (regrettable, anyway, in long retrospect) forces Siegfried, that wild child, to embark on a civilizing process under her tutelage. In Wagner's Germany, such tutelage was understood to be maternal;[26] here, in the wake of the "Heil der Mutter" passage, its maternal character is absorbed into an eroticism that, among other things, frees Brünnhilde to retrieve some of her earlier godhead in the figurative embrace of "leuchtende Liebe, lachender Tod" (radiant love, laughing death). Even though the retrieval is, for the time being, figurative and no more—Brünnhilde is still chained to her rock—it sets the terms for its more than figurative realization in the immolation scene of *Götterdämmerung.*

Meanwhile, Brünnhilde's sexuality gives her the power to intervene in the symbolic order. At the same time as this sexuality requires the sacrifice of her autonomy and turns her into a mere sign of Siegfried's mastery, it endows her with mastery of the signifying process itself. The result is to lay a foundation for the transcendent act of interpretation by which she will ultimately right the wrongs of the entire *Ring.* When the good Siegfried enters the ring of magic fire, he receives from Brünnhilde an identity that the bad Siegfried, thug and shill in the same place, cannot wholly revoke. She makes him a bard, the oral historian of his own exemplary saga, over before it begins but never over at all. Sculpted in her mind, he arrives as a male Galatea and leaves as a young Prometheus molded by the discovery of her body. She receives and sanctions him as his destined Molly Bloom, as she who alone can bear true witness to his story; without her nothing can happen, nothing have meaning. Brünnhilde's rock, ratio of fire and water, is literally the bedrock of Siegfried's legend as he knows it—and as he comes to sing it, to venture down the Rhine to sing it, to die singing it. On this rock is founded the circle of myth that Wagner's national culture claims as its universal origin; from this rock spring the arts—as fire? as water?—that glitter with voice and proclaim their return to that origin on the mythographic-phantasmatic stage at Bayreuth.

This return, however, is "magnificently equivocal." As soon as Siegfried descends from the rock, the legend with which Brünnhilde endows him must be reiterated in order to endure. It must be signified in the leitmotifs of the Rhine Journey music, narrated in fragments by Hagen and Siegfried at the Hall of the Gibichungs and in toto—the fragments now stitched together in a bizarre semipsychoanalytic dialogue between Hagen/Freud and the Wolf Man/Siegfried—in the forest during Siegfried's death scene, and renarrated by the combined voice of Brünnhilde and Wagner's orchestra in the closing double threnody. But with each reiteration except the last, the legend draws closer and closer to sentimental nationalist rant. Siegfried himself wakes up to the fact when he recovers his memory of Brünnhilde under Hagen's sadistic tutelage.[27] The only countervailing force, in terms of the Nietzschean allegory I am enfranchising here, is the radicalized sexuality that emerges in the rapture on the rock and that really belongs to Brünnhilde, not to Siegfried.

Far from merely reinscribing the clichés of nineteenth-century femininity (from which, admittedly, it is by no means free), this sexuality is an impossible, indecipherable formation. It is conceived in sympathy with incest, and awakened only insofar as Brünnhilde is a woman whose body arouses homosexual desire for her—literally for *her*—in a boy who through knowing that desire becomes a man. It is a sexuality, also, consumed by its one and only consummation and thereupon redirected entirely into Brünnhilde's imaginary register, her construction of Siegfried as hero, whether as free spirit or nationalist shill. The result is that the most erotic moment in the *Ring* is the nuptial conclusion of the immolation scene, an imaginary reversal of the abduction scene and an imaginary reprise of the original rapture on the rock:

> helles Feuer das Herz mir erfaßt,
> ihn zu umschlingen, umschlossen von ihm,
> in mächtigster Minne vermählt ihm zu sein! . . .
> Siegfried! Siegfried! Sieh!
> Selig grüßt dich dein Weib!
>
> [bright fire seizes my heart,
> to embrace him, be enfolded by him,
> to be wed with him in the mightiest love! . . .
> Siegfried! Siegfried! See!
> Blessedly greets you your bride!]

The musical eros that arises from and envelops this cry transforms the unmistakably false consciousness of the immolation scene, the dialectical reclamation of the bad as the good Siegfried, into something we—I—could wish to believe.

The origin of this transformation predates even the rapture on the rock, though Brünnhilde's rock is indeed where it starts. The origin lies at the close of *Die Walküre*, in which Brünnhilde, resisting her own Promethean punishment of helpless exposure on the mountain peak, proposes the magic fire. In so doing, she constitutes the man who will be Siegfried as a Promethean figure, he who takes control over a fire struck by a god. Crucial here is the fact that the idea originates with Brünnhilde, not with Wotan.

Even in abjection, Brünnhilde, firebrand to Valhalla, is the wellspring of moral agency in the *Ring* cycle. (Abjection, indeed, may at one level be little more than the raw material of her own Promethean creativity, which is merely displaced onto the more conventional figure of the masculine hero.) The fire, limned so pictorially in the music, can be taken to symbolize all the cardinal aspects of the heroic but terrible destiny that Siegfried-Prometheus will find in and through entering this *other* Ring, Brünnhilde's Ring: desire, ordeal, betrayal, immolation:

> The only hope, or else despair
>   Lies in the choice of pyre or pyre—
>   To be redeemed from fire by fire.[28]

At this point a certain deconstruction is no longer premature: the magic fire music already has its full symbolic density long before Siegfried masters it and renders that symbolism active, explicit, present, just as Wotan's deeply lyrical threnody of farewell to Brünnhilde contains a moving eroticism, as unactable as a dream, that can be enjoyed only by the free spirit who awakens Brünnhilde. The close of *Die Walküre* indicates that Siegfried is always already an imaginary form, projected out of a woman's defiance and desire.

No longer Wotan's instrument but a human subject, half woman and half phoenix, the Brünnhilde of the farewell scene usurps Wagner's place as Siegfried's librettist and composer, and she never relinquishes it. Her fantasy of a fire-fangled Promethean hero becomes Siegfried's destiny. When the magic fire music first flickers to life in the orchestra, it rings her with the power of her own thought. In the farewell scene, it haloes her body to prepare her once-in-a-lifetime union with the man her thought has sculpted. Later, in the immolation scene that closes *Götterdämmerung*, it reignites to prepare her fiery reunion with the man her thought has doomed.

The return of the magic fire music begins the immolation scene's long climax. The renewed flickering of orchestral flames impels Brünnhilde to sing her redemptory signature motive by Siegfried's pyre (example 3). This motive is not a familiar strand in the melodic web of the *Ring*. Sung only once before, by Sieglinde to Brünnhilde in *Die Walküre*, it reappears in the orchestra during the immolation scene with its significance, even its identity, still undetermined. Brünnhilde virtually plucks the motive out of the air, claims it as her own, and endows it with the meaning it lacks. Her unconditional melodic action corresponds to the unconditional interpretive action by which she reclaims the bad Siegfried as a free spirit. Both actions, moreover, gain credibility (more exactly, suspension of disbelief) from another

EXAMPLE 3. Wagner, *Götterdämmerung*, act 3: immolation scene ("Fühl' meine Brust auch").

EXAMPLE 3 *(continued)*

Brust auch, wie sie ent - brennt, hel - les
bo - som, how it doth burn; glow - ing

Feu - er das Herz mir er - fasst,_____
flames now lay hold on my heart;_____

ihn zu um - schlin - gen, um -
fast to en - fold him, em -

- schlos - sen von ihn, in mäch - tig-ster
- braced by his arms, in might of our

(continued)

EXAMPLE 3 *(continued)*

feature of the redemptory motive. Although it is almost a nonpareil, the motive bears some resemblance to a more familiar one used elsewhere to mantle Brünnhilde in lyrical pathos (example 4). When she claims the redemptory motive, Brünnhilde also disclaims the pathetic one. Her claim is not only that she has moved from low to high, from pathos to sublimity, but that all of her former abjection has been burned away.

The words sung to the motive say just this, that Brünnhilde is on fire, that she is the fire: "Fühl' meine Brust auch, wie sie entbrennt, / helles Feuer das Herz mir erfasst" (Feel my breast, too, how it flames up, / bright fire seizes my heart). The focal point of this supreme act of self-recognition, by which Siegfried is consumed without remainder, even more fully than by the pyre on which he burns, is the key word "entbrennt." When Brünnhilde sings her redemptory motive, she does so only twice. "Entbrennt" solders these two motivic statements together, beginning the second by ending the sentence otherwise given in the first. The signifier of flaming up, of catching fire, often used in the sense of becoming inflamed with love, thus be-

EXAMPLE 4

a. Brünnhilde's lyrical motive (transposed
   to E major).

b. Brünnhilde's redemptory motive.

comes identified with the continuation of the melodic process that Brünnhilde has kindled with her motive. Brünnhilde herself soon entrusts that
continuation to the orchestra. She goes on to seek a final, irrevocable, rapture, urging her voice upward along a chromatic chain of climactic high notes
to a high A at "vermählt ihm zu sein" (to be wed with him). The orchestra,
which has meanwhile begun braiding the most intense segment of her motive into a rising sequence reminiscent of Isolde's transfiguration (the so-
called *Liebestod*) in *Tristan und Isolde*, breaks through this pitch ceiling even
as Brünnhilde reaches it.[29] The orchestral process validates her longings, not
by satisfying them, but by projecting their satisfaction beyond her voice and
her life. Brünnhilde responds decisively. After a brief apostrophe to Siegfried,
her voice descends toward a climactic cadence that accompanies her leap into
the last ring of magic fire and, in so doing, releases the all-consuming tongues
of flame in the orchestra.

A great singer can invest this cadence with enormous authority, but it is
important to recognize that she cannot invest it with closure. The cadence
is of the kind technically known as deceptive, involving the resolution of
melody but not of harmony; Brünnhilde's immolation falls just short of
fulfilling her desire. Fulfillment, it turns out, must wait until her imaginary
relationship to Siegfried has been replicated in the listener's relationship to
her; the fulfillment can occur only in someone else's conception of it. The
music offers to model that conception some moments after Brünnhilde's
death, when the orchestra, now singing for her (on her behalf, in her voice)
as well as about her, reprises her redemptory motive in counterpoint with
the water music of the Rhine that emerges from murky depths of the *Rheingold* Prelude at the very beginning of the *Ring*. The annulus of aesthetic
closure thus becomes the metaphorical equivalent of Brünnhilde's bridal

consummation—not a mere sublimation (though one can choose to hear it that way) but an expansion, a reinscription, a redaction. Her wedding band becomes a ring of fire mirrored in a ring of water.

Didn't Wagner lose faith in his national and social ambitions in the rapturousness of scenes like this one—and like Wotan's farewell and the rapture on the rock? Might it have been for the sake of these moments that he took such care to excise his anti-Semitism (meticulously restored by modern scholarship) from his musical theater? Here, if anywhere, is an answer to the case of Wagner: not that the music surmounts or falsifies its dire ideologies, but that it yields on our behalf to their allure—an allure often cached, a guilty secret, in the psychological back pockets even of those who most passionately reject it. Having yielded, the music carries the logic of that allure to the point where it shatters, and in shattering releases an even stronger allure than the dire one lost. We do not have to forget the direness to enjoy the music; we enjoy the most when we best and most cunningly remember. We discover that we can solve, if not resolve, the case of Wagner by learning to hear how one of his most famous formulas, the line "Redemption for the redeemer" that concludes *Parsifal* and was blazoned on a wreath at Wagner's funeral, is continually subjected to travesty variations. The music drama compels us as it does because it ultimately betrays its own betrayals: seduction for the seducer . . .

Redaction for the redeemer: the wordplay is an act of ironic negotiation with Wagner's ghost, but it is also more. As the word's prefix indicates, a redaction is never simply the production of something in textual form, but always a re-production. For that reason, what the redaction fashions is not simply a text in the sense of an inscription, but always a text in the Derridean sense of a network of differential traces. The redaction is always the *différance* of the legend, narrative, image, or precursor text that it re-renders, and vice versa.[30] Wagner's scenes of rapture, especially the concatenation of the funeral music and the immolation scene in *Götterdämmerung*, are redactions of the music dramas that supposedly embed them. They resignify the dramatic action so that its erotic, ideological, and narrative components fly in different directions, their official or subtextual meanings disseminated toward unexpected and barely articulable regions. This process, moreover, seems to ground itself in next to nothing, a mere quivering in the air: in the power of the music to invoke beautiful figures we know to be false because we have seen the ugly truth of them: figures like the loving father Wotan, Siegfried "the free-spirit and immoralist" (Nietzsche), and above all the transcendental Siegfried who returns from the dead in Brünnhilde's final conception.

Nor is it an accident that the sequence of these scenes, each of them ringed by, bathed in, fire, traces a vocal passage from depth to height, a transcendental passage that also runs from masculine to feminine. First there is Wotan's baritone apostrophizing the sleeping Brünnhilde, then the commingling of Siegfried's tenor with Brünnhilde's awakened soprano, and finally the apostrophe to Siegfried by Brünnhilde's soprano alone. The descent of the bad Siegfried is countered by the ascent of Brünnhilde's voice.

This ascent, however, cannot settle the case of Wagner all by itself. The rapture of which Brünnhilde is the voice and portal is ambivalent to the core, always compounded of the elements of debased fact and supreme feeling (or is it really the reverse?). Its home ground, invoked throughout this chapter by the leitmotivic phrase "the rapture on the rock," delineates its character: hard, isolated, barren, elemental, lofty—elevated both literally and figuratively, that is, sublime. This is rapture in the root sense of being rapt, seized, and carried off to a condition not one's own. For Wagner this is the condition of redemption, a condition that surmounts but paradoxically does not diminish the abjection that it redeems. The question is whether, or rather in what conditions, we hear the song of this redemption as itself either debased or supreme: a mere vehicle for ideological desire, or (and?) a fictional rapture that almost induces a real one, that seems to transmit the Real in the Lacanian sense of that which lies beyond symbolic accommodation.

Everything depends here on the agency of the listener, on the intervention of the act of hearing. It is more than possible to hear Brünnhilde in the immolation scene voicing a nationalist promise that if modernity will only discorrupt itself, the next Siegfried will not have to die in squalor. Part of Wagner calculated on an uncritical form of this hearing. It is equally possible to hear the final Brünnhilde voicing an ostensibly philosophical pessimism that turns out to be a thinly veiled form of sentimental nationalism. That is what Nietzsche heard: Brünnhilde, who was "initially supposed to take her farewell with a song in honor of free love . . . now gets something else to do. She has to study Schopenhauer first" (CW 164). The Schopenhauerian Brünnhilde produces a false profundity, a "counterfeiting of transcendence" (CW 183) that flatters the narcissistic German penchant for "the idea" (CW 178). The immolation scene monumentalizes the spirit of the first (1876) Bayreuth festival at which the *Ring* was unveiled and at which Nietzsche made the dismayed discovery that "Wagner had been translated into German!" (EH 284) and thereby into complicity with "[the] most *anti-cultural* sickness and unreason there is, nationalism, this *névrose nationale* with which Europe is sick" (EH 321).

But it is also possible to hear something more, not something that supplants these critical hearings, but something that burns through and partly consumes them. It is possible to claim that the final Brünnhilde preserves and enhances what Nietzsche himself recognized, but not for publication, as the power of Wagner's music to "persuad[e by a] secret sexuality [wherein] one found a bond for a society in which everybody pursued his own *plaisirs*" (EH 285n). Consummating the scenes of fire-fringed voice that precede it, Brünnhilde's voice at the peak of its intensity in the immolation scene burns through the scheme of calculated redemption that Nietzsche excoriated. Conjoined with the funeral music and orchestral peroration, this voice constructs a Siegfried utterly at odds with the boorish farceur depicted in *Götterdämmerung*. It apostrophizes the partner of a desire even less subject to rationalization than the one that prompts the rapture on the rock. It shrills and croons, this voice, from within a zone of untranslatable, uncompromising, unredactable pleasure—a zone for free spirits:

> Fire and foam. Music, veerings of chasms and clash of icicles against the stars.
> O bliss! O world! O music! And forms, sweat, eyes and long hair floating there. And white tears boiling,—O bliss!—and the feminine voice reaching to the bottom of volcanoes and the grottos of the arctic seas.
>
> (ARTHUR RIMBAUD, "Barbare")[31]

The woman's voice in extremis rends the veil of our subjectivity, the veil that *is* subjectivity. We become subjects sometime in childhood by simultaneously identifying ourselves with the symbolic order of language and hiding our genitals: subjectivity arises between the logos and the fig leaf. If the hidden real of art is so often sexual, that is because sexuality is the prototype of reality in hiding. And if singing, especially operatic singing, is the most sexually real of the arts, that is because the singing voice, naked beneath its words, throbbing, sinking, soaring, assaulting, caressing, half understood, half not needing to be, the unconstrained singing voice simultaneously sexualizes utterance and utters forth sex.

Always feminine whether a man's or a woman's, that utterance at its peak shatters the mirror in which nationalist or other ideologies reflect, and so support themselves upon, sexual desire—the mirror in which such ideologies thereby constrain and normalize sexual desire. Nietzsche's betrayed utopia revives, if only for a little while, in what always seems the once-only sound of this voice, and above all in the genuinely once-only sound of Brünnhilde's self-immolating voice and its orchestral counterpart or continuation. The voice opens an invisible breach through which all "wayward and unproductive" sexualities (Foucault's phrase)[32]—sexualities otherwise policed, idealized, or disavowed—pour forth and are heard. The sexuality that once upheld and suffused national identity now scatters both itself and it.

Of course, this is not the only possible outcome. Indeed, the opposite is equally likely, perhaps even more so; one can find it realized in such latter-day Wagnerian artworks as Leni Riefenstahl's *Triumph of the Will*. But in Wagner himself the process goes in one direction only: an ignited eros burns out the thanatos of nationhood, even at the cost of becoming the thanatos of itself. The further that sexuality—or feminine sexuality, here Brünnhilde's—moves from conventionality (the bedroom farce of *Götterdämmerung*) to free love (the rapture on the rock, its reenactment on the pyre), the more the narrative movement is utopian rather than redemptive, universalizing rather than nationalizing.

At this point a caution is in order. I do not want to identify uncritically with this mode of hearing and in so doing to mystify sexuality as a source of liberation from the oppressions of culture. Rather, I want to recognize that Wagner, or Wagner heard via Nietzsche, is able to mobilize a trope of sexuality capable of disrupting all normalizing structures, including its own—a trope that, placed at the climactic moments of the *Ring*, can disseminate that disruption though and across the entire body of the opera, pleasurably shattering the nationalist ideologies that have otherwise found in a certain sexuality a far less pleasurable support. What I'm imagining for Wagner is a kind of anti-Foucauldian deployment: not a putting of sexuality into discourse, but a putting—a casting—of ideologically loaded discourse out of sexuality, the production of a counterdiscourse of eros that successfully masquerades as pre- and postdiscursive.

Not wanting to turn a deaf ear to this sonoric rapture, I decided to embody, not merely to recommend, a course of listening. I began to construct a "musical," expressive text in place of a sober linear statement of a thesis. (The case of Wagner requires thinking through, but the thought must be personal, figurative, and associative as well as conceptual.) If statues, I wanted to ask, if statues in fountains could talk, or, better, sing, wouldn't they tell us that the shape of the waters of Prometheus circulating around and through them was the ever-returning presence of the sensibility—desiring, contingent, material, vulnerable—denied by and to their marble bodies? Wouldn't their song proclaim that the shape of the waters was not a sublimation of that sensibility but a channel for it running all aglitter without walls? Nor could such a shape stand as a monument to hero, statesman, soldier, or nymph; the politics of exclusion would drown in the shimmer of unabatement. So I delight to imagine Brünnhilde as Molly Bloom, Molly as Brünnhilde, kindling and quenching the great pyre with her indelible dying voice. We need to hear more from the garden of the Blooms:

> The trajectories of their, first sequent, then simultaneous urinations were dissimilar: Bloom's longer, less irruent, in the incomplete form of the bifurcated penultimate alphabetical letter who in his ultimate year of High School (1880) had been capable of attaining the point of greatest altitude against the whole concurrent strength of the institution, 210 scholars; Stephen's higher, more sibilant, who in the ultimate hours of the previous day had augmented by diuretic consumption an insistent vesical pressure. (703)

The light in the window is doubled by the celestial fire of a falling star, the trajectory of which is again doubled by the double trajectories of Bloom's and Stephen's streams of urine. Each man proves an artist in water, and side by the side the two make art together, love together, each in liquescent calligraphy intimating a letter in space, Y and S respectively, and thereby forming together an alphabetic couple that Molly Bloom will conjoin with an E to produce the enraptured last word on which the novel ends: "and then he asked me would I yes to say yes my mountain flower . . . and his heart was going like mad and yes I said yes I will Yes" (783). The parabola of each Promethean stream traces the curve of its author's history, Bloom's with a positively Siegfried-like reminiscence of parabolic splendor, and, like the track of the meteor from Vega in the Lyre (for the poet Stephen) to the constellation Leo(pold), the parallel streams preserve as form the fiery energies they consume as material. Could it be that this glittering urinary epiphany traces the fulfillment of that most Wagnerian of ideals, the total work of art, in which the fusion of signifying media configures the audience into a single and, despite itself, a denationalized polity, whose united and divided halves, Adam and Eve, Siegfried and Brünnhilde, Leopold and Molly, Jack and Jill, continually live and die in each other's fiery streams of song?

4 Enchantment and Modernity

Wagner the Symptom

for PHILIP BRETT

During the heyday of Wagnerism, Wagnerian opera was for many music lovers the decisive event of European modernity. This was true in both a critical and a utopian sense. Wagner became both a symptom of what was wrong with modern life and a force for what might be made right with it. He both encapsulated the widespread diagnosis of modernity as a heartless juggernaut and represented the means of transforming it into the motor of an advancing civilization.

Wagner's rise to preeminence in the second half of the nineteenth century overlapped with the decisive arrival of modernity in the cities of the West. For at least one key figure in the history of city planning, Camillo Sitte, Wagner's operas suggested the best model for a modern life not dehumanized by its own economic and technological machinery. Sitte unveiled that model in a lecture to the Vienna Wagner-Verein (Wagner Union) in 1875. City building should pattern itself after the idea of the *Gesamtkunstwerk*, the "total work of art"; the city should give material form to the unifying myths by which modern culture could overcome the ever-present danger of social and psychological fragmentation.[1] A year later the first Bayreuth festival consolidated Wagnerism as a material as well as a cultural institution. In the same year, 1876, the exposition held in Philadelphia to commemorate the centennial of the American republic also identified the spirit of progressive modernity with Wagner, from whom it had commissioned its theme music, the Grand Festival March.

During the heyday of Wagnerism, Wagner represented what was transcendental about the new. Stéphane Mallarmé, writing in 1885 with *Parsifal* in mind, celebrated the bursting forth of "the god Richard Wagner radiating a consecration" that could no longer be obscured by dated forms of thought or faith, those "hieroglyphs by which the thousand rouse themselves / To spread on pinion a familiar thrill."[2] Thomas Mann, looking back from the fateful year 1933—the fiftieth anniversary of Wagner's death and the first year of Hitler's Reich—recalled his experience of similar consecrations with gratitude and regret: "My passion for the Wagnerian enchantment began with me as soon as I knew of it. . . . All that I owe to him, of enjoyment and instruction, I can never forget: the hours of deep and single bliss in the midst of the theatre crowds, hours of nervous and intellectual transport and rapture, of insights of great and moving import such as only this art vouchsafes."[3] Mann is openly nostalgic for the warmth of a nineteenth-century modernity that has since been battered by war and depression into skepticism and disillusionment, a decline whose best hope of reversal, if only at the symbolic level, is still Wagner.

Of course, Wagner also elicited intense hostility, most famously, exuberantly, and creatively from Nietzsche. But as Mann observed, Nietzsche's "immortal critique . . . [was] like a panegyric with the wrong label, like another kind of glorification. It was love-in-hate, it was self-flagellation. Wagner's art was the great passion of Nietzsche's life. He loved it as did Baudelaire, of whom it is told that in the agony, the paralysis, and the clouded mind of his last days he smiled with pleasure when he heard Wagner's name." Nietzsche himself conceded the point: "The last thing I want to do is start a celebration for any other musicians. Other musicians don't count compared to Wagner."[4] Without Wagner, Nietzsche's philosophical project is inconceivable, regardless of whether he writes as a disciple or an apostate.

During the heyday of Wagnerism, you could love Wagner or hate him, and very often both, but if you cared anything about music you could not take him lightly.

Baudelaire, Mallarmé, Nietzsche, and Mann form a distinguished if obviously somewhat arbitrary group of spokesmen for many others. The phenomenon they describe as enchantment or epiphany, as something interior or numinous, has a definite social character. It constitutes an aestheticized form of the experience of being touched at the quick, seized in one's very essence, that constitutes symbolic investiture. As we saw in the prologue, the "performative magic" of this fundamental social process fixes the character of my social world, fixes my place in that world, and fixes its place in me, that is, its "internalized" forms and values. Starting with naming, it traverses the whole field of ritualized behavior. As theorized by Pierre Bourdieu, symbolic investiture is a rite of initiation. But it is a peculiar sort of initiation whose effects can wear off; it has to be periodically renewed. Some such process is necessary for there to be any social world at all, and therefore for there to be any determinate form of individual subject at all. Yet for Bourdieu, as perhaps for Nietzsche, this necessity is a dire one. As noted in the prologue, symbolic investiture as Bourdieu conceives it is coercive to the core. The essence that it seizes is an essence it assigns. My essence is imposed on me as a fate and as such is, in another sense, fatal. Yet those who speak, like Mann, of gratitude and rapture, liberation and discovery, tell quite a different story, and it would be glib, even cynical, to write their testimony off as mere false consciousness.

These more affirmative witnesses tend to locate symbolic investiture primarily in art, not in the public forms of ritual and rhetoric that Bourdieu favors. Artists all, they are agents or heirs of the familiar nineteenth-century tendency for art to fill the void left behind by the collapse of other symbolic forms, whether moral, political, or religious, the collapse understood at the time as a defining trait of modernity.

This would settle nothing for Bourdieu, who regarded art as a form of symbolic capital. Besides, the larger quarrel of coercion and liberation probably has to be settled more by faith than by reason. But the stakes of this opposition, and of its shift in venue to art, to Opera, and to Wagner, are open to investigation. And the stakes are high.

The experience of symbolic investiture runs the risk of acquiescence in ideological fictions, of believing that choices arbitrarily made for one are the choices one has made. But experience in the absence of investiture runs the risk of committing one to a world deprived of genuine meaning and resonance. It is the dialectic of these two risks to which Wagner dedicated Opera, and to which his operas, over and above their specific dramatizations of that dialectic, were dedicated by the culture that received them.

That, perhaps, is one reason why the distinguished witnesses on our roster locate the musical mode of investiture less in a general conception of musical art than in the historical watershed defined by Wagner. "What a difference Wagner made in the world, after all," exclaims a character in Willa Cather's story "Uncle Valentine" (1925), moved by a blend of moonlight, memory, and the sound of *Das Rheingold* on the piano. In the earlier "A Wagner Matinée" (1904), Cather extends "this power that had kindled the world" to the reanimation of a soul nearly destroyed by the spiritual waste of hardscrabble life on the prairies: "It never really died, then—the soul which can suffer so excruciatingly. . . . [I]t withers to the outward eye only; like that strange moss which can lie on a dusty shelf half a century and yet, if placed in water, grows green again."[5] The trigger for this recrudescence is the prize song of *Die Meistersinger,* which draws its power from the twin magics of music and memory; Cather's protagonist has heard this song before, from the voice of a "German tramp cowpuncher who had sung in the chorus at Bayreuth when he was a boy" and for whom the protagonist, now old, had entertained a brief and futile love when young.

Cather's train of associations looks forward to Proust, and Proust himself provides a close analogy. The narrator of *In Search of Lost Time* defines the historical impact of Wagner as the discovery of an intimacy without boundaries, more resonant than the romantic love to which it is closely akin. Not music as such, but this music in particular is capable at times of becoming "so pressing and so close, so internal, so organic, so visceral, that [it seems] like the reprise not so much of a musical motive as of an attack of neuralgia." With this Wagnerian touch at the quick in mind, the narrator observes that "Music . . . helped me to descend into myself, to discover new things. . . . [T]he harmony of a Wagner . . . enable[s] us to know that essential quality of another person's sensation into which love for another person does not allow us to penetrate."[6] Wagner's music, above all *Tristan* and *Parsifal,* induces a kind of interior mutual nakedness that constitutes the self in the musical image of the Other.

But something is missing here. Proust is a writer; all my witnesses are writers, even if Nietzsche did compose a little. How does the Wagnerian enchantment play itself out among *musicians?* Or rather, in their music? That is my question here. It is not, emphatically not, the question of Wagner as an "influence" on compositional technique either in or out of Opera. Rather it is the question of Wagner as a cultural trope, as a charismatic voice, as a figure both *of* symbolic authority and *for* symbolic authority. Not all musicians, of course, have felt called on to address this question, and those who have form only an accidental group. The attitude within that group, however, seems more than just accidental, and it departs strikingly from the writers' adulation. At least in certain works by Debussy, Poulenc, Shostakovich, and Henze, Wagner assumes a disconcerting ambiguity. He represents not the continuing power of symbolic investiture but its recession into the dead past. Yet at the same time he also represents the uncanny persistence of investiture, its return to life in inverted form, like a panegyric with the wrong label. Wagner's symbolic effectiveness both intrudes on modernity as a relic and haunts it with a piercing, even dangerous, nostalgia.

This ambiguity seems to be bound up with the actual sound of Wagner's music, again regarded not as a model or influence, but as an acoustic object, a symbolic presence realized by quotation. The question is not one of sounding like Wagner, but of Wagner sounding, not what to do after Wagner but of what to do with him. The results are fraught with ambivalence, a quality that Mann, among the writers, finds endemic to Wagner himself. As well he might: for the question of whether symbolic investiture is alive or dead in the modern world is very much Wagner's question, his answers to which are as fraught with ambivalence as he is.

A further perspective on this question can be drawn from what seems an unlikely source, the delusional system of a nineteenth-century jurist, Daniel Paul Schreber, whose *Memoirs of My Nervous Illness* (1903) inspired a case history by Freud. Schreber became convinced that the redemption of fallen humanity was dependent upon his transformation into a woman as a result of his bodily penetration by the "rays of God." He is of interest here partly as the object of a study, not by Freud, but by the critic Eric Santner, who sees in Schreber a figure for the secret history of modernity based on the collapse of symbolic investiture.[7] No symbolic power can seize Schreber in his essence—either as man or judge—so he must fantasize a counteressence that can be seized literally, bodily, by the ultimate referent of all symbolic forms. The result is also of interest here because it is so strikingly Wagnerian. The theme of world redemption through feminine sacrifice is about as Wagnerian as one can get. The only thing missing is the music, which is supplied, ironically, by the most unmusical of thinkers, Freud, who compares Schreber's "end of the world fantasy" to the "climax of a lover's ecstasy" in *Tristan und Isolde*.[8] Schreber himself did no less. When he and his wife moved into a new home in 1901, after he had won release from involuntary confinement, he had Siegfried's horn call from the *Ring* cycle inscribed over the threshhold.[9] Freud's analogy and Schreber's inscription not only link Schreber's secret history to a pair of the nineteenth century's most representative, most symptomatic works, but also testify to the century's increasing identification of music with the primary terrain of symbolic investiture and its performative magic.

Wagner is pivotal in this development by means of a kind of doubling whereby his operas not only turn on dramas of investiture, but themselves for this very reason also become performatives of investiture. They form magical anticipations of a future redemption, realized in a musical present that revives the premodern past. They create a perennially transitional space that is symbolized by Schreber's threshold. This is the portal of Proust's intimacy, Mann's bliss fused with insight, Mallarmé's consecration, Baudelaire's smile. One might describe these performative effects in classical aesthetic terms by invoking the Kantian analysis of aesthetic judgment as a subjective universal. For Kant, who is not thinking of music because he doesn't think very highly of it, the judgment that something is beautiful demands universal assent in the full knowledge that such assent is unlikely to be given. The demand is a purely formal property, though not the less strongly felt for that.[10] In music heard with post-Wagnerian ears, and above all in Wagner's own music, this purely formal property of the aesthetic becomes an actual social force that seizes the subject in his or her essence.

Just why this happens is hard to say, perhaps impossible to say. It could be part of the hypnotic effect so often associated with Wagner's dilatory harmony and motivic web-spinning. It could stem from his conjunction of long, continuously evolving stretches of music with premodern narrative images, a coupling that enabled him to reverse—symbolically—the collapse of symbolic authority marking the advent of modernity. The historical fact is that it happens. With Wagner, after Wagner, music becomes the wellspring of performative magic. And because this happens, Wagner, too, encapsulates a secret history of modernity. But unlike Schreber's, this history is allegorical, not delusional, unless you are a perfect anti-Wagnerite for whom the two in the case of Wagner are the same thing.

Unlike Schreber's, too, the secret in Wagner's secret history is an open one, as allegorical secrets always are. As Walter Benjamin observed, with nineteenth-century modernity in mind, "[a]llegory recognizes many enigmas, but it knows no mystery. . . . To touch on things means, for it, to violate them. To recognize things means, for it, to see through them."[11] Wagner's impulse might be described as the desire to replace the allegory of modernity with the music that embodies it. The allegory points to a void of symbolic investiture; the music fills it. Wotan cheats; the music pays in full. The subsequent fate of this desire, which is my topic here, depends on how Wagnerian modes of investiture are cited, troped, adapted, and travestied, from Debussy's satire of the *Tristan* mystique in "Golliwogg's Cakewalk" to Anna Russell's travesty of the *Ring* as stand-up comedy, from the ubiquity of "The Ride of the Valkyries" on television commercials to the allegorical woodcuts and photographs by which Anselm Kiefer depicts German history after the Holocaust as an ironic repetition of the *Ring* and *Parsifal*.

Debussy offers an emblematic starting point for this phenomenon, in which Wagner becomes a symptom of modernity under the sign of negation. Where Wagnerism in its heyday was opera's, and music's, philosopher's stone of symbolic investiture, the relentless course of modernization effected a reversal whereby Wagner becomes the site of the modern failure of investiture. The reversal begins as something faintly comic but develops into something decisively tragic, even catastrophic.

The comedy begins with a doll and a dance. "Golliwogg's Cake-walk" is a very popular piece, the subject of innumerable arrangements. And it's common to observe that Debussy repeatedly makes irreverent quotations of the opening of the *Tristan* Prelude while evoking the European vogue for the cakewalk through the lens of child's play; "Golliwogg" concludes the *Children's Corner* suite (1908) dedicated to Debussy's daughter, Claude-Emma, whose playthings included both a golliwogg doll and several of the illustrated books on which the doll was patterned. It's not common, however, to remark on what an odd combination all this makes. What do the erotic and harmonic ferment of *Tristan* have to do with the buffoonery of the cakewalk, originally a dance by which African American slaves mocked their masters' manners, much to the latter's amusement, and subsequently to the amusement of fin-de-siècle Europeans, who enjoyed a toned-down version as a kind of do-it-yourself minstrel show?

Perhaps this incongruity is the whole point. Debussy does not so much write a cakewalk as portray one; he distances and miniaturizes it, wraps its signature syncopated rhythm in impressionistic harmonies, makes it the object of affectionate mockery. After all, this is Golliwogg's cakewalk, and a golliwogg is a grotesque object: a bug-eyed, thick-lipped, coal-black little man in fancy dress—hence the cakewalk connection—that is repellent today, but once struck many white people as endearing. It was meant to be a fashionable trifle. And by inserting *Tristan* precisely in the context of such trifles, Debussy suggests that Wagnerism, too, is just an exotic fad, amusing but ultimately just a debased puppet show.

The mockery here is not so affectionate, probably in proportion to resentment at Wagnerism's cultural authority. Deflating Wagner was no cakewalk. But "Golliwogg's Cake-walk" smilingly relativizes Wagner into insignificance. It puts *Tristan* cheek to cheek with music doubly primitive, being both American and African American. The point of the jibe does not, I think, include Wagner's racial ideology and anti-Semitism. Debussy, who remained noncommittal throughout the Dreyfus affair, who came to believe in pure (French) blood, and whose own anti-Semitism was not much affected by his second marriage to the Jewish Emma Bardac, is not the best source for that.[12] The point is to expose the social underpinnings of Wagner's musical metaphysics. The dancing doll shows up the sacred *Tristan* mantra as a social ritual, half affectation, half-fantasy: Golliwogg's lovedeath.

In this way Debussy teaches Wagnerism a lesson in modernist aesthetics, which is also a lesson in cool detachment and cultural sophistication. The effect, though Debussy loathed the term, is cosmopolitan. "Golliwogg's Cake-walk" reflexively demonstrates that it can absorb both a popular style and the Wagnerian afflatus, commit itself to neither, and thus achieve a fully modern identity. To that end, the piece takes pains to make Wagner inaudible at the very core of *Tristan*. There are no true quotations here. In Debussy's version, the melodic phrase that begins the *Tristan* Prelude is repeatedly stripped of its harmonic support; each time the phrase closes, it is deprived of the symbolically all-resonant *Tristan* chord and handed a substitute. Not that the chord is abolished; it's pilfered. Its pitch content turns up as one of the harmonizations of the cakewalk tune, but without Wagner's distinctive spacing in superimposed fourths. As golliwogg harmony, the rejiggered chord shows its true lack of metaphysical gravity; it adapts all too easily to witty banter. The seeming quotations thus mark not so much the recurrence of the *Tristan* Prelude as its disappearance, its impossibility in the modern era.

Yet the phrase from the Prelude is stubborn; it is heard four times, marked "with a grand emotion."[13] Its persistence seems to acknowledge that there is not only yearning in the *Tristan* Prelude, but a yearning *for* it. Debussy's cocktail-piano version of this music is not a rejection of Wagner as such but of the supine worship of "the god Richard Wagner" prominent among French composers, artists, and critics after 1880. The project of French Wagnerism was to reconcile Wagner's aesthetic with French national identity.[14] For Debussy the only means of doing that was ironic distance; his parody sinks German *Schwärmerei* beneath Gallic sophistication. "Golliwogg's Cake-walk" thus claims a progressive modernity for France, one that no longer requires Wagnerian symbolic investiture and that acquires its wit and energy precisely by enacting the obsolescence of the Wagnerian enchantment, its permanent, if always haunting, failure.

But the gesture is suspicious for being so slight: one really can't dispose of *Tristan* and the Wagner mystique in a two-minute piano piece. It's not so easy even in a full-length opera, as Debussy had discovered when he rewrote *Tristan* as *Pelléas*. The force of symbolic investiture has a way of reaffirming itself willy-nilly, as we will discover again in Poulenc. And this happens all the more when the failure of investiture involves events of more than musical significance, as we will see subsequently with Shostakovich and Henze. The symbolic forms broken by modernity survive in allegorical fragments that then proliferate, ever less animate, less numinous, but still indestructible.

Poulenc's citation of Wagner was the inspiration for this chapter. It came to my attention in a typically brave and brilliant paper by Philip Brett, sadly the last he lived to write.[15] Brett observed that a "café tune" strangely morphs itself into a fragment of Wagner's magic fire music in the finale of Poulenc's 1932 Concerto for Two Pianos in D Minor. This happens fleetingly but unmistakably, more or less bisecting the movement. The orchestra paraphrases the motive for the radiance of the fire, after which the two pianos parody the motive depicting the flickering flames. More distanced versions of the same allusions return, in reverse order, just before the abrupt conclusion. What does it all mean?

It could be another lesson in modernist aesthetics: a sophisticated satire, a cosmopolitan assimilation of Wagner on the understanding that he is as obsolete as he is inevitable. Or it could be a satire on cosmopolitan sophistication itself, a brief recognition that you are likely to run smack into Wagner just when you think you've escaped him forever. Either way, the little metamorphosis is a sign of modernist cool; it makes common cause with "Golliwogg's Cake-walk," which, as we've just noted, performs the converse gesture, converting the opening phrase of the *Tristan* Prelude to a café tune.

At another level, as Brett's paper suggests, Poulenc's citation may put a gay spin on Wagner's phrase, drawing it into the orbit of ironic mimicry characteristic of certain gay subcultures and consistent with the "nonseriousness" and stylistic pluralism of the concerto as a whole, which incorporates Mozart, Javanese gamelan, and neoclassicism as well as Wagner and café tunes. One might even suggest that the citation serves to "out" the broader queering of Wagner that flourished in the early twentieth century.[16] The suggestion is particularly resonant in connection with the magic fire music: the music, that is, for the barrier Siegfried must cross to find Brünnhilde at the defining moment of both his sexuality and his identity. As we saw in the preceding chapter, the object of desire that he finds sleeping amid the flames initially appears to him as male. But the appearance is deceiving, and so is that of the magic fire music in Poulenc, which is both a silly joke and an almost compulsory acknowledgment of the sneaking resemblance between Poulenc's tune and Wagner's motives. The citation is clear; what it means is not.

As with the incongruity in "Golliwogg," this semantic indeterminacy may be just the point. Highlighting the status of the motive as an unfixed, roving signifier gives the index of modernity. More particularly, it poses the question of what makes up the discourse of modernity. For this allusion is not just a subversion of Wagner. It is, so to speak, a subverted subversion. It is an invocation, in spite of itself, of Wagnerian seriousness, Wagnerian desire, as the condition that artistic modernity must either embody or travesty, and more often both at once.

T. S. Eliot produced an analogous situation a few years earlier in *The Waste Land* (1922) with the cries of the Thames maidens—Wagner's Rhinemaidens in shabby modern dress. When the Thames maidens speak, telling tales of seduction and abandonment, they represent the descent of Wagnerian allegory into lower-class realism. But their language is stately, its idiom a relic of Jacobean tragedy:

"Trams and dusty trees.
Highbury bore me. Richmond and Kew
Undid me. By Richmond I raised my knees
Supine on the floor of a narrow canoe."
(ll. 292–95)[17]

And when the Thames maidens' cries are transcribed with the vocables that Wagner devised for the Rhinemaidens, what we see on the page are the empty syllables "Weialala leia / Wallala leialala," but what we are supposed to hear in the mind's ear is the music by which Wagner turns these syllables into a haunting vocalise.

Poulenc's thematic metamorphosis represents a reflective form of the same dilemma. Its recycled motives retain much of their power, even their magic, but they have lost their epiphanic value. Poulenc's magic fire music is a throwaway in which the discarded object, Wagner's original, contains the modernist whole that ejects it. This is especially true of the initial quotation, where the element of travesty is minimal. Embedded in Poulenc's score, the magic fire music is no longer an enchanting fragment of Wagnerian allegory; it is a fragmentary allegory for the Wagnerian enchantment itself.

The whole question of modernity condenses here into a Wagnerian remainder as to its preordained destination. Such moments testify to the authority of symbolic investiture by investing in its reversal: they are moments of symbolic divestiture. They catch the sublimating movement that elevates the modest (not even the trivial: the modest, the ordinary, Poulenc's café tune) to a value beyond reason, a value that burns and flickers in defiance

of reason. And we hear this in the music itself, which is, of course, not itself at all.

The lightheartedness of Debussy and Poulenc did not survive the accumulating tragedies of the twentieth century. Moving forward to 1972, just over
a hundred years after the premiere of *Die Walküre*, we find the Fate motive
introduced in that opera recalled to service in the finale of Shostakovich's
last Symphony, the Fifteenth, a characteristic exercise in regret and lamen-
tation. This citation contains nothing of the spirit of cosmopolitan assimilation; spirit of any kind seems to have drained out of it. The music culled
from Wagner retains its expressive meaning only to deny that meaning to
the music that incorporates it. This denial is systematic and uncompromising. At first, without preamble, we hear Wagner's motive, the brass fanfare
that precedes both Brünnhilde's annunciation of death to Siegmund in *Die
Walküre* and Hagen's stabbing of Siegfried in *Götterdämmerung*. This is
followed by a variant of the timpani motto associated with the motive and
carried over into the beginning of Siegfried's funeral music. These quotations are stated twice, separated by a brief "heartbeat" figure on pizzicato
strings. Then what seems to be a third statement segues from the Fate motive to the opening phrase of *Tristan*.

But the burden of *Tristan* is too much to bear. At just the point where
the phrase would be harmonized by the *Tristan* chord, Shostakovich, like
Debussy, withholds it. So we are right back at "Golliwogg's Cake-walk," but
recomposed on a grand scale in postcosmopolitan, posttragic, postapocalyp-
tic mode. The *Tristan* phrase becomes the transition to a sad, straggling,
faintly folklike tune that seems to have nowhere to go. The tune is not at
home in a Wagnerian universe, and certainly not in the worlds of heroic or
ecstatic death invoked by the chain of quotations: worlds in which seemingly meaningless deaths—the murders of Siegmund and Siegfried, Tristan's self-destructive tearing at his wounds—are transfigured by the performative magic of music.

Shostakovich's quotations suggest a "reading" of Wagner which defines
that magic as the possibility of transcendentalizing death by love and love
by death: the first the case of Brünnhilde's immolation, the second of Isolde's
transfiguration. Nothing of the sort is possible in Shostakovich's world,
which has had too much death for any symbolic power to manage. The symphony's second movement, much of it devoted to a disconsolate funeral
march, has already made that clear. The movement even begins with a

solemn, semi-ecclesiastical brass chorale prefiguring the Fate motive that begins the finale. Quoted with the twentieth century behind it, that motive is no longer a portent but a memory, and the doom it remembers is abject, not exalted. Brünnhilde's words, "Only those doomed to die can see me; / Who looks on me must part from the light of life," hover in the air with discomfiting new meaning. The same logic bears down on the *Tristan* phrase, which no longer speaks of desire unto death but of the death of desire. The question thus posed by the finale is how to deal with the twentieth century's legacy of death—the superabundance of deaths, of persons, of hopes, of ideals—in the absence of symbolic support. The long remainder of the movement tries to find an answer without the support of Wagner, to whom its quotations form a final farewell.[18]

The world introduced by the sad little post-*Tristan* tune is one in which expressive value survives the loss of symbolic power, but at the risk of making the survival meaningless. Love is absent, and heroic death impossible, because the world is no longer one in which meaning is credible, even allegorically. All that is left is unheroic life, which does go on, just like the tune and the music that trails after it. But that is not really enough to live on, to live on with, and after traipsing along fecklessly for awhile the music is called to order by a restatement of the Fate motive. The heart of the movement follows: a long passacaglia which is also a long crescendo mounting to a violent, militaristic outburst, the only loud climax in the movement. The passacaglia constitutes an extended act of mourning for the world in which love and death could still be concentrated in the exemplary fates of a Siegfried or an Isolde: in "character isolated by a deed," as W. B. Yeats once put it.[19] The melodic contour of the Fate motive haunts the mourning process, which is in part an attempt to exorcise its memory.

What follows, after the fury of the climax has been allowed to dissipate, is a reprise of the opening in which the Fate motive is rejoined by the *Tristan* phrase, which has long been silent. But there are telltale changes. The timpani motto associated with the motive does not return. In Siegfried's funeral music, a "quickening" of that motto becomes the kernel of the musical narrative that redeems Siegfried's debased death by retelling the tragicheroic story of his life. There are no such stories to be told in this symphony. Meanwhile, although the *Tristan* phrase returns, it does so in distorted form. Lame echoes of it permeate the full reprise, which gradually winds down and gives out.

The rest is a long epilogue: not a coda, but a distanced reflection on things past. Here the music comes to a standstill in the midst of its own ruins. A quiet pedal point begins in the form of an open fifth on the strings: A–E, a reduction of the A–F–E of the *Tristan* phrase to an empty skeleton. The pedal goes on for a very long time. Over it rises a faint chatter and clatter of percussion: snare drum, wood blocks, triangle, xylophone. This is at once a meaningless sound, the rattle of dry bones, and a kind of Cheshire smile that lives on stubbornly when all the rest of the music has disappeared. At the last moment a few taps on the xylophone create a little whimper of A major in lieu of closure. Then the bare fifth does a quick fadeout, the last vanishing sound of a genuine farewell symphony.[20]

Of course, the prototype for this loss of enchantment is Wagner's own. The moment that announces it is a famous self-quotation, a moment of nostalgia for a Wagnerian enchantment already lost even to Wagner himself. When Hans Sachs, in *Die Meistersinger,* realizes he has to renounce his incipient desire for Eva, the orchestra strikes up the *Tristan* Prelude. Sachs must renounce the fatal and transcendental magic of this music in the interest of social harmony. What he accepts in its place is a public, ceremonial image of medieval Nuremberg as the ideal organic society. But there is much more to the problem than this one emblematic moment of reflection. As intimated in the Prologue, the issue of symbolic investiture is basic to the technique, the theme, and the effect of Wagner's work in general. It runs the gamut from *Der fliegende Holländer,* where investiture, in the form of Senta's interpellation by a picture, is the uncontested premise of the famous Wagnerian topos of redemption, to *Parsifal,* where the ceremony of investiture is the much contested goal to be attained only after a lifetime of penitential suffering. The distance between these works is in part a reflex of growing modern skepticism. And the theater of that skepticism is the *Ring,* named for an object that epitomizes the conversion of symbolic power into instrumental force. It remains an open question whether the cycle's acts of symbolic restitution are sufficient to counter the acts of debasement fomented by the Nibelung's ring.

Whatever the answer, the question is Wagner's legacy to modernity. Although he came too early to share the sweeping loss of faith that later generations endured or embraced, that loss is implicit in all of Wagner's works from *Tristan* onward. It is enunciated dramatically even earlier, in *Rheingold,* at the moment of that opera's most stunning coup de theatre, the eruption of Erda onto the scene of Wotan's haggling with the giants over what it will cost to buy back Freia. Wotan has refused to add the Nibelung's ring to the mounting hoard; Erda sternly admonishes him to do it. His compliance marks the defining moment of modernity for Wagner, as also for Marx:

the exact equation of human and economic worth, the alienation of Freia's subjectivity, without remainder, into the commodity form. The social consequences immediately become apparent in Fafner's murder of his brother. And the general loss finds its own revelation in the irony of Erda's warning. She herself is an unassimilable remainder of the premodern world, but her appearance as such is the surest sign that her world is already lost. The damage is done, whatever Wotan does. She has come too late.

Rheingold also supplies a musical image for the subjective destitution of modernity that anticipates both the percussive close of the Shostakovich Fifteenth Symphony and the mechanical imagery basic to nineteenth-century conceptions of the modern. As Wotan and Loge descend to Nibelheim, we hear the sound of hammering on anvils, a true anvil chorus, and nothing else. Music reduces to mere noise; the sonoric image embraces both the metallic drive of modern industry and the clinking of coin, a wealth of machinery and the machinery of wealth. George Bernard Shaw memorably described the allegorical value of the scene: "This gloomy place need not be a mine; it might just as well be . . . a whitelead factory, or a chemical works, or a pottery, or a railroad shunting yard . . . or any other of the places where human life and welfare are daily sacrificed [on behalf of] some greedy foolish creature."[21] The *Ring* thus becomes a prototypically modernist work in its opposition to the condition of modernity, and specifically to the failure of symbolic investiture that increasingly defines modernity. The crux of *Rheingold* both exemplifies and diagnoses this failure and puts it into dramatic and ideological play.

Wagner's anvil chorus reduces the possibility of symbolic investiture to zero so that the possibility can be recovered over the course of the next three operas, to be regained at last, after Wotan's corruptions and Siegfried's betrayals, by Brünnhilde's sacrifice. Melody and harmony collapse into raw rhythm, the pounding of matter without meaning, so that the remainder of the tetralogy, with its vast web of repeated, varied, and proliferating motives, becomes the antidote to this reduction. The "organic," "visceral" life of the motives repeals the possibility of lifeless mechanism.

The same pattern of reduction and recovery occurs again, almost exactly a century after the first complete *Ring*, in Hans Werner Henze's *Tristan* (1973, roughly contemporary with Shostakovich's Fifteenth Symphony). This polymorphic work, subtitled "Preludes for Piano, Tapes, and Orchestra," is perhaps the most thoroughgoing musical confrontation with the figure of Wagner that we have. It is a piece driven not only by the forces of alienated modernity that Wagner opposed, but also by the forces of destruction that his legacy served. Henze's attitude is akin to that of Serenus

Zeitblom, the narrator of Mann's postwar novel *Doctor Faustus* (1948), for whom the endgame of the Nazi era was an immolation kindled by the refusal of the Germans to relinquish symbolic anointment: "Yes, we are a completely different nation . . . whose soul is powerfully tragic; our love belongs to fate, any fate, if only it is one, even a doom that sets the heavens afire with the red twilight of the gods."[22] Zeitblom's language is too elevated; it is complicit with the madness it condemns. But Mann shares the stubborn love of Wagner that makes the metaphor of *Götterdämmerung*, then fresh, now almost a cliché, painful and shocking. Henze is not caught in this snare. "I had always avoided Wagner's work," he wrote, "out of a certain antipathy"[23]— the antipathy of a passionate man of the left who grew up during the Third Reich and devoted much of his music to issues of suffering and injustice. Yet given Wagner's musical rather than his political legacy, and especially his extraordinary gift for expressing suffering, some kind of reckoning was perhaps inevitable.

It was perhaps inevitable, too, that the opera chosen for this purpose was *Tristan*, the one of Wagner's mature works seemingly least affected by his toxic politics, the opera that for many is the very acme of Wagner's performative magic. "I am well aware what Wagner signifies," wrote Henze, "wherein his greatness lies; *Tristan*, which I have never seen, although I have studied the score in detail, has subsequently become a kind of bible for me" (144). For a Nietzsche, a Mann, a Proust, this music has the capacity to supersede and subsume all other music. Proust's narrator bears witness to that capacity by recalling an occasion on which he acted it out allegorically. He has been playing the piano sonata of the fictional composer Vinteuil and thinking of how "every great artist . . . gives us so strongly that sensation of individuality for which we seek in vain in our everyday existence." At once he is struck by a familiar passage in the sonata which he suddenly sees in a new light: "although Vinteuil had been trying to express a fancy which would have been wholly foreign to Wagner, I could not help murmuring *Tristan* . . . [S]o, on top of Vinteuil's sonata, I set up on the music rest the score of *Tristan*, a selection from which was being given that afternoon, as it happened, at a Lamoureux concert."[24] Suddenly, the murmur of *Tristan* is everywhere; it is the matrix within which all other music is heard.

So, too, with Henze's set of preludes, the score of which is figuratively set atop Wagner's on the music rest. There are six movements, unfurling in two waves. The first two preludes form a pair and pose a problem, to which the third reflectively seeks a solution; it fails, and the remaining preludes repeat the pattern in intensified form. The problem is the old one of the

"Wagner case" made new by the immolations of recent history: what do you when the Wagnerian enchantment becomes the Wagnerian horror?

That is just what happens in the first pair of preludes, "Prologue" and "Lament." "Prologue" is scored for solo piano with occasional interjections by the winds. According to Henze, the music is "cool, as if it were early morning, and the questioning and longing are expressed with muted voice." The questioning and longing are those of *Tristan*, which, Henze tells us, his own music "distantly recalls" with its harmony in search of an "incommensurate goal" and its vocabulary of "semitonal steps and sixths, chords of fourths and, in particular, diminished fifths" (222). But the distance is more moral than musical. The winds in particular tend to break it down with *Tristan*-esque moans, intruding the questioning and longing on the piano's cooler reflectiveness; the sound of *Tristan* permeates the prelude, all the more palpable a presence for never quite condensing into an exact quotation. This "absent presence" carries over into the second prelude, where the full orchestra and tape erupt into action. With them come unwelcome things: darkness, heaviness, violence. The enhanced texture is harsh and chaotic, and relentlessly worsens with each new layer of sonority.

The third prelude, "Preludes and Variations," is an attempt at coping, the first essay in what Henze identifies as the larger work's underlying effort to form "a vehement act of will against this chaos that threatens to break in from all sides" (225). The attempt is premature. "Everything," Henze writes, "is in a state of unrest and agitation, as if a gust of wind had blown through the house" (226). The music even forgets its Wagnerian identity and blunders into a quotation of the vehement C-minor opening of Brahms's First Symphony, with its pounding timpani and uncanny melodic resemblance to the Desire motive of *Tristan*.[25] The prelude eventually ends in fragmentation, "blinded and stumbling."

Then things get worse. The fourth prelude, "Tristan's Folly," is a prolonged essay in mounting cacophony, centered emblematically on a taped deformation of Chopin's Funeral March described by Henze as being of "an overpowering hideousness." Paired with the fourth, which segues into it, the fifth prelude initially makes a retreat to the safe haven of all modern alienation, parody and pastiche. It unreels a series of burlesque dance pieces—a waltz, an *alla turca*, a march squeezed between the abstract panels of two ricercars. But there is no playfulness here; this is not Poulenc. And the bad faith behind the parodies eventually succumbs to a resumption of monstrous cacophony, worse than before. Henze's description is, as usual, eloquent: "[the end is] a scream of death [*Todesschrei*], no longer simply that of Isolde or Tristan, but of the whole suffering world, which seems to burst the bounds of concert music. What can be heard on the tape is an electronic elaboration of the scream of a Wagnerian heroine, broken up into many voices and colours. The utmost volume in the orchestra: weeping, howling and bird-calls, and the sound of flexatone and foghorn, all of which slowly ebb away" (227).

The entry of the human voice, deformed beyond recognition into a physically assaultive mass of inarticulate sound, far harsher than Wagner's anvils, threatens to mark a zero point, a point of no return. Henze reduces the voice to dead matter, much as Anselm Kiefer, in a roughly contemporary woodcut, reduces Brünnhilde's warhorse, Grane, to a skeleton exposed as by an X-ray by the flames of a general immolation; the animal can be identified only because its name is written across the top of the picture. But as the sixth and final prelude is about to reveal, the Wagnerian death cry of the fifth is a turning point, albeit one still inchoate.

"Epilogue," the sixth prelude, seeks a resolution by recreating Isolde's transfiguration in a non-Wagnerian setting. After a few moments of reflection, we hear the taped sound of a human heartbeat. Then an articulate voice, high and sweet, intervenes: the voice of a boy intoning, in lightly accented Cockney English, a fragment of the twelfth-century *Tristan* by Thomas of Britain: "She takes him in her arms, and then, lying at full length, she kisses his face and lips and clasps him tightly to her. Then straining body to body, mouth to mouth, she at once renders up her spirit and of sorrow for her lover dies thus at his side."[26] Medieval austerity replaces romantic lushness; the innocence of a child, reciting with at best a partial understanding, replaces adult sexuality and world-weariness. But the effect is not to escape from Wagner but to recover him: to restore to Wagner's *Tristan* the transfiguring value that has become tarnished, precisely, by Wagner himself. Henze constructs the moment as a temporal palimpsest or polyphony in which Wagner can still be heard. Beneath the medieval words in the modern music, we hear "in extreme augmentation the Wagnerian *Tristan*-sounds from [both] . . . the beginning of the third act" and the song that Wagner regarded as a sketch for it, *Im Treibhaus*.[27]

But what is recovered in this prelude, now a postlude, is only the performative magic of the original, not its content. Henze's transfiguration of love and death is not a scene of rapture like that of Wagner's Isolde. That Isolde is almost rescinded here; a small boy reciting a text in Cockney English is about as far from her as one can get. And the deeply lamenting music that begins the opera's third act is predicated precisely on Isolde's absence. What Henze recovers in this scene—again quite unlike Shostakovich in the Fifteenth Symphony—is sorrow without irony. He does so by putting the third act lament in the place of Isolde's transfiguration, but not to oust it: to become it, rather, as befits the modern age. The rehumanized voice of the final prelude brings with it the capacity to mourn, to let grief overflow, and so to replace horror by lament and at the same time reconcile history and tragedy. The remainder of the music, a long second epilogue, seeks just those ends. Henze's description cannot be bettered: "Bells chime . . . and are accompanied by taped electronic transformations of this old music, waxing and waning, chaconne-like, glistening like the sea on an autumn evening. . . . In this light, and these sounds, this weeping and falling mute, everything that has accompanied this work comes together: places and people . . . deaths and varieties of death, and the dead whose passing has impoverished humanity while the fascists' goose-step resounds through empty buildings."[28]

One reason for the power lost and recovered—yet still lost—in Henze's *Tristan* is the completeness with which Wagner's music has been felt to negate, to make disappear, the materiality of the modern world that intrudes the erosion of symbolic power on everyday life. Henze's transfiguration scene does the same thing in a latter-day context almost in spite of itself. The theater at Bayreuth, with its covered orchestra pit that turns the stage into a quasi-immaterial fantasy screen, successfully sought to institutionalize this dematerializing effect and invest it with cult value. But the music proved able to produce a like effect just about anywhere. It was an effect much sought after in the era of nineteenth-century modernity, what I think of as the "middle" modernity shaped by technological transformation and the icon of the machine. Contemporary observers of this phenomenon such as Max Nordau and Georg Simmel emphasized the corrosive effects of speed and steel, the acceleration of time and reorganization of space, the penetration of daily life by robust and impersonal force.[29] Surmounting the material world of middle modernity, if only in virtual terms by morphing it into its own antithesis, was the paramount alternative to embracing it. The result was an abstract imagery, an allegorical dreamworld, everywhere informed by a modernity it nowhere acknowledged.

While they still had novelty value, at just about the height of the Wagnerian enchantment, both the phonograph and urban electric lighting were important media for this effect. The phonograph was initially regarded primarily as a means for recording not music but voices, which were widely felt to acquire an uncanny disembodied life that escaped the device that conferred it.[30] The machine became a cocoon for the ghost. This phenomenon still lingers in "historical" recordings of famous singers; opera stars were, of course, among the first to be recorded. The recordings, laden with a sense of their own pastness and often of their technical obsolescence, serve to perpetuate not so much the music sung or even a particular rendition of it as the voices that sang it: not a performance of Brünnhilde or Isolde, far less of Wagner, but the vocal trace of Olive Fremsted or Kirsten Flagstad.

Meanwhile, the new wonder of nighttime illumination turned cityscapes into Bayreuth-like dreamscapes. At world's fairs and trade expositions in Paris in 1889 and 1900, and in Chicago in 1893, massive shows of electrification were received as "fairytale spectacle[s]"; at an automotive trade show in Paris in 1904, the Grand Palais built for the 1900 exposition was illuminated by 200,000 lights that turned the building into "a radiant jewel." As one observer noted, this was no more than a heightened form of the everyday magic that turned the urban night into an antidote for modernity: at nightfall "[the] trifling or irritating profiles [of the city] are melted into a conflagration of apotheosis."[31] Tristan's abnormal longing for a night to obliterate day once and for all was translated into a normal and punctual event. This systematic doubleness, not to say duplicity, marked these technological effects as Wagnerian and at the same time marked Wagner as quintessentially, symptomatically, modern.[32]

This symptomatic value was largely atmospheric, but it could become explicit. In the final volume of Proust's novel, the narrator talks with his friend Saint-Loup about the aesthetics of aerial combat over Paris in World War I. "I spoke of the beauty of the aeroplanes climbing up into the night," he says, comparing the distant squadrons to constellations; then asks: "'Don't you prefer the moment . . . of *apocalypse*, when even the stars are hurled from their courses? And then the sirens, could they have been more Wagnerian? . . . One had to ask oneself whether they were indeed pilots and not Valkyries.'" "'That's it,'" Saint-Loup replies, "'the music of the sirens was a 'Ride of the Valkyries'! . . . The Germans have to arrive before you can hear Wagner in Paris.'" The narrator continues: "In some ways the simile was not misleading. The town from being a black shapeless mass seemed suddenly to rise out of the abyss and the night into the luminous sky, where one after another the pilots soared upwards in answer to the heart-rending appeal of the sirens, while . . . the searchlights strayed ceaselessly to and fro. . . . [E]ach pilot, as he soared thus above the town . . . resembled indeed a Valkyrie."[33] The Wagnerian spectacle both carries the morphing effect of the electrical fairyland to its uttermost extreme and strangely anticipates the famous scene in Francis Ford Coppola's film *Apocalypse Now* when American army helicopters attack a village in Vietnam while blaring "The Ride of the Valkyries" from loudspeakers.

But America got into the act much earlier. The country was a hotbed of Wagnermania in the late nineteenth century—for instance, at Chicago's Columbian Exhibition of 1893. This hugely popular world's fair based its morphing effect on what would later become the principle of the Hollywood movie set. The fair's buildings and midway were constructed of a plaster-board-type material to give the illusion of an imperishable utopia, the famous "White City," a newly built Valhalla unbesmirched by Wotan's dirty dealing. The scene could be observed as a whole from the heights of a rotating mechanical image of the modern world, the giant wheel designed by George W. G. Ferris to rival the Eiffel Tower. Wagner was very much on the soundtrack for these images. Under the direction of Theodore Thomas, the conductor of the Chicago Orchestra, the exposition offered a series of concerts meant to provide "a full illustration of music in its highest form, as exemplified by the most enlightened nations of the world." (It was Thomas who had conducted the Grand Festival March in Philadelphia at the Centennial Exposition.) Wagner was the composer most often performed in the White City, and the series of concerts began, in fine allegorical fashion, on his birthday.[34]

For Proust, Wagner's power of dematerialization stemmed from a self-division typical of the greatest nineteenth-century art, a hovering self-contemplation from which the artist drew "a new form of beauty, exterior and superior to the work itself."[35] In their "quality of being—albeit marvelously—always incomplete," Wagner's operas insist that any image of closure or totality in the modern era is necessarily false. Benjamin assigned the same power to allegory, which, he said, is to the mind what ruins are to history. For Georg Lukács, allegory in Benjamin's sense combines with modern self-contemplation to produce nothing less than "the disintegration of the world." Objectivity dwindles; immanent meaning disappears; time dissolves into pure subjectivity: "The individual, retreating into himself in despair at the cruelty of the age, may experience an intoxicated fascination with his forlorn condition. But then a new horror breaks through. . . . By separating time from the outer world of objective reality, the inner world of the subject is transformed into a sinister, inexplicable flux."[36]

Lukács might just as well be describing Wagnerian time, that slow-motion passage through a medium like the depths of the Rhine, which, in combination with Wagner's "close," "organic," "visceral" style, creates an alternative materiality that envelops the listener—an embrace for some, suffocation for others. Wagner's operas as early as *Tannhäuser,* but especially from *Tristan* onward, constitute allegorical rejections of modernity and its materialities to which the enveloping mode of Wagnerian time and sensation stands as a surrogate for the worldly redemption still to come. In contrast to later listening—the Wagnerian listening that demands to be enchanted—later music found itself unable either to make the same rejection or to offer the same surrogate. It could, however, occasionally let itself be haunted explicitly by Wagner's power to do both.

Which leaves us where? The story of modernity may have entered its late or "post-" phases, but the story is not yet over, and Wagnerian symptoms are still a part of it. The Wagnerian enchantment is still possible even today, when we all know better than to be fooled by it. A few years ago, the Metropolitan Opera put on a brilliantly sung production of—what else?—*Tristan und Isolde.* During the love duet in the second act, the two lovers, seated side by side, were rendered invisible by a shadow that fused and enveloped them at the center of a nearly bare stage—a narrative image that realized Tristan's dream of a nocturnal world swept bare of all phenomena. The staging may have been meant in part to cloak the large physiques of the principals (Ben Heppner and Jane Eaglen), but regardless, the staging, by Dieter Dorn, was pure performative magic. What one saw was the void into which the whole material, the whole phenomenal world had fallen, a void that was also the oracular depth from which the interlocked voices led the music forth to replace that world. What became noticeable only after the duet had reached the interrupted climax that shatters it was how silent the house had become until that point: not a program rustled, not a throat cleared. It was as if the entire audience had been holding its breath. No one even had to murmur *"Tristan."*

5 Modernity's Cutting Edge

The Salome Complex

From Flaubert to Richard Strauss, male artists in late-nineteenth-century Europe were fascinated by the figure of Salome. The fascination, indeed, amounted to a genuine craze. One representation sparked another: J.-K. Huysmans fantasized about paintings by Gustave Moreau, Oscar Wilde expanded on Huysmans, Aubrey Beardsley illustrated Wilde. Fine editions of Wilde's *Salome* with Beardsley's illustrations remained cult objects well into the twentieth century. Like the science and medicine of its day, on which it drew, the Salome craze reflected a growing preoccupation with femininity as an object of fascination, study, and control. The processes of modernization threatened traditional forms of social order, a key barometer of which was the norm of inequality between the sexes. Containing the damage visited on that norm by recalcitrant modern forms of femininity and effeminacy, often associated with notions of degeneracy and/or exoticism, became a key project for both science and art. What follows revisits this well-known episode in cultural history with special focus on Richard Strauss's opera *Salome*, perhaps the climactic instance of the fin-de-siècle compulsion to retell the Salome story with lavish attention to misogynist imagery—those quivering female bodies and gory male heads. What is the cultural logic of that compulsion, that fascination, that craze?

Arriving at answers to these questions will require two chapters, one focused more narrowly on the question of femininity, the other more broadly on problems of modernity and technology. The two areas, of course, constantly overlap, but it should not be surprising that the full significance of the first will not emerge until we have worked our way through the second.

128

1

Salome is everyone's favorite fin-de-siècle dragon lady. As commonly understood she stands, or rather dances, as the extreme personification of the era's fears of female sexuality, fears so disruptive that they compulsively played themselves out in scenarios of fetishism and castration.[1] I want to suggest, however, a different way to read the Salome of nineteenth-century literature and art. Not that reading her as a castrating femme fatale is unpersuasive; who could avoid it? It seems clear enough that the Salome craze constituted an effort to normalize, by means of aesthetic pleasure, what Freud identified as the dominant sexual disturbance of the age, the coupling of masculine potency with the debasement of women.[2] But behind this reading, perhaps screened by it, may be others that are even more disturbing to the masculine subject addressed by representations of Salome. As Peter Conrad has observed, Salome can easily become risible, as she does in Aubrey Beardsley's elegantly obscene series of illustrations to Wilde's play.[3] Wilde himself opened the door, willfully playing off the florid but cool style of Huysmans's descriptions by raising the temperature to the point of self-parody. Oscar Wilde was not the man to miss a joke.

Besides, the erotic anxieties invested in the figure of Salome abundantly overlap troubles of other sorts. Emily Apter connects Flaubert's description of Salome's dance to his representative experience as a tourist in Egypt seeking "an 'eyeful' of cultural alterity balanced on a Eurocentric pin." Françoise Meltzer suggests that Huysmans's *A Rebours* uses its descriptions of two paintings of Salome by Gustave Moreau to interrogate the "logocentric" repression of writing. Sander Gilman argues that Strauss's *Salome* shares in the discourse of both theatrical and political anti-Semitism.[4] Salome in her heyday was, in short, a kind of all-purpose cultural symptom. I will therefore treat her in what follows less as a monstrous sexual icon than as a focal point for a bundle of instabilities produced in and around the fin-de-siècle gender system. Questions of sexuality, both masculine and feminine, are certainly involved, but so are questions of gender, writing, and cultural authority.

The earliest important Salome narratives, by Flaubert and Huysmans, establish a fundamental two-part pattern that persists in later versions of the story. The first part culminates in Salome's dance before Herod; the second dramatizes her relationship to the severed head of John the Baptist. These two parts are antithetical. The first leads to a scene of motion, the second to a tableau; the first focuses on Salome, the second on the severed head.

Each of these reversals strips Salome—sometimes literally—of her sexual charisma, leaving behind a degraded and marginal figure. In the process, each reversal also yields an affirmation of indestructible masculine power. Thus Salome comes to appear, not as the personification of castrating feminine sexuality, but as the reverse, a figure for precisely those threatening aspects of the feminine that the masculine can subjugate.

The instrument of this subjugation is John the Baptist's head. In Flaubert's 1877 version of the story, "Herodias," the appearance of the severed head tellingly coincides with the disappearance of Salome. When she receives the head, Salome scampers up to a balcony where two carved lions seem to be biting her mother's shoulders, as if to declare the self-consuming nature of feminine violence. The head is then returned to Herod by an old woman, and Salome is heard of no more. It is as if the head has produced a narrative metamorphosis in which the sexually overpowering young virgin is changed into the desexualized old woman. This process is anticipated early in the tale when Herod, looking at a rooftop, catches sight of the same old woman casting a shadow with a parasol—a curiously phallic parasol with a handle "long as a fisherman's rod."[5] The shadow half-hides a "supple" and "delicate" young girl whom we guess, correctly, to be Salome: a Salome whose sinuous movements already excite voyeuristic desires that foretell the effect of her dance, but who is quite literally overshadowed by phallic authority from the moment she enters the text. As for the head, once severed it alters from an object of dread to an object of fascination. Though gory enough, its blood-spattered mouth drawn into a rictus, the head is also beautiful enough to compel the gaze of everyone—more exactly, every man—who sees it. "The closed eyelids," writes Flaubert, "were as pale as shells, and rays of light fell on the face from the candelabras all around" (124).

It is important to note the specifically visual disposition of this shift in value. When she dances, Salome assumes her power by subverting the visual pleasure she is supposed to give: she disrupts the male gaze. This point should not be passed over lightly; the fact that the gaze has been talked nearly to death in recent years does not make it any less fundamental as a social institution.[6] In the nineteenth century especially, the traditional privilege of men to scrutinize women's bodies—as aesthetic objects, as sexual surfaces, as virginal enclosures—assumes unprecedented importance. Hence the period's extraordinary proliferation of erotic writing, photography, and painting, a proliferation that traverses both high culture and low. Foucault may have been right when he argued that the era sought tirelessly to put sex into discourse, but it was even more tireless in trying to make sex visible, to render the field of vision an intrinsically sexual space.[7] For nineteenth-century men, the pleasure of looking can plausibly be said to have rivaled that of physical penetration as the chief means of satisfying sexual desire. Free of overt anxiety, susceptible to sharing among friends, grounded in the exercise of a power represented as assured, the gaze was something like the nineteenth-century version of safe (or maybe just safer) sex. Unpenetrated, the gazed-at female body is instead subjected to and by a "penetrating" look: a sustained, transfixing look that, as Norman Bryson has suggested, renders whatever it sees a "disposable term—object to be held in position, term of subservience, submission."[8] There is, to be sure, an element of pretense in all this. Recent studies have rightly emphasized the fictitiousness and vulnerability of the gaze, attributes that will also figure importantly in what follows here. Such emphasis, however, is important only because the gaze was and is socially efficacious, false pretenses or no; like the Terminator, it tends to keep on working no matter what you do to it.[9]

The interrelations of the gaze, gender, and the head-body economy of the Salome complex appear with telling clarity in Baudelaire's poem "Une Martyre." The martyr of the title is a decapitated woman, evidently a prostitute, whose body lies stretched out on a bed. The poem begins by literally setting her head aside like a potted plant on a night table:

> La tête, avec l'amas de sa crinière sombre
>   Et de ses bijoux précieux,
>
> Sur la table de nuit, comme une renoncule,
>   Repose.[10]

[The head, with its mass of dark hair and its precious jewels, rests on the night table like a buttercup.]

A remarkable description of the woman's body follows: remarkable because it candidly attempts to gratify the reader's voyeuristic desire. The horror of the situation is simply ignored, because in some sense there *is* no horror: the woman's head is simply a disposable term:

> Sur le lit, le tronc nu sans scrupule étale
>   Dans le plus complet abandon
> La secrète splendeur et la beauté fatale
>   Dont la nature lui fit don;
>
> Un bas rosâtre, orné de coins d'or, à la jambe,
>   Comme un souvenir est resté;
> La jarretière, ainsi qu'un œil secret qui flambe,
>   Darde un regard diamanté.

[On the bed, the naked trunk shows off, without a qualm, with the most complete abandon, the secret splendor and the fatal beauty with which Nature gifted it; a rosy stocking, adorned with clocks of gold, clings to a leg like a souvenir; the garter, like a secret eye that blazes, casts a diamond look.]

In their Salome narratives, Flaubert and Huysmans establish that a decapitated man is all head. Baudelaire completes the gendered logic of this representation by establishing that a decapitated woman is all body. Such a body, moreover, is the ideal object of the gaze, because it is totally abandoned (étale / Dans le plus complet abandon) to being seen.

It is precisely this abandonment that the body of Salome denies, or, to be more exact, defers. When she dances, Salome turns the gaze back against itself by making it impossible for the male spectator to structure the visual field. Though she remains the object of the gaze, she usurps control of it; she subjugates the eye that subjugates her. Flaubert presents Salome's dance as a form of motion that the eye cannot frame: polymorphous, continuously changing, often divided into simultaneous currents. The result is a kaleidoscopic series of erotic images that raises the gazer's desire to an unbearable pitch even as it denies him the pictorial stability by which the gaze takes possession of its object and appeases desire. "With her eyes half-closed," writes Flaubert, positioning Salome on the uncertain border between seeing and being-seen, "she twisted her body backwards and forwards, making her belly rise and her breasts quiver, while her face remained expressionless and her feet never stopped moving. . . . [From] her arms, her feet, and her clothes there shot out invisible sparks" (appropriated fragments of the gazes that fall on her) "which set the men on fire" (121).

Salome's appropriation of the visual field depends on a shared, tacit awareness that the man who gazes can also be seen to gaze. The visibility of the gazing eye is also its vulnerability. As Flaubert's description of her dance proceeds, it becomes clear that Salome has taken the goggle-eyed Herod as a choreographic center, the axis of her every move. To bring the dance to a climax, she whirls around Herod's table "like a sorceress's spinning top," confounding his view of her, conflating the visible with the invisible. This disruption of the visual field empowers Salome to end her dance by violating a basic law of visual domination: the prohibition against returning the gaze. Literally inverting the visual order, Salome stands on her hands and gazes up at Herod. Her eyes, veiled at the start of the dance and later exposed half-open, now open wide under her "black eyebrows" to become "well-nigh terrifying": terrifying, it would seem, because Salome's upside-down position sets her eyes—open things fringed with hair—in the place of her genitals, which male fantasy traditionally perceives as the site/sight of castration. What follows completes Salome's visual triumph, and Flaubert portentously allows it a paragraph to itself: "She did not speak. They looked at one another" (122).

Both literally and figuratively, then, Salome turns men's heads, which in the calculus of the gaze is to say that she severs them. With the appearance of a real severed head, however, the masculine order at once recaptures its power over the gaze. All eyes turn to the head; the rays of light that fall on the face merge the image of a saint's halo with an emblem of the drawing back of visual power into an offended masculinity. John the Baptist's head becomes a talisman, an apotropaic charm that turns away Salome's visual power and reclaims the scattered light in which that power flourished. Unlike the head of Baudelaire's martyr, this head of a man is anything but disposable. Flaubert's tale underscores the point in its final image, which shows three men carrying the head to Galilee; they are constrained to carry it in turn, "as [the head] was very heavy."

The same point is made more emphatically by Gustav Klimt's painting of 1901, *Judith and Holofernes* (figure 1). As Carl Schorske has observed, Klimt's Judith, "fresh from her love-slaying of Holofernes, glows in quasi-maternal voluptuousness."[11] Holofernes's head is bisected by the lower right-hand corner of the canvass; it forms a dark mass that the brightly illuminated Judith seems to be trying to push out of the pictorial space, her stiff right arm—tensed with its talon-like hand against the stubborn mass of head—in striking contrast to the languorousness of her face and body. Holofernes's head, in other words, cannot be disposed of, and Klimt's painting, which overtly inscribes Judith's triumph, covertly inscribes her subjugation. Holofernes's own gaze has been shut down, but it is transferred to the viewer for whom Judith's provocatively half-naked, sexually charged body has become available as spectacle. The inconvenient head remains as a blot on what would otherwise be the clear field of Judith's desire.[12]

With Huysmans's reflections on Salome (1884), Flaubert's structure of reversal grows more explicit, not to say more blatant. Of the two Moreau paintings that Huysmans describes, the first, *Salome Dancing*, is said to show Salome in polymorphous motion, usurping on Herod's visible gaze just as she does in Flaubert. Salome's body again radiates its power in the form of light, which scatters from the jewels that "glitter against her moist flesh"; her cuirass "seems to be ablaze with little snakes of fire, swarming over the mat flesh, over the tea-rose skin, like gorgeous insects."[13] The second painting, *The Apparition*, shows the saint's head as the virtually self-willed agent of Salome's undoing. Its halo is a weapon that turns the light back against

FIGURE 1. Gustav Klimt, *Judith and Holofernes* (1901). Photo: Galerie Welz, Salzburg.

Salome, "holds her nailed to the spot," and takes over the center of the visual field from the halted dancer. Floating in the air, glowing in triumph, the head transforms Salome into a passive, subjugated object of the gaze. The implicit fate of Klimt's Judith is here spelled out with undisguised masturbatory involvement: "She is almost naked; in the heat of the dance her veils have fallen away and her brocade robes slipped to the floor. . . . [A] girdle encircles her hips, hiding the upper part of her thighs, against which dangles a gigantic pendant," and so on for two paragraphs of striptease (67–68). Salome is displayed to gratify whatever gaze "dangles against" the painting (or the text): the unseen gaze of which the unseeing head is the instrument.

There is no need to delve further into the lurid details of Huysmans's account, but two points do deserve mention. For Huysmans, the dancing Salome is purely an object of desire, the very personification of "accursed Beauty . . . like the Helen of ancient myth" (66). The "nailed" Salome, however, is also a subject of desire, "a true harlot, obedient to her passionate and cruel female temperament" (68). As such, she is also subject *to* desire, that is, to male desire, which her own desire arouses all the more strongly. Her overthrow by the head is caused by, as it is revealed in, her own lust. A further source of her subjugation also looms behind some hints that Huysmans throws out about the nature of the Baptist's talismanic head. Dark clots of blood, we discover, form at the ends of the hair and beard; Salome, "petrified and hypnotized by terror," is assimilated to an imagery of stones, jewels, coal. Petrifaction and a horrible hairdo quickly suggest the Medusa. Does Huysmans's saint achieve his final incarnation as a male Medusa's head?

Later depictions would take this hint to heart, as they would make still more literal Salome's defeat by the loss of visual power under the weight of her own desires. In Aubrey Beardsley's 1893 drawing of the close of Oscar Wilde's *Salome,* a drawing done before Beardsley turned the story to obscene comedy, the identification of the saint's head with the Medusa becomes explicit (figure 2). Salome's hair is coarse and vegetative; it thins into a mass of tangled, weblike lines that envelop half the picture, as if to conjure up the common association of women's hair with a spider web.[14] John the Baptist's hair, however, is unmistakably snaky, and as Salome stares at it her face appears masklike and rigid, while a strange stole with a phallic tip encircles her body. If we accept Freud's famous reading of the Medusa's head as an image that both expresses male horror at the supposedly castrated female genitals and mitigates that horror with the profusion of phallic snakes,[15] then what we have in John the Baptist's head is a male appropriation of the very core of female power. The severed head changes from an image of castration to an image of that detachable, all-powerful signifier of law, culture, authority, and potency, the phallus itself. And in particular, this is the phallus of visual pleasure: the instrument by which the unseen gaze (again betokened by the head's closed eyes, as by the secret eye of Baudelaire's poem) transfixes its object.

In Wilde's *Salome,* the triumph of this visual phallus is carried a step further. Salome, here as in Huysmans the inflamed subject of desire, not only surrenders the visual power that she has wielded in her dance, but specifically mourns for it. She is tormented by the longing to command the gaze; her monologue to the head is punctuated by variations on the complaint "If you had looked at me, you would have loved me."[16] Her desire for Iokanaan, meanwhile, takes the form of a further longing that punishes, in Dantean fashion, the first. Salome desires to look, in her own right, from the forbidden masculine perspective: to take Iokanaan as the object of visual love. She apostrophizes his absent body: "Your body was an ivory column on a silver base. It was a garden filled with doves and silver lilies. It was a silver tower decked with ivory shields. Nothing in the world was so white as your body" (294). This slavish worship of Iokanaan as the phallus petrifies Salome in her monologue and turns her into an erotic spectacle for the punishing gaze of the theater audience. Eventually, that retributive and self-pleasuring gaze materializes onstage in a ray of moonlight, which illuminates Salome as she is crushed to death (295).

Wilde also endows the severed head with the male Medusa's phallic snakes, which appear in the form of a "red viper" invoked three times in rapid succession as a metaphor for Iokanaan's tongue. Salome, in the gesture of final abasement that marks the apex of her desire, ecstatically kisses this phallicized mouth. I will shortly suggest that this action is equivocal, but its initial impact—especially in the theater where the image of Salome is fleshed out by a real woman—can only be to identify feminine desire as uncontrollable penis envy.

The fin-de-siècle Salome story, then, at least as told so far, is not only the anxiety-dream it is usually supposed to be; it is also a classic wish fulfillment. (The Freudian terms, here and elsewhere, are historically resonant: this is exactly the kind of culturally specific fantasy structure that influenced Freud's theories by presenting itself for explanation.) The story reorients the opposition of (male) head and (female) body that permeates its era from a terror of separation to an assurance of transcendence. It turns what is threatening in the sight of the female body into a righteous aversion that harbors a secret pleasure.

FIGURE 2. Aubrey Beardsley, *Salome with the Head of John the Baptist* (1893), illustration of the final scene from *Salome* by Oscar Wilde. Aubrey Beardsley Collection, Manuscripts Division, Department of Rare Books and Special Collections, Princeton University Library.

But there is also another story to be told: one which in some sense does not involve women at all, though femininity is basic to it. In his study *Romantic Image,* Frank Kermode suggests that the fin-de-siècle dancer, Salome preeminently, forms an emblem of the perfect work of art that fuses sensuousness and thought into one.[17] In all the versions cited here, however, Salome appears not as a kind of art but as a kind of artist. In Flaubert she is an erotic illusionist, depicting different forms of desire in the phases of her dance; in Huysmans she is a specialist in adornment and ornamentation, using her clothing and jewelry to form a prolific vocabulary of gestures and figures; in Wilde she is a love poet who speaks in an incantatory stream of similes, of which the seven veils of her dance form visual emblems. (The elaborated similes are reduced to compact metaphors in her monologue, the rhetorical equivalents of reducing a whole man to a head.)

In each case Salome's style as an artist is the same. It is decorative, intricate, figurative, and arcane; it is self-absorbed in its richness of imagery and highly colored detail, antireferential even where it most seems to betoken things outside itself. It is, in other words, very much the evocative fin-de-siècle style of Flaubert's "Herodias," Huysmans's *À Rebours,* and Wilde's lyric poetry and fairy tales.

Salome, accordingly, would seem to form a self-portrait of the artist as a woman—perverse, desirous, and castrated. In Wilde's case, the portrait extends to the artist as homosexual, a figure whose artful language is (in this cultural setting) impelled by a hopeless love. The first such love in the play is that of Herodias's page for a young Syrian captain, who in turn loves Salome, who in turn loves the "very young" Iokanaan. The sequence suggests that love is not in the first instance a relation between the sexes but an attitude toward the unobtainable; the proliferation of one-sided longing seems to act here as the very form of desire, a dramatic equivalent to the proliferation of erotic similes in Salome's language about Iokanaan. But some love objects are more unobtainable than others, and it is more than suggestive that the sequence both begins and ends with a young man as the object of unavailing desire. Evoking the late-nineteenth-century theory of sexual inversion, Salome in this context would represent a theatrical "coming out" of the woman's soul hidden within the aesthete's male body. The desire she embodies has a cross-sex form and a same-sex content. Hence Beardsley's 1893 Salome, who resembles nothing so much as a man in drag. Hence, too, perhaps, Wilde's choice of Sarah Bernhardt as the ideal star for his play. As Marjorie Garber has noted, Bernhardt was famous for her cross-dressed roles; Bernhardt playing a woman would be no less a fantasy figure than Bernhardt playing a man.[18]

This feminization of the artist, and in particular of the artist who works in a certain evocative fin-de-siècle style, provokes a good deal of male anxiety. For one thing, it attacks the stability of gender on which the privileged definition of masculinity depends. For another, it threatens to degrade the status of art itself, which in a culture based on masculine privilege can possess authority only if it is thought of as man's work.[19] The feminized artist is a symptom of decadence in the pejorative sense of the term, as Nietzsche, for one, attests in a polemic against Wagner's *Parsifal*. "Never," he writes, "was there a man equally expert in . . . all that trembles and is effusive, all the feminisms from the *idioticon* of happiness!—Drink, O my friends, the philters of this art! Nowhere will you find a more agreeable way of enervating your spirit, of forgetting your manhood under a rosebush."[20] In artistic terms, feminine desire turns out to be indistinguishable from the desire to create a luxurious, suggestive, highly wrought style. It is a desire that thrives on its own "multiplicity, abundance, and arbitrariness," to call once more on Nietzsche's description of Wagner (178): a desire, a lust, to revel in an excess of imagery that continually postpones the illusion of reference, or to reduce the Word—Iokanaan's medium, the vessel of the idea and the ideal—to the sensuous friction and proliferation of words.

This mode of desire helps to explain why Wilde's Salome is so obsessively concerned with kissing Iokanaan's mouth. Her true monstrousness in the play does not attach to her dance but to her style of speech, her promiscuous weaving together of erotic similes in the service of her desires. The dance, it is true, usurps male visual power, but it is at least isolated from the more vital cultural power of, and over, language. For Salome, the dance serves as a means to gain what her rhetoric has repeatedly sought and failed to gain: control over the prophet's organ of speech. (Strauss's opera creates a telltale inflection of this desire by giving Salome the habit of elongating the second syllable of Jochanaan's name, as if to take his vocalic spirit into her throat.) Salome's kiss, therefore, carries a double meaning. Understood erotically, reduced to the discourse of the body apparently encoded in the dance, the kiss is a gesture of submission, a symbolic act of fellatio performed on the indestructible phallus. Understood culturally, however, the same kiss represents a triumphant incorporation of the male power of speech, with its corollary, writing: an appropriation of the movement of the tongue/viper/pen/penis. It is precisely when Salome turns to celebrate this appropriation, ecstatically repeating, "I have kissed your mouth, Iokanaan, I have kissed your mouth," that Herod—and Wilde—have her killed. She is, as we say, rubbed out: blotted to death like a blood or ink stain under a mass of shields.

(Under armor: a traditional metaphor for a condom. And a shield, of course, is a weapon of defense.)

In my second story, then, a story not perfectly consistent with the first, Salome's punishment at the hands of the male artists whom she fascinates— themselves half Herods, half Baptists—is a gesture of artistic vindication. It puts forth the claim that an art disencumbered of its traditional responsibility to represent, its phallic duty to point to what arouses its interest, is still a manly art, and still, therefore, worthy of the reward of cultural authority. Lost in one place, the ruling phallus will be found in another, disguised as its greatest antagonist, castration itself. So the moral of this story, perhaps of both stories, and certainly of this first phase of my argument, is simple: you can't keep a good man down.

2

Richard Strauss's *Salome*, a setting of an abridged but otherwise unaltered German translation of Wilde's play, was completed in 1905. Like its literary antecedents, the opera pivots on the structure of reversal that traverses Salome's dance and her monologue to the severed head. The two scenes are linked melodically, but more importantly they are linked by the fact that they, and they alone, suspend the dramatic action and present Salome as an erotic spectacle for the audience.

The notorious Dance of the Seven Veils was widely regarded as a striptease long before sopranos actually began disrobing to it. The music's flagrant hootchy-kootchy style signified as much no matter what the staging; one reviewer of the American premiere complained that the dance alone "ought to make it impossible for any Occidental woman to look" at Strauss's handiwork.[21] The remark may have been only slightly less silly in 1907 than it is now, but it is not just irrelevant. Even after a century of modernism and decades of sophistication about visual pleasure, the role of erotic spectacle in musical theater is still bemusing, as can, so to speak, be seen in a recent takeoff on the Dance of the Seven Veils, John Eaton's "pocket opera" *Salome's Flea Circus* (2003). Anthony Tommasini's *New York Times* review of the premiere fumbles tellingly at the problem of spectatorship. The text wavers easily between aesthetic and erotic appreciation:

> [This] was a 10-minute showpiece for the admirably versatile clarinetist Jean Kopperud, here portraying the Biblical Salome in later life, who has sunk to touring the circuit with a flea circus. Dressed as an exotic belly dancer, the limber, long-haired and fearless Ms. Kopperud alternated playing insinuating lines on the clarinet with speaking text in a raspy Sprech-

stimme style, all the while twisting, gyrating, and falling to her back on the stage floor with her legs kicked up. Eventually she executed a bedraggled version of Salome's dance, as the pianist . . . yanked off one of Salome's seven veils with his teeth.[22]

Critical distance gyrates with the dancer; the imagery of twisting and gyrating even recalls Flaubert. As to the seven veils, invoking them allows both the performers and the reviewers to make a suggestive connection between revealing and orality (a prophecy is also a revealing), but they also lead the review into a—revealing—slippage. The veils do not belong to the "Biblical" Salome at all but only to the exotic dancer of Wilde and Strauss. The accompanying photo of Jean Kopperud, as described, belies the *Times's* customary description of itself as a "family newspaper"—unless the family happens to be Herod's.

The question of who ought to look, and at what, is one that no production of *Salome* can evade. Salome's dance challenges the ability of opera to contain and control spectacle. The music for this episode is notorious for flirting with a sleazy orientalism (the flea circus may well be on its circuit), but it nonetheless affords Salome a chance to achieve by dancing before Herod the seductive power, the compelling union of thought and expression, that she could not manage by singing to the still-living Jochanaan. Like her counterpart in Flaubert, she turns everything upside down. Her dance constitutes a generic disruption after which, as Peter Conrad observes, "Salome ceases to be a character and becomes an image, and opera turns simultaneously into a symphonic poem, into a ballet, and into a painting" (154).

With Salome's monologue, a fourth form can be added to Conrad's list: the tableau vivant. By centering her movements on Jochanaan's severed head, this scene strips Salome of the gestural freedom of her dance and exposes her to the full power of the gaze, of which the unseeing head is paradoxically the instrument. By singing to the head, Salome sings for the gaze, which invites everyone to take a good, long look at her. Much longer than the dance, Wagnerian in its luxuriant nonaction, the monologue scene exaggerates the capacity of music to stretch time out like taffy. It uses its music as Moreau's "The Apparition" uses the light that radiates from the head, to nail Salome to the spot. Strauss's Salome sings out her ecstasy and torment for nearly eighteen minutes before the combination of her perversity and her orgasmic intensity makes Herod, who has finally seen enough, have her killed where she stands.

The instrumental music that accompanies—envelops—this episode is lush and sensuous, a gorgeous mass of orchestral color. It is music whose expressive character simultaneously works to mirror Salome's desire acous-tically and to isolate her, even repudiate her, visually. The nub of this effect is the dissonance between the music's romantic beauty—a term I mean de-scriptively, generically, not evaluatively (though it is that, too)—and the per-verse spectacle on stage. As with Klimt's Judith, the head of Jochanaan forms an indelible blot on what would otherwise be the clear field of Salome's de-sire. It is precisely the impossibility of reconciling the ear and the eye that keeps the eye riveted and the ear baffled—and vice versa. An equivalent ef-fect is even possible with the mind's eye. After hearing this scene in class, one student of mine, a German as it happens, told me that she wished she had not understood the words: "The music is so beautiful."

Salome's means for navigating this treacherous territory is her voice. When she sings, her voice and the desires she voices urge a "transcendence" of the dissonance between music and image, which nevertheless continu-ally absorbs her, much as her voice itself is sometimes absorbed as merely one thread among many in the rich, dense orchestral fabric. One reason she serenades the head so long before actually kissing it may be to build up a kind of vocal capital as a hedge against the monstrousness of the act. She sings as if knowing that only her voice can sustain the equivocation that even she needs in order to rationalize her desires.

Like Flaubert, Huysmans, and Wilde, Strauss narrates the failure of that rationalization in a style that Salome herself has seemed to author: sensu-ous, incremental, highly wrought, resistant to closure. He indulges in a ra-tionalization of his own by refiguring the "effeminacy" of the fin-de-siècle style as antifeminine. As the embodiment of that style, with its impulse to detach both art and desire from the hidden moralism of "natural" feeling, Salome forms a mobile alter ego for fin-de-siècle artists. But to the extent that such artists—Wilde and Strauss notably among them—want to rein-stall a moral center as a means of claiming cultural authority, Salome must be sacrificed, debased, abjected. From the sphere of identification, she has to be relegated to the sphere of desire, where she can become the object of both enjoyment and disgust, in keeping with the standard routines of fin-de-siècle misogyny. As we'll see later, she may not stay where she is sent; but there she must go.

Her exile is epitomized in a photograph from the first Viennese pro-duction of the opera (1907) (figure 3). The photo presents Salome (Fanchette Verhunk), with Jochanaan's head raised before her, as a double erotic offer-ing to the eye. Her own eyes are fixed on the head, whose upturned but un-seeing gaze seems to have frozen her in place; her face is a blank. The up-per body of the performer is an ample plateau of casually punished flesh:

FIGURE 3. Fanchette Verhunk as Strauss's Salome in the first Viennese production (1907).

bare shoulders under narrow straps, bare arms ringed by tight circlets rising to the level of the bosom, bosom set off by a tight, low-cut bodice. The
stance of the lower body symbolizes what its sumptuous clothing conceals.
Salome stands with her legs wide apart, one foot on a high step; her cos-
tume falls so as to bisect her lower body along a visual path that ends with
a bejeweled ornament at her pelvis. A pendant dangles from the ornament.
From the top down, this gazed-at woman is an object of sadomasochistic pleasure, symbolically in bondage; from the bottom up she is a fetish, an object
of aesthetic pleasure elaborated out of the phallic ornament.[23]

As a cultural icon, the monologue scene of Strauss's *Salome* is unusually resonant, perhaps just because it does not, contrary to the claims of its
early admirers, transcend its material. The resonance begins with Oscar
Wilde's play. In writing the original version of Salome's monologue, Wilde
gave the theater audience precisely what Herod is condemned to lack: an
unseen position from which to gratify voyeuristic desire on the body of a
real woman. (In both Wilde and Strauss, Herod is a pointedly incompetent
gazer; real visual power rests with the audience.) Despite the likelihood that
Wilde's Salome is largely a kind of prosthesis for male same-sex desire, his
play was widely received and adapted as a vehicle for the erotic display of a
woman's body, a vehicle taken up appropriatively by such dancers of the era
as Ida Rubinstein and Maud Allen. The site for such display had become
latent in the theater sometime after 1803, when the introduction of gaslight
made it possible to illuminate the stage without illuminating the house; darkened theaters were universal by the mid-1880s.[24] It is arguable that the in-
visibility of the theatrical, and later the cinematic, gaze, has been decisive
in (re)shaping the erotics of drama and film. If so, the monologue of Wilde's
Salome is scandalous only because it makes explicit the voyeuristic basis of
modern performance.[25]

The same thing can be said of Strauss's scene, but with a critical difference. As we have noted, Wilde's monologue is not perfectly straight in
any sense of the term. Hinting at a homosexual subtext and stylizing Salome's repetitive, florid language to the point of self-parody, the scene uses
outright staginess as a defense mechanism to limit its voyeuristic appeal.
Its ultimate success at this can be measured in theatrical history by the
gradual replacement of hetero/sexy performances and adaptations with
stylized, ritualized, or outright drag versions. Strauss's scene takes exactly
the opposite course. In line with other contemporary treatments, the opera
as a whole overrides Wilde's homosexual evocations with heterosexual display. The process begins by straightening out the subplot of the Syrian
captain and the page, the latter of whom is cast as a trouser role for con-

tralto; it ends, and culminates, in the kinky love scene between a singing body and a silent head. Sensationalist rather than stagy, Strauss's monologue obliterates Wilde's defenses with song. The scene melts down the artifice of Salome's language into an extravagantly sensuous vocal line: a line supple and continuous rather than repetitive, a line shot through with superslinky, more-than-*Tristan*-esque chromaticism, a line that imitates the accents of feminine desire in both low croonings and high climactic outcries and projects that desire onto the illuminated body and breath of the singer.

The result is a distorted *Liebestod*—distorted in a very particular way. Whereas Wagner's Isolde bears audible witness to a splendid sight, the resurrected Tristan, that she alone can see, Strauss's princess "with the voice of Isolde" visibly serenades a gruesome sight that everyone can see. And whereas Tristan's silence is the medium of Isolde's transfiguration, Jochanaan's silence is the mark of Salome's debasement. Earlier, the sole encounter between Jochanaan and Salome has ended with his curse and her silence, a long moment of speechless erotic anguish that is filled out with an orchestral interlude, a rarity in this opera. Salome's final monologue is her attempt at both vocal recovery—the chance to sing her desire better, more compellingly, than she had done before—and, through that, of erotic supremacy. But just as Jochanaan's head is a blot on the visual field of Salome's desire, his silence in the face of her long apostrophe is a blot on the field of her voice. Her monologue really is a vocal recovery: indeed, like Isolde, she never sounds so splendid as she does here. But her voice keeps pouring itself fruitlessly into the void of Jochanaan's silence. The sight of this sound, to steal a phrase from Richard Leppert, struck many people as both torrid and degenerate to a degree that Strauss himself found disconcerting.

He had no one to blame but himself: even the orchestral music he wrote for Salome's monologue is a virtual gaze. As I have already remarked, the scene is an extreme instance of the musical dilation of time; it prolongs a single image far beyond the capacities of nonmusical theater. Music circulates through this static visual field, enveloping and transfixing the figure of the singer. Concentrating the style of the opera as a whole, melodic motion obsessively recurs in its two extreme forms, sometimes in juxtaposition, sometimes intermingled. At one extreme, especially at the beginning of the scene, runs and other rapid figurations ripple almost continuously across the orchestral texture; at the other, especially at the end, lengthy trills, tremolos, and pedal points sustain a kind of vibratory nimbus. The result is nothing less than a musical model of the unseen gaze of the audience: the gaze as a fluid, all-embracing motion, later to be realized by the movie camera, that continuously refreshes itself with the (ungratified) desire of its (feminine) object and ends as a kind of shimmer or flickering around the desire-laden body—the gaze as magic fire.

This modeling effect is confirmed by the outcome of an interlude late in the monologue, during which Herod and Herodias take the position of unseen gazers and argue about the spectacle Salome presents to them. Herod, who no longer wants to look, orders his attendants to extinguish the torches; the stage, already darkened by the clouding of the moon, grows darker still. Salome sings the consummating moments of her monologue, jubilant at having kissed Jochanaan's mouth, from amid this darkness— depending on the production, a darkness that may gather as she sings. At the last moment, however, as Salome stands silent amid a mass of trills on woodwind and percussion, the moon, according to Strauss's stage direction, "breaks out again and illuminates" her. The consummation of her monologue is not only her last, high-pitched, melismatic cry in the dark, but also her sudden appearance in the midst of the light. As the music fades around the sight, Herod gives the order to have Salome killed. The orchestra responds with a paroxysm of violence, anticipated by a pungent chord that interrupts the fadeout; the eye so long held open now snaps shut.

This climactic play of light, sight, sound, and silence is charged with ambivalence. On the one hand, the closing passage of the monologue is the only one that gives the voice uncontested primacy in the texture. If Salome's voice can be associated with the agency or subjectivity that her presentation as spectacle denies, then this passage replaces sight by sound and belongs to Salome alone, not to those who can no longer see her clearly. From this perspective, the final illumination gives her back to the pleasure of those observers, restores what the sound of her voice in the dark makes them, more than ever, want to see. At the same time, Herod's savage reaction suggests that at this point Salome has wrested the gaze away from the orchestra and audience alike; she registers for the eye only as something too bright to see. It may be that what triggers the violent close is the discrepancy between the demand to see Salome one more time and the suddenly revealed power of the Salome thus seen (no matter how she is seen) to repel the eye that sees her. In Lacanian terms, the final moments of the opera tear open the gap between the eye and the gaze: a gap that takes dramatic form in the antithesis between music that pulsates and music that hammers, and structural form in a corresponding change of key, a wrench from C♯ major to C minor.

By combining the zenith of Salome's vocal eloquence with the nadir of her visual debasement, the monologue scene sets up a kind of destructive feedback loop in which each extreme struggles for breakout dominance. From within the ideological world that the opera inhabits, this contest represents an important insight into the antithesis of art and reality and the mystery of desire. Its status as insightful also furnishes a rationale for the opera's subject matter, permitting it to be regarded as daring rather than just decadent or sleazy. Similar considerations would apply several decades later to W. B. Yeats's reworking of Wilde's, if not Strauss's, *Salome, A Full Moon in March* (1935). Yeats's protagonist is a kind of composite of Salome and Turandot who ritually sullies her moonlike purity, combining the dance and the adoration of the head into a single action:

> What do[es she] seek for, why does [she] descend?
> —For desecration and the lover's night. . . .
> What can she lack whose emblem is the moon?
> —But desecration and the lover's night.[26]

Step outside the ideological envelope, though, and such "insight" changes its spots. It becomes more a signifier than a signified, an expressive form rather than a content, and one about which certain questions cannot help but cluster. From this perspective, the issues of the monologue scene, and beyond it of the opera, are why the polarity of supremacy and debasement seems like such a natural source of insight; why its focal point seems so naturally to be a female body and feminine desire; and why the insight is sustainable only as long as Salome can sing, so that when her voice is stopped—especially by kissing Jochanaan's mouth, the very act the consummates her desire—the whole system totters toward becoming pure spectacle, a debased image in a sticky entanglement of sound.

Strauss's transformation of the orchestra into a phallic eye during Salome's monologue also resonates beyond the theatrical and even the aesthetic context into the field of what Naomi Scheman calls "epistemic modernity."[27] Starting with the Renaissance, Western knowledge itself comes increasingly to be identified with visual power. The ideal of knowledge becomes the occupation of a vantage point from which, in Stanley Cavell's formulation, "our natural mode of perception is to view, feeling unseen." Thus situated, "We do not so much look at the world as look out at it, from behind the self."[28] In this visual dispensation, the knowing subject is necessarily at a distance from the object known. The achievement of such distance—of perspective, detachment, independence, objectivity, clear-sightedness—is projected as a heroic task, and, as Nietzsche suggested in Essay Three of *On the Genealogy of Morals*, an ascetic one. It is also a task strongly coded by gender. As Scheman suggests, the career of the epistemic hero coincides with the accomplishment "of the normative male tasks of separation and empowerment based on dissociation from everything maternal and, by extension, everything female" (85). In this context, it is likely that Strauss's monologue scene exalts, by aestheticizing and eroticizing, the visual ideal of epistemic heroism. Following the music, the unseen gaze of the audience reenacts the drama of separation and empowerment, the triumph of masculine art over feminine style, of masculine culture over feminine nature. If Catherine Clément was right to claim that nineteenth-century opera thrives on the "undoing" *(la défaite)* of women, then Strauss's monologue scene may be one of those exemplary instances ("best examples") that embody in their realization of the pattern a glimpse or echo of the reason for it.[29]

Not surprisingly, the monologue scene is also the formal crux of *Salome*. As my account so far tacitly acknowledges, the epistemic modernity of the opera is in the first instance a matter of broad stylistic and theatrical effects. But it is also a matter of detail. Especially at moments of crisis or transition, Strauss represents Salome structurally as well as theatrically; he asks thematic and harmonic patterns to (re)produce cultural meaning. When they do, however, the meanings produced do not always behave themselves properly.

An important leitmotif associated with Salome is shown in example 5. It consists of a little wriggle and a dying fall. The notes involved are those of a simple triad, but so arranged as to end with the "top" note of the chord, its fifth, on the "bottom." (In other words, the motive is essentially an arpeggiated six-four chord—a common formation, here put to uncommon uses.) The close on the fifth evokes a restless feeling, a touch sultry, a touch high strung. Most tonal melody takes the fifth scale degree as the site of expectancy or demand; here the melodic motion is so pared down, so abstracted, as to suggest some sort of essence of demand. The motive takes up the triad in pure form, the heart of musical order, and sets it awry, much as Salome's desire for Jochanaan is set awry. Intimations of this last analogy appear in a striking musico-dramatic reversal. Salome's Desire motive (as I will call it) first arises early in her confrontation with Jochanaan when she says that he is "horrible . . . really horrible" (Fig. 76.1–2).[30] Its next four appearances (Figs. 77.1–3, 80.1–2, 89.6–7, 92.1–2) trace a gradual movement from disgust to desire, culminating with the statement "I am in love with your body, Jochanaan." The recurrence of the motive embodies the unbroken continuity, the latent identity, between the two extremes. (Salome subsequently switches back and forth between the two before committing herself to de-

EXAMPLE 5. Strauss, *Salome:* Salome's Desire motive.

sire.) The process is like the shape of the motive itself writ large, a sheer insistence on going against the grain.

Taken as a commentary on Salome's character, the Desire motive most obviously dwells on that insistence, investing it with qualities of mindlessness and self-absorption that might recall Huysmans's description of Salome as an "indifferent, irresponsible, insensible" incarnation of lust.[31] Like the woman, the motive is preoccupied with one untoward idea; virtually every time it appears, the unstable little phrase reduplicates itself exactly. One might even say that the real motive is just this reduplication. The effect becomes almost absurd in the confrontation scene as Salome, faced with Jochanaan's violent bouts of ranting, repeatedly responds by contemplating his body to the imperturbable sound of the self-mirroring motive. The Desire motive thus suggests that Salome, again in Huysmans's words, is "thrust by a fateful power, by an irresistible force, into the alluring iniquities of debauch."

Yet there is also a countersuggestion available, something that eventually crystallizes as the motive emerges against a sensuous, richly ornamental instrumental backdrop at the critical juncture of the Dance of the Seven Veils.[32] Obstinately returning to the unstable fifth degree, the Desire motive may also affirm its own imponderability on Salome's behalf. Its intransigence gives the measure of her resistance to being incorporated into the tonal order—a department of the overstabilized symbolic order of centrality, normality, hierarchy, spirit, paternal law.[33]

This equivocal association with the fifth scale degree reaches a point of crisis as Salome waits in a fury of impatience for Jochanaan's decapitation. The moment also involves strange twists of sonority that put both her voice and her character in a troubling new light.

As Salome stands by the cistern in which the prophet is imprisoned, a low E♭ pedal point emerges on four tremolo double basses. A bass drum roll blends into the sound, giving it a thick, lower-bodily character, as much felt as heard. Salome has a special affinity with these sounds from the bottom of the acoustic spectrum: after her rejection by Jochanaan, she conceives her desire for his head to the ruminating sound of a solo contrabassoon, and when she subsequently exclaims to the head, now severed, that the sight of the living Jochanaan caused her to hear "mysterious music" *(geheimnisvolle Musik)*, an organ behind the scenes sounds a pair of single tones in its lowest register. Salome is the figure through whom these visceral, mysterious depths become articulate, and in whom articulate sounds are revealed as a gloss on the visceral and mysterious depth of subjectivity. But this articulation has its limits, as some other double basses are about to prove.

Over the drum roll–tremolo pedal, four other basses gradually combine to execute a series of *sforzando* attacks on a high B♭ (Fig. 303.5 and following, example 6). This note, the score instructs, is to be attacked with a very short stroke while the player pinches the string between thumb and forefinger, "so that a tone is produced that resembles the suppressed moaning and groaning of a woman" (sodass ein Ton erzeugt wird, der dem unterdrückten Stöhnen und Ächzen eines Weibes ähnelt). The most obvious suggestion made by this sonority is erotic. The music simulates the pulsing of Salome's body in a state of distinctively feminine sexual excitement, and at the same time exposes such excitement as "horrible . . . really horrible." More than iconicity, the sound aspires to virtuality: at first spaced widely, the pinched B♭'s soon come thicker and faster; just as they do, Salome lets slip a cry—*ach!*—in which "the suppressed moaning and groaning of a woman" briefly rises to the level of her voice.

Beyond its overtly lurid associations, the pinging of the B♭'s becomes disturbing for its automatism, its mindless, perfectly regular insistence, its absorption of desire into the mechanism of sheer drive. The sound is less something wrung from Salome's subjectivity than it is the realization of an impersonal force from which her subjectivity is elaborated. This impression resonates with accounts of femininity widely known at the fin-de-siècle; it is consistent both with Otto Weininger's view of women as subrational desiring bodies and with Freud and Breuer's account of hysteria as a splitting of consciousness subtended (for Freud, at least) by disturbed sexuality.[34] By catching Salome at a moment when the voicing of her desire must be "suppressed" because she has not yet taken possession of its object, the scene at the cistern, with its B♭'s, "reveals" that desire as the hidden truth of her nature, perhaps of feminine nature at large. The suppressed voice breaks through to audibility not as an utterance but as an object, an excrescence that interferes with Salome's attempt to express herself, the inert voice of a heedless Other who speaks senselessly at the same time as she does. This presence of this Other is the truth that declares itself to everyone but Salome as, singing largely "out of tune" with the E♭–B♭ fifth, she begins her

EXAMPLE 6. *Salome:* decapitation scene.

(continued)

EXAMPLE 6 *(continued)*

EXAMPLE 6 *(continued)*

death vigil for Jochanaan by imagining herself crying out—he, of course, does not—in his place.

Once again, however, a countersuggestion is available. The "moaning and groaning of a woman" can refer to birth pangs as well as to sexual abandon, an association that shows indirectly in Strauss's choice of the verb *erzeugen*, which means to engender or bring forth as well as to produce in the general sense. Perhaps the sexual form of Salome's desire is itself only a kind of suppression. Desiring Jochanaan's head, the locus of phallic and oracular power, Salome is arguably in labor to bring herself forth as a subject, which is, in figurative terms, to give herself birth. From this standpoint, the syncopated, increasingly breathless pulses on the fifth scale degree affirm her resistance to being bounded by either rhythmic or melodic norms. And the utterance of these pulses by the voice-as-object suggests a surplus of subjectivity that will not even observe the boundaries that are nominally its own.

This affirmative reading finds dramatic expression when Salome, no longer "out of tune," cries out to Naaman, the executioner, to strike (see example 6). The melodic motion of her utterance mimics both the death stroke and its effects. Singing "Schlag' zu, schlag' zu" (Strike, strike!), Salome ascends through the tones of the E♭-minor triad from the first degree to an urgent statement of the fifth. Her vocal "stroke" on B♭ falls on the same pitch, B♭' that the basses have been voicing as a woman's *Stöhnen* and *Ächzen*. It does so, moreover, just as the basses have fallen silent after a sudden new acceleration of their pulse strokes. Salome's voice literally takes their place, or more exactly reveals that they have been holding hers. From that place, after a transitional "off-key" call to Naaman (remote from her desire, yet the agent of her satisfaction), Salome reattacks the fifth degree and carries her triadic motion into the upper register ("schlag' zu, sag' ich dir" [strike, strike I tell you]), breaking off just as the sound becomes brilliant. This second statement upends the triad to Salome's characteristic six-four position. Backed by an outburst of "short and hard" strokes on the tympani, she has, yet again, entered the space of the triad to set it awry in an access of desire. Taken as a whole, her exclamation, anchored by the vocal strokes on B♭', momentarily fuses together the two outcries Salome yearns to hear, one knowingly, the other not: the death cry of Jochanaan, for which she waits ("Warum schreit er nicht, der Mann?" [Why doesn't he cry out, this man?]), and the moan of self-generation through which she seeks new life.

As if to arrest Salome's tendency to appropriate the fifth degree, Strauss forms an important link between her Desire motive and the melodic figure

EXAMPLE 7. *Salome:* the Body motive in the monologue (a) and dance (b).

a.

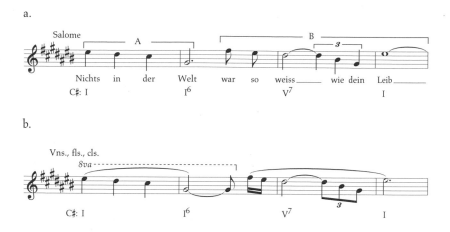

shown in example 7a. This is the setting for one of the climactic phrases of the final monologue, "Nichts in der Welt war so weiss wie dein Leib" (Nothing in the world was so white as your body); the first half of the still-unvoiced phrase also makes a series of dramatic appearances during the orchestral interlude following Salome's encounter with Jochanaan, while a version of the full phrase forms one of the climaxes of her dance.

As a comparison of musical examples 5 and 7 will show, the first half of this "Body" motive, marked A, consists of a slightly ornamented version of the Desire motive's descent through the tones of the six-four chord. The second half, marked B, recalls and retards the characteristic opening rhythm of the Desire motive. (The monologue version is more deliberate, more languorous, than that of the dance; compare examples 7a and 7b.) The Desire motive, we might say, generates the Body motive by breaking apart, desynchronizing its melody and rhythm. For Salome, desire finds its object in a lyrical self-negation; what begins in the indeterminacy of psyche or spirit twists and extends itself to end in the fixity of body or matter. And in this disassembled new form the Desire motive surrenders its fixation on the fifth scale degree. In both the dance and the monologue, the second half of the steadily descending Body motive ends with an ascending leap to the third of the triad at the place reserved for the charged word *Leib* (body). The note assumes a striking brightness when approached this way. Absorbed in Jochanaan's body, Salome experiences something like bliss. Yet the cost of this bliss is the more challenging sound of her very desire for bliss.

The collapse of Salome's Desire motive into the Body motive can be taken to suggest that Strauss, like Huysmans, defines Salome as a subject solely by her desire for Jochanaan, and at the same time, again like Huysmans, projects that desire as the means by which Salome as a subject is broken and dispersed. In the monologue scene, Strauss's Salome loses herself musically in the act of imagining the absent body, the phallic tower of ivory, she can never possess. That she does so while apostrophizing Jochanaan's severed head suggests a new wrinkle to the familiar symbolism. What Salome discovers to her own undoing is that sometimes a head is just a head. It only works as a phallus on behalf of a male subject—which is precisely what it does in this scene by causing Salome to "make a spectacle" of herself and her desire. The head forms the inescapable focal point of a series of gaps that open in the final monologue and that are in some sense its true subject: gaps between head and body, fetish and person, what Salome sees and what the audience sees her see, and above all—as already remarked—between the grotesque, Grand Guignol stage image and the lavish sensuous beauty of the music that envelops it.

Strauss's elaboration of that contradictory beauty is primarily textural—the orchestral fabric is conceived as a kind of gigantic Art Nouveau skein of seven veils swirling around the action (see the next chapter)—but it also extends to the expressive use of tonality. At a series of transitional moments, changes of harmony coincide with strongly marked moments in the drama, revealing a symbolic subtext to the prevailing harmonic volatility.[35] It is questionable how clearly these relationships can be heard as such, even by a listener who knows the score well, but they can nonetheless be understood as means provided for thinking about the opera; their symbolic value does not require an exact acoustic equivalent, and may even thrive on the absence of one.

Like many things in music, this tonal allegory begins with C major. Traditionally the "purest" of keys, C is associated here with the voice of Jochanaan as the medium of prophecy. (It is, by the way, literally Jochanaan's voice that I mean here. Since Jochanaan sings from his cistern much of the time, his voice is a character in itself—the character, indeed, that Salome most desires.) The voice both enters the opera and departs from it in C major (from Fig. 11.3 to the full cadence at 12.1, completing the phrase "Nach mir wird Einer kommen, der ist stärker als ich"; from Fig. 244.1 to 245.2, where the impending cadence is significantly aborted). When Jochanaan himself appears for the first time, an orchestral cadence on C major confirms his emergence from the cistern, thus mediating, so to speak, between the voice and its incarnation (Fig. 65.8–14); when Jochanaan's voice resumes singing from the depths of the cistern, its first utterance ends with

EXAMPLE 8. Salome seizes on C♯ major.

a C-major cadence (Fig. 184.4–185.6, completing the phrase "Sieh', die Zeit ist gekommen, der Tag von dem ich sprach, ist da").

As for Salome, she is associated with C♯ major, a tonal level she chooses for herself (as a nonresolving dominant!) in response to the sound of Jochanaan's voice. Diversified by changes in mode, the allegorical polarization of C and C♯ assumes dramatic form at the close of the opera, furnishing the hinge for the major turning points of Salome's monologue. Something is being said by this.

To hear just what, we might think of Salome herself as a listener, since it is precisely what she hears that impels her desires; Jochanaan's voice is "like music in [her] ear." During Salome's face-to-face encounter with him, Jochanaan's savage denunciation of her mother carries him from the environment of C minor (Fig. 83.8–11) to that of C♯ major (Fig. 85.1), into which he seems to blunder in his fury. Salome immediately seizes the new key from him as her own (example 8). Her tonal center, she seems to be saying, will be his set awry by one semitone. Her key will be his turned the wrong way, the Latin for which is *perversus*. Her desire, which she will satisfy without regret on his severed head, is to raise him from his C and to kiss and possess him in her C♯.

By the end of the encounter, the terms of that desire have been clearly set. Jochanaan, driven shortly before to utter Salome's name for the first and only time, is clearly in a state of panic, out of control. He ends the scene with three increasingly hysterical curses, the last of which cadences to C♯ minor, where it is greeted by several full-bodied statements of Salome's Desire motive. The difference between her desire and its gratification emerges as the difference between the minor and major modes of C♯; all that remains is for Salome to accomplish the mode change, which she will do—twisting the curse into a blessing—in the course of her monologue. The logic is inexorable, and she is no more in charge of it than he is. Like Huysmans,

Strauss thus interprets Salome less as a person than as something more tractable: a personification of her own "passionate and cruel female temperament . . . whose charms are those of a great venereal flower."[36] His Salome is not merely perverted; she is Perversion.

Just what this means for Strauss bears some looking into. To continue with C♯ major: the choice of key is both obvious and odd. Obvious, because as Hugh Macdonald has shown, the nineteenth century increasingly associated "remote" keys with "sensuousness and mysterious ecstasy," qualities reinforced by the sensuous "feel" of these keys on the piano.[37] Odd, because C♯ major is a notationally difficult key; it requires seven sharps. The same pitches can more easily be specified by D♭ major, which has five flats. D♭ also has specific associations that would make it the key of choice for Salome; most pertinently, it is the key of the love duet in Saint-Saëns's *Samson et Dalila*.[38] Of course, from the point of view of a listener who lacks a score, the difference between C♯ and D♭ is purely academic, and there are D♭ episodes in the opera. Strauss, however, regularly ascribed concrete expressive significance to particular keys at an early phase in his compositional process.[39] From his point of view, Salome's characteristic key is C♯, *not* D♭. The reason why, I would suggest, is to be found in the Salome complex.

If we think of C major and C♯ major in terms of their notated scales rather than of their pitch content, the two keys become radically incommensurate. A single difference governs both the C and C♯ scales taken as wholes and any pair of same-letter notes drawn from them: one sharp. In German, one cross, *Kreuz:* the sign of cancellation, defacement, and crucifixion. Strauss's notation, then, articulates a symbolic division between saint and dancer, word and flesh, (masculine) Purity and (feminine) Perversion. As the avatar of C♯, Salome stands revealed as the absolute Other of the musical and spiritual order signified by the voice of Jochanaan and its originary C major. Repeating, in musical terms, the gesture of Baudelaire's "Une Martyre," Strauss first sets aside Salome's head by identifying her with a key, C♯, that is all body, then seeks a dramatic/erotic climax, the monologue, that exposes her body to the gaze "dans le plus complet abandon."

This gender-specific logic of head and body, C and C♯, is supported in *Salome* by a stylistic division between the music assigned to Salome and the music assigned to the voice of Jochanaan. With local exceptions, the one is sensuous, sinuous, and mercurial, the other solemn, austere, and obstinate. (The music sung by Jochanaan in his own person varies between these extremes; Jochanaan tends to sound more like Salome the more he talks with her—she gets, in this sense, her tongue in his mouth.)[40] In Wagnerian terms, it is as if Isolde had fallen in love with Parsifal. This split, however, also points

EXAMPLE 9. Salome's monologue: "Ich lebe noch" in C major.

Nun wohl! _____ Ich le - be noch
C⁶

to a certain instability in Strauss's expressive rhetoric, which, like Wilde's, is only equivocally successful in its triumph over Salome.

Strauss's emblematic polarization of C and C♯ can be understood as a diffuse form of chromatic saturation. Its effect is to suggest that Salome and the voice of Jochanaan form an inevitable couple. Each fills the tonal space that the other leaves void; each, as the rigid logic of head and body demands, personifies what the other lacks. One measure of this complementarity is a telling difference in the relationship of the two parties to their signature keys. C major frames the appearances of Jochanaan and his voice, but the prophet does very little singing in the key. His relationship to it is abstract and spiritual, paralleling his status as precursor to the true redeemer whom he never names except as the Son of Man. Salome, by contrast, comes to do a great deal of singing in C♯ major, to which her relationship is both sensuous and phantasmatic.

Much of that singing takes place during the monologue, which, as already noted, is charged with turning the C/ C♯ saturation from an inferential pattern to a dramatic series of events. The crucial episode begins with Salome telling the severed head, "Nun wohl! Ich lebe noch" (Well now! I'm still alive) to the sound of a pristine, diatonic C major chord (Fig. 329.3–4, example 9). C minor sounds next, after which the tonal level lapses for several measures. It resumes in the form of a pedal point deep in the bass, sinking from *forte* to *piano* and swelling again in a gradual crescendo while the rest of the orchestra, together with Salome's voice, spins out a fantastic chromatic tapestry. As the crescendo peaks, a chromatic descending tetrachord in the bass shifts the pedal from C to G♯, which the teeming upper voices gradually establish as the dominant of C♯. This transition accompanies Salome's ecstatic phrase "Ah! ah! Jochanaan, Jochanaan, du warst schön" (you were beautiful); the final word ushers in the full cadence to C♯ major. The cadence itself is hushed and serene, the culmination of a *diminuendo* lead-in; given the agitation and volatility of the passage it concludes, its arrival has the force of an emotional homecoming. What follows immediately is a sustained lyrical outpouring in C♯ major, begun by the Desire motive heard *sehr singend* on the oboes, and consummated by Salome's ecstatic and despairing outburst on "Nichts in der Welt war so weiss wie dein Leib," which takes off from one C♯-major cadence and closes with another.

The meaning of this episode cannot be fixed; it shuttles between interpretations favorable to Salome on the one hand and the voice of Jochanaan on the other. From the perspective of the voice, for which C major is a centering point of origin and C♯ a locus of extremity, Salome's tonal activity constitutes a radical disruption. Her gesture of chromatic saturation is histrionic, if not hysterical; it undercuts the unifying, centralizing force of tonality—the abstract, "masculine" quality on offer when the voice of Jochanaan booms out one of its many pious cadences—in favor of a weakly structured display of harmonic color, a "feminine" style that characteristically disguises lack as plenitude. Salome's consummating passage from a C major chord to a C♯-major cadence is a triumph of the senses over meaning. It first veils an almost lost C major in a swirling mass of dissonances, then casts off the veils to reveal C♯ in all its perverse purity.

From Salome's perspective, however, which centers not on an origin but on the ends of desire, the effect of the C/C♯ saturation is profoundly stabilizing. It negates rigid oppositions, affirms the constructive value of sonorous pleasure, and transforms a lack into a plenitude. The cadence in the monologue does not cast off the dissonances that swirl above the C pedal there; it absorbs them, distills them in a spasm of pleasure that is pure just because it is perverse, the musical name for which is C♯ major. By appropriating the key of Jochanaan's voice and linking it to a cadence in her own, Salome assumes—tries to assume, fantasizes about assuming—the authority of prophetic speech on behalf of a female subject and her desires. From the first, she has referred his efforts to utter the Word as logos or spirit to the sound of his voice, and the sound of his voice to the body that houses it. Now, at the last, she makes that word flesh in her own voice and body. It is a purely, radically, allegorically modern gesture of secularization: the reduction of spirit to Opera. Salome transposes the "strange music" that is Jochanaan's voice into her own register, literally into her own key. Her most uninhibited cry—"Ah! ah!"—sounds in three ascending chromatic steps precisely as the descending chromatic bass determinedly transmutes the C to the G♯ pedal (example 10). Salome's perversity becomes regenerative in this passage; the C-major Word from which she begins is not "Ich lebe noch" for nothing. It must, of course, come to nothing: but that judgment is not imposed by the music, or not by the music alone. Its catalyst is the lurid theatrical spectacle called forth by the severed head, which we have to see no matter what we hear: the curse of the male Medusa.

EXAMPLE 10. Salome's monologue: climactic cries over chromatic bass descent, C to G♯ (V/C♯).

(continued)

Strauss has no wish to rescind that curse, but in the long run he follows Wilde in granting Salome more power over the means of expression than he is able to control. If nothing else, Salome's musical language is more modern, more "progressive" than that of Jochanaan's voice. In fact, its climactic perversions—its dense texture, chromatic slithering, and overelaborate orchestration—cannot be told apart from Strauss's own musical signature. Salome appropriates too much of the composer's own voice to be fully negated. But more is at stake in this than some facile notion of Strauss saying "Salome, c'est moi." The open secret of his stylistic identification with

EXAMPLE 10 *(continued)*

her spills over into the wider field of culture. As Susan McClary points out, Salome is a vessel for "the treacherous chromaticism to which European composers and audiences had become increasingly addicted [and that by 1905] could no longer be rationally contained." The figure of addiction is telling: musical pleasure, and more broadly aesthetic pleasure, had become dependent on expressive excess, transgressive desire. In this context the excess embodied musically by Salome is that of the fin-de-siècle as a whole. Her expurgation is the mark of her era's bad conscience—"a bit disingenuous," as McClary dryly notes.[41] Both the ambivalence of the gaze, which

EXAMPLE 11. Salome's monologue: dissonant apotheosis.

simultaneously enjoys and condemns Salome's addictiveness, and the final resort to violence when the gaze threatens to fail are symptomatic of a historical dysfunction. They mark the divorce of social and cultural authority from reason, in the name of reason: an accurate portent for the twentieth century, but not a good one.

The closing measures of the opera all but concede the point before the lid clamps shut. Although Strauss faithfully preserves Herod's attempt to blot Salome out, he does award her—after many vacillations—a final possession of C♯ major in tandem with the triumphant claim that she has kissed Jochanaan's mouth. The cadence at this point is followed by two C♯-major chords separated by a famous, very pungent bitonal dissonance (example 11) that seems to represent a distillation of Salome's entire experience. From the perspective of Jochanaan's voice, the chord is monstrous, the mark of desire gone as wrong as desire can go. From Salome's perspective, it is the ultimate spasm of dissonance as pleasure that feeds the luminous perversity of C♯ major. Neither point of view can prevail. The chord both blurts out the ugly truth of the spectacle as opposed to the seductions of the music, and offers the listener a fleeting moment of absolute sonorous bliss framed by the shimmer of C♯ major. Still, it is worth noting that the execution of Herod's petulant kill order, apparently prompted by this very sound, can reasonably be heard as the voice of *ressentiment*. Forcing closure in C minor, and crushing Salome to the rhythm of her own Desire motive, the death scene may stand as Jochanaan's revenge on a sonority—modern, decadent, sensuous, unintelligible, amoral—that is, in every sense, unthinkable within the traditional stringencies of his world.

Most productions of *Salome* are indifferent to these internal complications. Opera, occasionally a politically progressive form, is rarely progressive socially; it is too expensive for that. Nevertheless, a deconstructive performance of *Salome* would be possible: a like-minded singer and stage director could effectively bring out all the resistances that the figure of Salome offers to her debasement. Oddly enough, the first person to approve of such a performance would have been Richard Strauss. Strauss wanted Salome to retain a certain dignity and detachment even in the monologue scene; to that end, he prescribed only the "simplest and most aristocratic" of physical gestures for her, a prescription, as he ruefully noted, honored mostly in the breach. Strauss's reasons, though, were problematical, dictated largely by the logic of the Salome complex itself. Defensively inclined to regard his music as one thing, and titillating stagings of Salome's monologue as quite another, he complained, in a notable glass-house comment, that some performers took perversion and abandonment altogether too far, "exceed[ing] all bounds of propriety and good taste." He objected to the "excesses . . . permitted themselves" by "sleazy-cabaret types *[Tingeltangelleuten]* swinging Jochanaan's head through the air."[42] That is no way, Strauss implies, to treat a man's head: the phallus deserves more respect! Salome, no longer a dancer, should allow herself to be bounded, defined, by the frame of the final tableau. Otherwise, she might "arouse only horror and disgust rather than compassion."

There are, however, alternatives. A Salome who distanced herself from the compassion that Strauss offers would also be one who resists being assimilated into the discourse that makes a Baudelairean martyr of her. True, Strauss's "ranting and raving" music (his own description) makes a formidable obstacle against which to test that resistance. But since *Salome* remains the most popular survival of the fin-de-siècle fad, the effort might be worth a try.

It would not, in any case, be the first attempt to appropriate the Salome complex on Salome's behalf. In 1890 the American artist Ella Ferris Pell exhibited a strikingly offhanded portrait of Salome (figure 4). According to Bram Dijkstra, "Pell's Salome makes a revolutionary statement by being nothing but the realistic portrait of a young, strong, radiantly self-possessed woman who looks upon the world around her with confidence. . . . [Such a woman] was far more threatening, far more a visual declaration of defiance against the canons of male dominance than any of the celebrated vampires and viragoes created by turn-of-the-century intellectuals could have been."[43] What is perhaps most striking about the picture is the famous charger, which Salome holds negligently against her knee. The charger is empty. Confronted

FIGURE 4. Ella Ferris Pell, *Salome* (1890). Private collection.

with that emptiness, the observer may choose whether or not to fill it. *No one is compelled to imagine John the Baptist's head on that plate.* For those who leave the plate empty, the Salome complex begins to disintegrate. Salome remains in control of the visual field, which in Pell's painting is dominated by Salome's right shoulder, arm, and breast: an iconic affirmation of woman's body as a painter's body.

What I hope to have shown in my analysis of male-authored versions of Salome, Strauss's opera preeminent among them, is that Pell's kind of resistance to voyeuristic head-body logic is not only a concealed or repressed part of that logic, but one of its very premises. Wouldn't it be logical, then, to hope for future productions of *Salome* more Pell-like than the R-rated spectacle that so often slouches toward the opera house to be born?

6 Video as *Jugendstil*

Salome, *Visuality, and Performance*

Wie wird Moderne zum Jugendstil?

WALTER BENJAMIN

The question with which the last chapter ended is real, not rhetorical, but its answer is still pretty clear. The answer is "No." Regardless of latter-day critical ingenuity that has gone into imagining a Salome empowered by her singing or dancing, and regardless of the ambiguities offered by the opera itself, performances of *Salome* stubbornly keep reverting to the fin-de-siècle norm. If a "feminist" Salome were going to appear, she might have been expected during the last decades of the twentieth century, when awareness of the changing social status of women was at its height and when the re- lation of women and visuality, not least in *Salome* itself, was hotly debated. But the record suggests that this Salome largely remains unseen, precisely because the Salomes presented to us can still be seen all too well, and in step with Strauss's music, not at odds with it. The emancipated Salome is still a critical phantom; the real Salome is still a cheap date. She is a figure who, at certain moments in certain performances, may rise to the level of ambi- guity the opera affords her, but has not yet been able to rise above it. For some insight into why, I turn to performances in a medium that heightens the opera's own already intensive concern with the visual, and thus raises the question of visual pleasure in opera in an especially acute form. The medium is the opera video: a recording meant primarily for the television screen, regardless of whether its format is VHS or DVD.[1]

In its sets and costumes, the 1992 Royal Opera production of *Salome* at Covent Garden, as seen on video, strongly evokes the fin-de-siècle visual style associated with German *Jugendstil* and the Austrian Secession; the color and costumes seem specifically to allude to the style of Gustav Klimt. A video version of the 1990 production by the Deutsche Oper Berlin does much the same thing with Art Nouveau, using sets and costumes dominated by contrasts of black and white and clearly alluding to the style of Aubrey Beardsley. With this recourse to visual styles drawn from the opera's own day, these videos initiate a process of interpretation that works at two levels. First, they suggest that there is a connection between these decorative, highly detailed, deliberately artificial styles and the opera's music, and again between the ethos associated with those styles and that of the opera. Second, by alluding to recognizable styles of visual art, they mark the visual itself as an issue of special pertinence to this opera. It is no accident, they seem to be saying, that *Salome* depends so much on how the audience *sees* its protagonist: as she dances, as she waits by a cistern for a man to be decapitated, and as she sings a long serenade to that man's severed head. This is an opera, they seem to say, about seeing. It is therefore an opera especially suited for the unsparing, intimate kind of seeing proper to the video medium, a kind of seeing that also has something to do with the historical phenomenon of the visual styles I will lump together here under the term *Jugendstil.*

What follows is an attempt to hear the opera through looking at, looking through, and looking over these two videos, together with a third, with three questions, or clusters of questions, in mind. First, just what is the role of the visual in this opera, and what can be learned from it by studying its video renditions? What, more generally, does this approach to the opera have to tell us about the whole concept of a rendition, a version, a realization, visual and otherwise? Second, what do these visual issues have to do with the figure of Salome, and more particularly with the aura of perverse sexuality that she is commonly taken to represent and that in recent years has been the object of controversy in relation to the representation of her as a woman? Finally, what can we learn from the invocation, in both the opera and the renditions, of *Jugendstil*?

VIDEO AND THE VISUAL

At one level all opera raises the question of visuality. Since an opera must ordinarily be staged, imagery, gesture, and spectacle all figure into any production. But this figuring-in is remarkably loose. Although miscalculations are obviously possible, the range of visual realizations for any given opera is virtually unlimited. In part this is because music in opera is accorded primacy; the relation of subordination creates breadth of tolerance for visual realization (which includes productions that tinker with time, since the main mark of temporal change is the look of the mise-en-scène). Good singing easily outweighs bad scenery; good scenery never outweighs bad singing.

The situation in opera can be considered a mirror reversal of that in classical narrative film, where it is the image that holds primacy and music that stands in a subordinate, supplemental relation. In even larger part, though, music's visual tolerance stems from the semantic malleability or plasticity accorded to it as part of its very definition qua music. The music thus easily accommodates itself to a wide variety of visual representations. As a result, any particular operatic realization appears precisely as that, as a visual alternative linked to a body of music that is relatively fixed in form but highly variable in meaning.

What would it take, then, for an opera to raise the question of visuality in an acute or special sense, even in a critical or crisis-oriented sense? Something in the opera would have to raise the impression of visual realization from the level of assumption to that of dramatic event. The visual element would have to be made remarkable by literally being re-marked, in the Derridean sense of marked over, meaning marked both again and across, such that the effect of the re-marking is to put the normal primacy of music in doubt, whether or not an actual reversal of values, temporary or permanent, occurs. As a rule, out of what might be called operatic self-interest, this re-marking of the visual is more a product of experimental production than of operatic composition. But in *Salome*, Strauss makes it an immanent matter, and does so by the most simple, direct, and brutal means, a means consistent with Freud's near-contemporary claim about the origins of the drive to know, and with contemporary renegotiations of the field of vision in general. His means, of course, is the display of sexuality as located, by cultural mandate, in the female body. But this is supplemented by or supplements the obsessive thematizing of looking and being looked out throughout the opera. Still, perhaps we shouldn't speak carelessly about "his" means here. The lore surrounding the opera suggests that Strauss did not quite want it to be what virtually everyone has taken it for, an overripe expression of fin-de-siècle sexuality as mediated by a relay of gazes. Given the topic, given its cultural prevalence, the opera could virtually not be anything else; it just got away from Strauss, who never again, not even in *Elektra*, ventured into this territory.

In the theater, intimacy with the performer's body comes at moments of coalescence of vocal effort and dramatic crisis. But the face is missing. In a video, images of the whole body are by definition not intimate, so the result is the presentation of the fragmented body and especially of the face. One might have expected this to alter the equation in *Salome*, but what it does instead is extend the realm of visual pleasure into wider and deeper territories than are available in the theater. And this is particularly so in the three scenes in which Strauss (re-marking the issue) compels the audience to do what the opera says is so dangerous to do: to look at Salome, in the first two instances without hearing her at all: in the orchestral interlude following the encounter scene, in the dance, and in the monologue.

JUGENDSTIL AND MODERNITY

It is at this point that the question of *Jugendstil* becomes a factor. The approach to it I find most suggestive is scattered throughout Walter Benjamin's unfinished magnum opus *The Arcades Project* (Das Passagen-Werk), which repeatedly tries to come to terms, aphoristically at least, with *Jugendstil* as a symptom of modernity.[2] Benjamin, gathering notes rather than writing an argument, is necessarily unsystematic, and he tends to lump architecture, literary style, visual imagery, and advertising under the single umbrella term *Jugendstil*. The outlines of a theory have to be drawn by inference. Those outlines, however, have both an independent interest and a striking pertinence to *Salome,* and I will therefore sketch a portion of them here.

For Benjamin, *Jugendstil*—so called because of its association, after 1896, with the magazine *Der Jugend*—is "the stylizing style [der stilisierende Stil, 691] par excellence" (556); the priority it gives to ornament, a kind of fetishizing of technique, develops into three characteristic motifs that Benjamin labels hieratic, perverse, and emancipatory. This "technical" emphasis has historical roots. Benjamin claims that *Jugendstil* was

> the second attempt on the part of art to come to terms with technology. The first attempt was realism. There the problem was more or less present in the consciousness of the artists, who were uneasy about the new processes of technological reproduction. . . . Jugendstil no longer saw itself as threatened by the competing technology. And so the confrontation with technology that lies hidden within it was all the more aggressive. Its recourse to technological motifs arises from the effort to sterilize them ornamentally. (557)[3]

That is, by translating technology into ornament, the anti-organic, anti-human potential of technology, and hence of modernity, could be rendered harmless, "sterilized." Typically this sterilizing ornament takes the form of elaborate floral or vegetal motifs, the lines of which could equally well be drawn in the ink of a poster or by the wrought iron of a building. Benjamin compares the result to the identification of nerve and electrical wire, and describes this "vegetal nervous system" (das vegetative Nervensystem, 694) as "a limiting form to mediate between the world of organism and the world of technology" (558) (als Grenzenform zwischen der Welt des Organismus und der Technik vermittelt, 694).

The emblematic figure to whom such a nervous system belongs is a perverse and sterile woman: "The extreme point in the technological organization of the world is the liquidation of fertility. The frigid woman embodies the ideal of beauty in Jugendstil. (Jugendstil sees in every woman not Helen but Olympia.)" (559).[4] Removed from her traditional reproductive function and wrapped around with ornament, the *Jugendstil* woman embodies the marriage of organism and machinery, and, in her perversity, further embodies both its appeal and its dangers. Benjamin traces the "line" of perversion specifically from Baudelaire to Wilde to Beardsley, thus specifically implicating the figure of Salome without actually naming her. The figure he does name is Ibsen's Hedda Gabler: "Just as Ibsen passes judgment on Jugendstil architecture in *The Master Builder*, so he passes judgment on its female type in *Hedda Gabler*. She is the theatrical sister of those *diseuses* and dancers who, in floral depravity or innocence, appear naked and without objective background on Jugendstil posters" (551).[5] Hedda Gabler does not make a bad parallel to that notorious dancer, the Salome of Wilde and Strauss. Salome might be said to be Hedda without the bourgeois constraints: like her sister of the drawing room, she is overwhelmed by desires for which her world has no room and no name, and quite willing to displace their satisfaction into the savage destruction and mutilation of the man who embodies them.

Also notable in this context is Benjamin's invocation of the poster, the mechanically reproducible form, used above all for advertising, that is the defining medium of *Jugendstil* imagery. "Advertising," says Benjamin, "is emancipated in Jugendstil" (176) (Die Reklame emanzipiert sich im Jugendstil, 238); and again, "In Jugendstil we see, for the first time, the integration of the human body into advertising" (186) (die Einbeziehung des menschlichen Leibe[s] in die Reklame, 250). The flatness, lack of background, and ornamental overlay of the poster renders the *Jugendstil* Beauty not only sterile but also one-dimensional, emptied of an interior subjectivity that is replaced by the pure exteriority of the ornamented body image. "Among the stylistic elements that enter into Jugendstil," writes Benjamin, ". . . one of the most important is the predominance of the *vide* over the *plein*, the empty over the full" (550).[6] The expression of this emptiness as a form of subjectivity is the vacuity—floral depravity or innocence—of the *Jugendstil* Beauty. For this vacuity Benjamin borrows a phrase, "deep, but without thoughts" (tief, aber ohne Gedanken, 694), used by Nietzsche to describe "flower maidens—an important theme in Jugendstil." Lacking content, the depth becomes a pure appearance, which is to say, a surface, marked by what Benjamin elsewhere describes as the "brittleness" *(Sprödigkeit)* of allegory, "the antithesis to the beautiful appearance in which signifier and signified flow into each other" (374) (der Widerpart des schönen Scheins, in welchem Bedeutendes und Bedeutetes ineinanderfliessen, 472). Nietzsche's phrase, Benjamin continues, "perfectly captures the expression [trifft genau den Ausdrück] worn by the prostitutes" in the Parisian sketches of Constantin Guys, the illustrator who inspired Baudelaire's essay "The Painter of Modern Life" (559). And it does so as part of a broad historical trend: "Just as certain modes of presentation—genre scenes and the like—begin, in the nineteenth century, to 'cross over' into advertising, so also into the realm of the obscene" (173).[7] In the poster, what you see is what you get, and what you get is the coalescence of the *Jugendstil* motifs of emancipation and perversion.

The figure of the poster Beauty brings us back to *Salome.* From its very first moments, Strauss's opera presents Salome as a fascinating and dangerous magnet for the eye, at once an inapproachable, "sterile" virgin, still almost a girl, and a perverse sexual predator. The climactic scenes of the dance, the vigil at the cistern, and the monologue to the severed head with its consummation in a necrophiliac kiss are all themselves visually magnetic. They are scenes of staring at which we are invited to stare, scenes of transgression we are lured to witness; they are scenes, too, that derive their visual energy from the haunting presence of something not heard—Salome's voice in the dance, the sound of the decapitation by the cistern, Jochanaan's answer in the monologue. The music we do hear, the elaborate "vegetal lines" of sound swirling around the poster-girl figure in these scenes, both sustains and embodies the force of visual magnetism; this is above all music to see by. The exoticism of the dance music invokes the imagery of orientalist fantasy; the bizarre squeals of the vigil place Salome's demand for the head of Jochanaan in the sphere of psychiatric fantasy; and the dense, glittering orchestral fabric and Wagnerian sensuality of the monologue fill out the sphere of erotic fantasy, in particular of the fin-de-siècle fantasy of the excited, dangerous female body wrapped or encrusted in ornament, organic tendrils, or jewels.

The dance and monologue musics, moreover, maintain what might be described as a strict position of exteriority with respect to Salome herself, in contrast to the music for the decapitation scene, which tries to get "inside" her mind and body. Unlike Strauss's Elektra and Wagner's Isolde, who at climactic moments hear the music around them as expressions of their inner truth, and unlike Elektra in particular, who can exclaim of such music, "It comes from me!" Salome is entirely self-absorbed, entirely aloof. Her dance is a calculated performance, not an expression—at least not a voluntary expression—of anything in herself, as we clearly see from her utter indifference after the dance is over. And her monologue is divided by the drastic contrast between her own concentration and the orchestra's expansiveness, her utter absorption in the head of Jochanaan and the complex, coruscating musical energies that surround and threaten to overwhelm it. She stands amid the music the way many women in Klimt stand enveloped, nearly consumed, nearly rendered inorganic, by glittering tiles of metallic color.

This is not to say, however, that the music of the monologue scene does not express Salome's subjectivity, that it does not "envoice" her in some way. It is to say, rather, that this subjectivity has become purely external; its putative depth has been emptied and its contents redistributed across the visual and auditory fields of the scene. This is a subjectivity that has, so to speak, been turned inside out to reveal the pulsing, shimmering, yearning surface that is both the music and Salome's body, the twin sources of the voice through which she sustains her obsession to the end. The Salome of the monologue scene is all surface, almost exactly like the women pictured on the *Jugendstil* posters recalled or imagined by Benjamin.

And here we return to the question of medium, of technology, as an essential rather than accidental component of the opera's effect and of the opera "itself," whatever that phrase might mean. In the opera house, the identification of Salome with a visible, purely "superficial" subjectivity realized through music is at best a figurative or metaphorical effect, qualified by the material weight of the singers and the stage and by the "live" auditory presence of the music. On video, however, the effect can become entirely literal: conjoined with recorded music, the flat, intimate, tightly framed image of Salome on the television screen becomes the *Jugendstil* poster brought to virtual life, which is to say, not to an organic-seeming "real" life (as might even be possible in a movie theater) but to the spectral, inorganic life of virtuality. And this is a life, I want to suggest, or a lifelike lifelessness, that is not added from without by the advent of a new medium, but inextricably a part of whatever we can credibly mean by the opera per se, as such, "itself."

ENTR'ACTE

This last remark leads naturally to a reflection on method that can also be taken as a caution. In reading the videos it is not always possible to distinguish between the layers of interpretation belonging to the production and to the video, nor again between either of these layers and the one belonging to the opera itself. As I've just indicated, I regard this indeterminacy not as a problem to be solved but as a welcome indication that the usual distinctions between a work and its realizations are unsustainable except as temporary conveniences. A similar indeterminacy arises from the necessity of describing what the video shows and how it shows; one may not be able to say for sure whether what is being interpreted is the imagery or its description. This, too, is a positive, not a negative, condition. The video cannot interpret itself, even while it is running; only if it is seen "under a description" can it come to hermeneutic life.

Two trains of thought, at least, seem to branch out from these recognitions:

1. The indeterminacy over what, exactly, is being interpreted is not unique to the video medium, but only highlighted by it. The highlighting allows us to question with some robustness the representational model whereby a work, understood as in some sense self-contained, may be interpreted, performed, realized, adapted, or otherwise presented in diverse media. We might want to speak, not of an operatic work that is represented in being realized, but of the ways in which the operatic work, the opera itself—whatever we intend by such expressions—may reveal certain dimensions or raise certain questions when realized *this* way that may not arise so vividly when it is realized *that* way. But there is no possibility of making a clean separation of an ideal opera to which its various renditions are external or supplementary.

2. The video medium in particular means that, by comparison to the opera house, we always see more than we are supposed to. Not only do we get too close, but we move too much; in reading the camera we must so to speak read around or through the convention that demands changes in angle and distance regardless of the subject matter of the scene. With videos the problem of how to look, how to show, is itself always literally on view. As a practical matter, these visual rhythms are so extensive that it is impossible to trace any of them in a linear fashion. In what follows, I will rely on two practical solutions to this problem: descriptions of the overall character of the rhythms in each video, and intensive focus on the treatments of a single scene—the first encounter of Salome and Jochanaan—from which com-

ments on the decapitation scene and final monologue, as well as cumulative comparisons among the various renditions, can branch out.

"ICH BIN SALOME, PRINZESSIN DER JUDEA": MARIA EWING

Maria Ewing's Salome in the video of the 1992 Royal Opera production is a regal, arrogant figure who seems instinctively to translate her desires into rituals; from the very beginning, her relationship to Jochanaan is as much symbolic and gestural as it is erotic.[8] Her style is the stylizing style par excellence. The rhythms of the camera extend this orientation across the opera as a whole. These visual rhythms parallel and underline the opera's large-scale dramaturgical design, which in its own right is already underlined by the pared-down version of Oscar Wilde's play that serves as the libretto. The design can be described as a prologue (all about looking at Salome) plus an ABA pattern consisting of three encounters: between Salome and Jochanaan, in which she seeks to kiss him; between Salome and Herod, in which, the kiss denied, she seeks Jochanaan's head; and again between Salome and Jochanaan, now reduced to his severed head, which again she seeks to kiss, and does kiss. Each of these encounters is bisected by an interruption— the suicide of Salome's admirer Narraboth, Salome's dance, and the colloquy of Herod and Herodias—to form its own smaller ABA pattern. The prevailing symmetry and formality contribute to an impression that is part ornamental and part ritualistic or hieratic—two of Benjamin's triad of *Jugendstil* motifs. The third, perversion, is of course pervasive.

Roughly speaking, the outer sections of the video's large-scale design concentrate on close-ups, the middle section on longer and middle-distance shots. The first section alternates close-ups of Jochanaan and Salome; the final section concentrates on Salome alone, which is also to say that it deemphasizes the presence of the head in her monologue, with, as we'll see, one notable exception. The outer sections also show a tendency for Salome to engross the viewer's gaze by filling the space of the television screen, but with a telling reversal of emphasis. In the first section Salome tends to lay claim to the screen space by extending her arms wide to touch its limits; the gestures are pictorial, and combined with Ewing's slimness and tallness they are vaguely evocative of Egyptian tomb painting. In the monologue, by contrast, the camera rather than the women is the principal agent. It seems to cram Salome into the screen space with tight close-ups, primarily of her upper body and face, as if she, too, had been truncated by Jochanaan's decapitation.

In the encounter scene, Jochanaan appears almost naked, clad only in a loincloth, as if to put the audience in Salome's staring position: his flesh rivets the gaze. Standing atop the housing of his cistern (an elevated structure with a stairwell) he draws the eye upward to his seminakedness, incidentally putting the onlooker into the viewing posture of the classical Freudian fetishist. But Jochanaan's body also repels the gaze. Whether from makeup or lighting or some combination of both, his body has a decided bluish cast that it seems to emit as a faint, sickish glow; the body is livid, as if Jochanaan were already a corpse. The real erotic spectacle here is the fully clothed Salome, in whom (especially on her face, of which more later) the audience is invited to recognize what it is really looking for, that is, the efflorescence of her desire. It is desire, not the body per se, that is the impossible object of erotic spectatorship. The gap between Jochanaan's actual appearance and the figure Salome evokes in her passages of adulation ("Your body is like a tower of ivory," etc.) is thus particularly glaring, and Salome's regular alternation between adulation and disgust ("Your hair is glorious," "Your hair is horrible," etc.) marks both the power and the futility of the desire that fills the gap—the desire the viewer can see only by scrutinizing Salome's face, body, and voice for traces of what she sees in Jochanaan.

The video realization of the scene dramatizes these relationships by alternating three types of shot: close-ups of Salome, close-ups of Jochanaan, and long shots in which both figures appear in the frame. These distanced, duo shots play out a miniature narrative based on position and power. The narrative sequence begins with Jochanaan at the screen's upper left, Salome at lower right, maximally separate, and concludes with the two figures almost overlapping; the sequence breaks off at just the point where Salome almost achieves a two-handed grasp of Jochanaan's head. The overall tendency is toward increasing proximity (with local hesitations and reversals) and involves several inversions of power and control depending on who stands and who lies or leans supine. Meanwhile, there is a complex negotiation among points of view. In the close-ups of Jochanaan, the point of view is Salome's; in the long shots it coincides with that of a theater audience. But since Jochanaan steadfastly refuses to look at Salome, the close-ups of her proceed from an "impossible" point of view, a floating intimacy, assumed by the viewer but belonging to no one, that sees the truth of her desire. All the close-ups, therefore, both now and later, and whether of Salome or Jochanaan, show the spectacle of Salome's desire.

More exactly, they *make* a spectacle of it, both in the literal sense of composing it as an image and in the idiomatic sense of compulsively showing something shameful or excessive. Ewing emphasizes this effect with a constant, very busy gesticulation with her arms and hands. The movements at

once form an extension of sight into touch, suggest an "exotic" Eastern posturing, and evoke a kind of inverse Galatea-Pygmalion relation as Salome
sculpts in air the object of her desire. Jochanaan's whole effort in this scene
is to repel Salome (or, failing that, to convert her), but the effort is obviously doomed. He cannot escape the tendrils of either her gestures or her
gaze (which he specifically tries to repel) as long as he remains visible—a
predicament that gives special force to the dramatic facts that he has had to
be *made* visible, drawn forth from his cistern, and that his visibility itself
is so glaring. Jochanaan is thus tethered to Salome's fantasy space. His tether
is made explicit in the rope that binds his hands and restricts his movements,
and that, at one point, when his handler is momentarily hidden, seems to
come to him directly from Salome's body like a perverse umbilicus.

When Jochanaan does redescend into the cistern, finally breaking the link,
the production has Salome fling herself down and writhe and roll in an erotic
frenzy. The music calls for something of the kind; marked "with extreme
passion" (mit äusserster Leidenschaft), it situates the display of Salome's response to Jochanaan's rejection of her in the opera's only substantial stretch
of purely instrumental music apart from the dance. What this means is that
the response is confined to the arenas of visuality and gesture; voice is, so
to speak, out of the picture. Salome's effort to overcome Jochanaan's rejection will ultimately coincide with the recovery of her voice as an instrument of desire in the final monologue.

In Ewing's realization, Salome's body is literally overturned by the force
of her passion, propelled down the stairwell of the cistern to a "low" point
of frustration and degradation. The camera accompanies her abjection with
a ternary visual rhythm: long shots (interspersed with a few close-ups) that
show her writhing on top of the cistern, close to the void that contains
Jochanaan; low-angled close-ups that follow her prostrate form down the
stairs as she turns over and over, with further emphasis on hand-wringing
and arm movements; and a sustained long shot that frames her against a
blue background—a visual rhyme for Jochanaan's skin tone—as she rolls
and writhes on the ground. The sequence culminates with Salome locked in
an extended full-body clench, her posture unnaturally curving, like a taut-
ened bow.

The posture suggests an extended orgasm, one that peaks with a triple-
forte C♯-minor cadence for full orchestra, but also one that cannot find true
release. The cadential tutti jolts home violently but vanishes in an instant,
leaving behind a C♯ tremolo in the violins. Against this background the brass
and winds mass together for a crescendo on a long chromatic auxiliary chord,
then twist, with a short wrenching stab, onto the C♯-minor triad. This "or-

gasmic" secondary cadence resounds through a slowly fading series of echoes; as the tremolo continues, the dynamics lessen, the register sinks, and the instrumental forces dwindle. The effect is one of sinking downward to the dark, as if to the heart of mystery and perversity—from which, as we will see later, the solo contrabassoon emerges with something to say. But Salome, as the tremolo keeps insisting, is anything but appeased. Midway in this passage, and just before the secondary cadences shift to her signature key of C♯ major, the music returns to the melodic motive with which the episode began, the little phrase associated with Salome's desire. The motive is now heard in a truncated form, unable to complete the descending motion that characterizes it. Meanwhile, the position of Salome's body—clenched, rigid, unnatural—remains unchanged, as if in Ewing's rendition Salome were simply impervious to the orchestra's surrogate eroticism, at least as long as her body remains visible. When the "Desire" motive appears, the camera averts its gaze to another part of the stage—an empty space dominated by the huge moon, the symbol of Salome's feminine nature, and here both her visual surrogate and a visual blank. Salome's physical release, if she has one, occurs off-camera, as if the depth of either her pleasure or her frustration would be unbearable to watch. The extreme of her sexuality has to be shunted away into the unseeing realm of its musical imitation.

This retreat of the camera also occurs at the end of the Dance of the Seven Veils. Ewing's rendition of the dance picks up several visual motifs from the encounter scene. It begins as a performance coolly calculated to arouse Herod. Its opening play with the veils themselves is impersonal, detached, and its choreography at first involves controlled, stylized forms of the seemingly involuntary movements—arm and hand motion, lying supine, writhing—that had overtaken Salome after Jochanaan's departure from that first encounter. As the dance proceeds, however, the impression of control and detachment is stripped away along with Salome's clothing. By the close, her stylized gestures have yielded to openly masturbatory touching, slightly displaced to her upper thighs, and to the unabashed display of full frontal nudity for which the Royal Opera production was briefly notorious. The turning point in this process comes when Salome mounts the cistern, a cylindrical projection with a gaping hole at its center, and frenziedly dances around the circumference of that hole. This motion around a lack, the gap at the core of desire and visibility alike, culminates when Salome falls prone onto the grate covering the hole. Her action refers back to her behavior in the first encounter: vainly trying to touch Jochanaan's hair, she has posed herself behind the grate, which at that point was in its upright position, its bars marking the prison of her desire. The message in the dance scene is plainly that Jochanaan should look at her and love her, just as she says in her monologue that he should have done.

The impossibility of this ever happening propels Salome into another frenzy, so that in the end she is no longer dancing for Herod at all but, vainly, for the unseen and unseeing Jochanaan. And once again the spectacle of this is too much for the camera eye to bear, or rather it must limit what it shows, must gaze askance, in order to enjoy the spectacle. At the end of the scene the camera turns prudish, as does the lighting, which dims to turn Salome's body a grayish blue, visually rhyming with Jochanaan's. Ewing's nude Salome stands in semidarkness, situated at the left rather than the center of the TV screen in a medium-long shot, as if it would be dangerous to look any closer or more directly. The danger might be thought of as cultural: a better look would make the spectacle more pornographic than aesthetic, and that would be Salome's triumph. The triumph is one that Ewing's Salome clearly claims by standing proudly for a long moment of self-exposure, while the camera at one and the same time censures her, censors her, and enjoys what its off-center view reveals. The camera may be accused of timidity here, but its timidity, even its cowering, has the cultural authority that Salome lacks: it, not she, controls what we see. Any power she may have had has been lost in the frenzy that increasingly overtakes her once she mounts the cistern.

In the final monologue Ewing's Salome appears, pointedly, clothed in a blood red garment, the sign of both Jochanaan's mutilation and Salome's incarnation of the scarlet woman, the Whore of Babylon. Ewing sings most of the scene on her knees before the head, which is itself rarely seen, and mostly seen from behind. At the point where the music makes a cadence to the phrase, "Jochanaan, du warst schön," Salome lifts the head, gazes at it, and hugs it maternally to her bosom. Shortly afterward, as Salome says that she had heard "strange music" in Jochanaan's voice, we see a shot of her face juxtaposed with the head's, the two filling the screen in extreme close-up in a travesty of romantic union. The head more or less vanishes after this. Salome's face, more than her now hidden body, is the key visual element in this scene: more intimately and at greater length than in the first encounter, her face is the medium in which her subjectivity appears and her desire is revealed. Ewing at this point acts a great deal with her face, modulating the expressions of longing and bliss with a fine detail visible only through the agency of the close-up camera. The effect is redoubled by the fact that she is also sweating at this point, more and more profusely, and the close-ups clearly catch the glint of perspiration on her face and neck. The image might be said to offer "the little piece of the real" in which, according to Slavoj Žižek, all symbolization and all fantasy must at some point be grounded.[9] The fictional body of Salome merges at this point into the actual body of Maria Ewing, as the physical trace of a taxing performance does double duty as the material manifestation of perverse desire.

THE IMP OF THE PERVERSE: CATHERINE MALFITANO

As noted earlier, the sets and costumes of the 1990 production by the Deutsche Oper Berlin suggest Beardsley rather than Klimt: they emphasize line and contour and contrasts of black and white.[10] The overall impression is spare, abstract, and harshly angled. There is also no cistern, which is most important: in the first encounter Jochanaan appears from on high, and it is some time before he descends along the white stripe of a long thin stair amid the prevailing darkness. He also has complete freedom of movement, and closes the scene by reascending to fulminate at Salome again from on high. Simon Estes, the Jochanaan, is shot here and throughout prevailingly from low angles, emphasizing his imposing size and stature. He is a full head or more taller than Catherine Malfitano's Salome, and also massive; as he steadfastly refuses to look at her, he stands straight and tall—which is to say, rigid and erect. Yet we do not see his body with the libidinal force that Salome does, as we do in the Ewing version. For the viewer, Estes's Jochanaan is above all a figure of authority, not of desire, and he is clothed accordingly: although he has a bare chest, he wears a majestic cloak and his lower body is concealed.

Faced with so formidable a figure, Malfitano's Salome shrinks both emotionally and physically, even as she pursues him with a relentless will. Malfitano never asserts her full stature when close to Estes, but always crouches and leans, constantly orbiting the figure of this Jochanaan, with whom she is photographed only in ways that subordinate her to his presence. When he curses her, shown from below reascending the stair while she cowers beneath him, she abjectly caresses his foot. The visual imbalance between the two figures is interspersed with prolonged medium shots of Salome that obscure the stage set, showing her against a black background and thus isolating her within the void of her desire. In the Ewing version, this fatal meeting of Salome and Jochanaan is a genuine dramatic encounter, though its outcome is predetermined: the characters interact. Here there is no interaction except during Jochanaan's conversion attempt—more gen-

uine here than in the Ewing version—which also allows Salome some il-
licit touching of Jochanaan's hand. This Salome has no power at all except
the power of desire. She is not only dwarfed by Jochanaan but also crushed
by the force of his voice—Estes being far "bigger" in that sense than the
Royal Opera's Jochanaan, Michael Devlin. This vulnerability perhaps renders Salome more sympathetic, since she has a real injury to avenge, whereas
Ewing's Salome almost literally chases her naked Jochanaan down the rab-
bit hole.

During the orchestral interlude following her rejection, Malfitano's Salome sheds her cloak for the first time, lies back, touches her breasts, and
then runs aimlessly here and there, not knowing what to do with herself.
At several moments she is pinned to the wall by a conspicuous spotlight
that rhymes visually with the image of the moon. Eventually she finds herself in a crowd of leather-clad bare-chested soldiers who emerge from the
wings as if they had just escaped from an S/M bar and who, leering, gradually encircle her. We see them obliterate the sight of her face and body in
medium shots, and eventually close like a dark shadow around her in long
shot, anticipating her death at the end of the opera. The scene ends showing what the other version does not, Salome's orgasmic spasm at the first
echo of the C♯-minor cadence, to which the subsequent echoes become af-
termaths. This physical literalism in her pleasure, unlike Ewing's strong-
willed insatiability, will reach a spectacular climax in the final monologue.

Before that, the same literalism manifests itself in the dance, as if
Malfitano were trying to translate Salome's sexuality into image and gesture to match Strauss's translation of it into music. The dance uses the full
logic of the veil and is much more sexually explicit than Ewing's: Malfitano
dances naked under a translucent drapery, makes deliberately provocative
pelvic thrusts, and displays her nudity front and center, not off to the side,
though only for a moment. Her self-display, however, is self-consuming: on
her knees, Malfitano's Salome falls violently forward onto her face, as if she
would be unable to withstand for more than an instant the gaze she has so
relentlessly called forth.

Later, at the climax of the monologue scene, she corrects that impression.
With extreme close-ups of her face used for the first time in the video,
Malfitano's Salome opens her mouth wide and plants a deep wet kiss on the
head of Jochanaan. The kiss seems to last forever—and then Malfitano repeats it. With her own head filling the screen, and her lips working hun-
grily, this Salome's kisses are flagrantly sloppy, visual realizations of the raw
physicality of her desire. The impression is reinforced by the sweat that
bathes Malfitano's face as it does Ewing's, but more as mere bodily secre-

tion than as the glistening substance of desire. So intense is the physical engagement that it is hard not to wonder about the state of mind that makes it possible. To act in character at so physical a level suggests, at least, a momentary surrender of separate identity. The union of bodies that emerges at the parallel point in Ewing's version seems in Malfitano's to extend, to be meant to extend, to a union of psyches. It may be that the person kissing Jochanaan's mouth here is, in a sense, not one Catherine Malfitano, but actually Salome, Princess of Judea.

The impression continues to the brink of Salome's death. At the very end of the monologue, we see Jochanaan's head perched on a column where Salome has placed it, the better to kiss its mouth. To this column Malfitano presses herself closely, clutching it between her knees in another pelvic thrust as she kisses the head yet again. The significance of the column is too obvious to require comment, and this Salome is uninhibited about presenting herself as a debased spectacle, without dignity or sense, and beyond redemption by the sound of her voice. Yet her death is so violent that we can certainly not identify with Herod's reaction to the spectacle, either. Salome's death is shown in shadow as a gang-stabbing, a thinly veiled gang rape, not as the crushing by shields that the text demands. The end is thus virtually nihilistic. It is aptly embodied by the famous horrendous dissonance that accompanies Salome's final ecstasy and by the orchestral violence that accompanies her death—musical gestures that now cast a retrospective pall over the opera as a whole.

BETWEEN ARTIFICE AND ORGANISM: TERESA STRATAS

If Malfitano's Salome is less "progressive" than Ewing's, Teresa Stratas's is much more so.[11] The term, though, is decidedly relative: none of these versions, and this is the point of comparing them, can establish an affirmative point of view of, or for, Salome. This version, too, directed by Götz Friedrich in 1974, with the Vienna Philharmonic under Karl Böhm, is perhaps the most highly organized in visual terms. It uses visual leitmotifs and quasi-ritualized rhythms to translate the dramatic "choreography" of the narrative.

One sign of this approach is the expanded role given here to a minor character, Narraboth's page. Played as a woman, not as the usual trouser role, the page gets a great deal of screen time throughout. Hopelessly in love with Narraboth, yet entirely unperverse, she seems to represent the feminine norm or ideal that Salome violates. The page is finally banished from view at the start of the decapitation scene, where the production interprets her as the person addressed by Salome's demand to repeat the kill order to the

executioner. Obeying, the page disappears into the cistern as Salome's transformation into a necrophiliac siren becomes complete.

Stratas's Salome, from the start through her encounter with Jochanaan
(Bernd Weikl), is both imperious and highly nervous: quicksilver, hysterical,
in continual motion. For example, as Jochanaan first approaches, she rushes
to the cistern, peers down in close-up, darts hither and yon. Her reaction to
Jochanaan's rejection, however, is to become composed, self-possessed. She
distances herself from her own hysteria in order to stage it as a kind of fiction
in her dance, only thereafter to yield to it progressively during the final
monologue, becoming ever more "natural" and "feminine" as she continues.
One of the visual leitmotifs traces this progress. Until the dance, Salome is
dressed in a white tunic, similar in color to the rocky walls of the set, the
most "primitive" of the sets under study, all roughhewn stone, with the cistern sunken at the rear of the stage. She also wears a tight-fitting white cap,
encrusted with "diamonds," that covers her hair—binds her in cold artifice,
like "the sterile woman's icy majesty" (la froide majesté de la femme stérile)
evoked in several poems by Baudelaire and linked there with the metallic
glint of jewelry or the impersonality of ornament.[12] At about the midpoint
of the dance, however, Salome sheds the cap to reveal her bound hair, which
she quickly shakes out. Her hair frames her face in soft curves until the
monologue, at which point it begins to become disorderly, rhyming with
the tangled, matted hair of Jochanaan. Close-ups of this hair, a key *Jugendstil* motif not mentioned by Benjamin, become increasingly prominent as
the monologue moves toward its climax.

This production also relies much more than the others on reaction shots
of characters other than Salome, including extras, and with emphasis on
Herodias and the page, the witch and the good girl, respectively. Like the
others, though, this video makes extensive use of reaction shots of Salome
as well, especially in the first encounter where, indeed, these shots domi-
nate more than in the other versions. The theme of looking could not be
more emphatically realized. One of the key instances is the reaction shot
showing Salome's becoming infatuated with Jochanaan as he emerges from
the cistern—before we see him for the first time. The encounter is marked,
further, by another visual leitmotif that tracks the realization of Salome's
hysteria as the product of repressed desire, a Freudian rendition, if you will.
There are many shots of Salome's head from behind, with emphasis on the
tight-fitting cap—shots that, as noted, give way after this scene to "normal"
frontal shots with flowing hair.

The ritualized rhythms of this scene, forming a set of narrative tropes,
involve Jochanaan's body and Salome's triple invocation of it as an object

of desire: first as a whole, then as broken down into "part-objects," to use the psychoanalytic term, the hair and the mouth that condense the force of the body and give Salome's lust for them a fetishistic intensity. We almost never see Jochanaan's body as a whole. Jochanaan appears to us first as a tangled mass of hair and beard, a dark, shaggy blot on the screen, in extreme close-up: like the cistern mouth in the Royal Opera version, this image displays the empty or blind spot at the center of visual desire. Jochanaan is seen shortly afterward in extreme long shot; framed by the massive set, he also appears dark, fully clothed in dark garments, unreachable. Except for two moments in the conversion episode, Jochanaan mostly appears to us in pieces from this point on, dismembered by the camera, which shows us now his head, now his arms, now his hands, and so on. When Salome sings that she is in love with his body, we see his face, a close-up of his mouth, the page, Narraboth, everything, in short, *but* his body, while Salome sinks to her knees, Jolson-style, as the camera draws toward her.

In sum, this Salome's Jochanaan is not ours, and he has none of the "objective" reality of his counterparts in the other productions. Nor does he have any objective relationship to Salome herself, in that respect being the opposite of Simon Estes's Jochanaan. He is always a figment of Salome's imagination, which the camera cannot translate, leaving it to the music to do so. This absorption of Jochanaan into Salome's subjectivity is clearest, perhaps, during the triple invocation. Each time Salome says, "I am in love with . . ." the camera gives us a close-up of the relevant part-object, thus identifying its own viewpoint with Salome's subjectivity. The first instance, where the object is the "body," substitutes Jochanaan's eyes for his body, thus once more engaging the whole question of Salome's visuality and ours. The hair appears, again, as a black close-up mass—the dark mass of the Real; and the mouth appears in conjunction with a flickering torch, suggesting the tongue of flame that Salome ideally seeks. The "Let me . . ." demands for physical contact that go along with Salome's invocations also follow a "motivic" pattern: with each demand, the desired touch or kiss does not happen physically, but does happen visually, symbolically, as the images of Salome and Jochanaan cross or seem to touch. By the end of the scene, Salome has become abject, crawling to Jochanaan's feet; his attempt at conversion, not sung "to" her at all, is directed to her prostrate form, at one point shown as all cap and bare arms. The slow pan that shows us Salome thus prostrated is the only point in the scene at which we see Jochanaan's body cohere into a whole (it happens twice), though we don't see the finished whole itself. When she says thereafter that she will kiss his mouth, she in effect sexually assaults him, even as he is in the processing of cursing her. When she is repelled, he exits as a shaggy indeterminate mass as she crawls after him: desire as abjection in pursuit of an object as impossibility.

The postrejection scene, with orchestral interlude, brings to culmination the domination of the encounter by reaction shots of Salome. Here, the whole episode of "extreme passion" is an extended reaction shot, focused in extreme close-ups of Salome's face, with wide open mouth, and of her arms and clasping hands; and in longer shots that show her crawling onto the lid of the cistern. She plays the sequence of musical "orgasms" with spasmodic gasping gestures, not blatant, but perceptible, and ends fallen prone atop the cistern. As she lies there, there is an extreme close-up on the symbolically fraught cap. Her face finally rises to view only as, to the accompaniment of the contrabassoon groaning at the bottom of its register, she discovers what she is about to do. One can almost see the idea as it crosses her mind.

Stratas's rendition of the dance requires less comment. It is highly structured around the removal of full-body veils in different colors, and slowly builds to its erotic climax, which shows her rolling and writhing, arching her back, and stroking herself. As the final veils drop, the camera gives close-ups of Salome's feet and face, but does not show her nudity (except in a brief, off-center glimpse from behind as she is covered) as if to avert its gaze more fully than its counterparts in the other versions. This will prove premonitory of something more important. The dance also involves a chorus line of four women in black with exposed legs, backs, and arms, and a few scenes of black drummers to orientalize the episode—a bit of casual racism in what is also the most crudely anti-Semitic of the three productions. (By contrast, the Ewing version generally avoids highlighting the racial difference between its Salome and the other characters—Ewing has a striking combination of light skin and African features—and indeed to subdue the exoticism of the opera, emphasizing instead the explicitly fin-de-siècle fantasy space created by the Secession-style costuming and stage sets, including a huge image of the full moon that presides over the whole. In the Malfitano version, Simon Estes's blackness is simply irrelevant, except perhaps as his particular vocal timbre might have gospel associations for some American viewers.)

The decapitation scene is rather underplayed here. Salome's reaction to its most striking feature—the series of pinched high notes on double basses meant to evoke "the moaning and groaning of a woman"—is shown in medium-long shot with the music at a rather fast tempo. Malfitano provides a point of contrast, as she twitches violently with the first four double-bass strokes. As her hysteria mounts, though, Stratas's Salome does address the cistern sexually, as Ewing would do later, particularly in relation to the overtly phallic rope that extends from the clasp of the lid.

But the real action is being saved for the monologue, which, like the encounter, is structured around specific visual rhythms. Jochanaan's head seems to emerge out of the "cistern" formed by the base of the screen, rising from the bottom line as a black mass that partially obstructs our view of Salome, who cowers a bit as she sees it. Recovering, she grasps the platter and lifts the head triumphantly out of the screen space; but when she draws it near for the much-deferred kiss, she seems to struggle with it—this head is too big, too heavy, too phallic. The scene centers on an extended sequence in which, in extreme close-up, Salome's head and Jochanaan's divide the screen, which is slit diagonally, each antagonist taking half the space, with Jochanaan below. The camera then moves slowly so that now the upper triangle, now the lower, crowds out the other, now her face and mouth, now his dark matted mass, enacting the irresolvable opposition between her fantasy triumph and her degraded exposure. The second half of the scene translates this simultaneity into a sequence. Much of it shows Salome in the bottom triangle or half of the screen, with the top half blank, as she sings some of her most lyrical effusions. One could almost forget the presence of the head (something impossible in the theater)—but the shift to Salome's face is prefaced by a frontal shot (the first) of the head on the plate framed by its Medusa-like locks, and is interrupted—at "you would have loved me if you'd looked"—by another close-up shot of the head with its closed eyes. Salome's face does regain its position after this, but the damage is done: no forgetting is possible, though it is true that the extreme intimacy of the scene does draw the viewer closer to her fantasy space than is the case in either of the other videos and closer in all likelihood than is possible in any opera house.

Toward the end of the scene, Salome's head hovers directly above Jochanaan's, as if they were doubles, and sinks toward his—is absorbed into the mass—at the point of the kiss, which, like Salome's body, is not shown, perhaps to deny the kind of visual pleasure and shock found in the Malfitano version, and/or perhaps to suggest that it cannot or must not be seen, only heard. After the interlude with Herod and Herodias, Salome's face slowly emerges from the matted tangled mass, a mass at first scarcely recognizable as two heads close together; even as her face pulls away, it is barely recognizable as a face for a long time. Salome may have decapitated Jochanaan, but she has in the end de-faced herself, plunged face-first into a repellent nonhuman mass, or mess. When her face finally emerges into the light, Salome is given a parody of redemptive visual rhetoric: shown from a low angle, with her head thrown back, mouth wide, light flooding in from the moon above her, she unites Benjamin's motifs of the perverse and the hieratic: she is a saint at prayer. At which point Herod orders her death, which is shown confusedly, with quick shots of stabbing phallic spears.

"THE MYSTERY OF LOVE . . . "

All of which shows us—what? Certainly that the camera eye in a video of *Salome* is highly likely to become personified precisely in relation to the act of looking, and more particularly of sexualized looking. The medium of sight will assume the identity of a virtual subject inescapably caught up in a network of sexualized gazes, by which it may be mesmerized or interrogated but over which it has ultimate control. Voice, however powerful or beautiful, becomes in this context primarily a means of address between two persons contending with each other over viewing positions. Since Salome is at the center of this network, the roles assigned to voice and vision suggest that the entire opera can be understood as an extension of its musically most "readymade" segment, Salome's dance. What the music does throughout is guide or, so to speak, choreograph the eye. And what the video medium does is transform the figurative or virtual choreography available in the theater into a literal, real-time series of movements and glimpses.

This personification of the viewing eye has a tendency to depersonalize Salome, much as the camera eye's control is bought at the price of Salome's visual debasement, or at least the invasion of her intimate bodily space. What Salome thinks of as her subjectivity is gradually exposed as an epiphenomenon, the by-product of Benjamin's triad of *Jugendstil* tropes: the perverse, the hieratic, and the emancipated. Each term in this series is bound to the others by an ironclad logic that is simultaneously narrative, musical, and technological. Narratively, Salome's perverse desire is a reaction to Jochanaan's mixture of sacred fury and physical magnetism, and its outcome is the "emancipation" from all law or restraint acted out in Salome's monologue. Musically, this pattern corresponds to the confrontation between Salome's post-*Tristan* and Jochanaan's post-*Parsifal* idioms, which ultimately produces the overripe, overornamented *Jugendstil* texture of the final monologue. Technologically, these musical changes correspond to changes in visual rhythm that become manifest in the video medium as the video eye develops an ever deeper, ever more invasive intimacy with Salome. Each of our three videos realizes this pattern differently, and with different ideological implications, but the end in each case is the same, and in each case finds its "ocular proof" in the same places: the postrejection orchestral interlude, the final moments of the dance, and Salome's final monologue, the last above all.[13]

Historically, this dimension of *Salome* corresponds to what Benjamin would identify as a new technology of spectatorship that becomes one of the defining conditions of modern subjectivity. The focus on the female body that goes along with this seems to derive in part from well-known and well-worn trends in sexual politics, but in part from an unexpected combination of technological and cultural forces. Regarded as a *Jugendstil* type, Salome is above all a feminine image that is mechanically reproducible—a poster girl. The sign of this unnatural, even unfeminine, reproducibility is her "sterile" sexuality, which leads on the one hand to her perversity and on the other to the general sexualizing of the image that is so basic to modern advertising. On the opera stage, Strauss's Salome is almost too alive, and therefore almost impossible to render convincingly. The music around her has the literalness, the overappropriateness, of the soundtrack to an advertisement, but the figure on the stage, especially when she sings, is the bearer of a material bodily presence that resists the flattening and distillation of everything into a posterlike image. The video medium removes this problem, not only by removing the singer's body in favor of an actual image, but of doing so on the small scale and with the relatively poor image quality of the television screen. The opera loses some of its potential ambiguity in video realization, but for just that reason the video is perhaps the ideal medium in which to realize *Salome*.

To close, let me speculate a bit on that suggestion. I said just now that music of *Salome* shares an overobvious pointedness with the music used on advertising soundtracks—soundtracks that did not, of course, exist when the opera was written, though department stores and trade expositions had certainly experimented with using music as a background to the display of goods for sale. The opera may thus have had latent qualities that had to await technological development to be rendered fully active. If Wagner's Bayreuth music dramas can be said to imagine the fantasy conditions realized in the twentieth-century movie theater, Strauss's *Salome* can be said to do the same for the quite different conditions of television viewing, commercials and all. The hypnotic, metaphysical, absorptive effect ascribed so often to Wagner's music, especially in the later nineteenth century, fosters the "suturing" of the spectator into the film image that is basic to classical cinema, and it is therefore no accident that so much classical film scoring has Wagnerian roots. Strauss's dense but highly discriminated style, at the acme of both qualities in *Salome*, is, so to speak, more secular. The pictorial quality so often attributed to it fosters what Benjamin would call the loss of allegorical "brittleness": the exact specification of commodity value that is basic to the public culture of the modern image. Perhaps the persistent feeling that Strauss's music suffers from an excess of technique over expression—that it is, so to speak, deep but without thought—finds some justification and explanation here. This quality, a flaw by nineteenth-century aesthetic standards, is the mark of the music's twentieth-century modernity—a modernity of which the apparently exotic and archaic Salome is one of the first embodiments.

7   Fin-de-Siècle Fantasies

Elektra *and the Culture of Supremacism*

In 1903 Otto Weininger, twenty-three, Viennese, Jewish, and an imminent suicide, published his misogynist manifesto *Sex and Character* and created an international sensation. "One began," reported a contemporary, "to hear in the men's clubs of England and in the cafés of France and Germany— one began to hear singular mutterings among men. Even in the United States where men never talk about women, certain whispers might be heard. The idea was that a new gospel had appeared."[1] Weininger's new gospel tied the spiritual progress of the human race to the repudiation of its female half. Women, said Weininger, are purely material beings, mindless, sensuous, animalistic, and amoral; lacking individuality, they act only at the behest of a "universalized, generalized, impersonal" sexual instinct.[2] For humanity to achieve its spiritual destiny, men—particularly "Aryan" men, who had not suffered a racial degeneracy that made the task impossible— must achieve the individualistic supremacy first revealed by the philosophy of Immanuel Kant. In order to do this, they must both rid themselves of the femininity within them and reject their sexual desires for the women around them.

Within a few years, Richard Strauss had twice put woman, in Weininger's sense, on the operatic stage—and created an international sensation. In 1905 there was Salome, inflaming desire through her sensuous dance before Herod, crooning and shrieking over the severed head of John the Baptist, raising the voice of her hysterical desires in contrast to the babble of the "stage Jews" who act as a chorus.[3] In 1909 there was Elektra, a dancer of another sort, sustaining herself on fantasies of blood sacrifice, eroticizing her kinship with her sister and brother, raising the voice of her hysterical desires in contrast to the shrill babble of the serving maids who act as a chorus.

Weininger provides an instructive bridge between Strauss's Salome and Elektra, who are in many respects contrary figures, at least on the surface: one fascinating, the other repellent; one a law unto herself, the other drunk on the idea of justice; one violently absorbed in eroticism, the other erotically concentrated on violence. It is striking how easily these contrary attributes can be flipped over so that each applies to both women. Salome and Elektra are sisters under the skin, the alluring and threatening faces of a feminine principle that—so it seemed—urgently needed to be explored, classified, and judged on behalf of human autonomy and cultural advancement.

The immediate context for this project, which clearly goes beyond garden-variety misogyny, and to which both Weininger's book (among many others) and Strauss's operas contributed, was a cultural formation that grew up in the nineteenth century and came of age in the fin-de-siècle. The categorical imperative of this formation, which I call supremacism, was the separation of what was "higher" and "lower" in human nature and society. Elaborate, indeed obsessive, systems of classification were deployed to the purpose, capable—like the Straussian orchestra—of combining great technical refinement with utter brutality. And the work was pursued in a climate of thought that made abnormality, as Strauss's *Elektra* made vocal shrillness and orchestral mayhem, virtually the norm.

The origins of supremacist culture lie partly in the rise of economic and social stresses on the middle-class family central to the organization of nineteenth-century life, and partly in the ideological impact of evolutionary science. Basic to the formation was a dualistic, not to say phobic, contrast between cultural progress and cultural regression, evolution and degeneration. Weininger's organization of this contrast is exemplary. The progress of civilization rested with northern European men; regression to the level of the "primitive" threatened from women (whom Darwin had argued were less evolved than men), from the urban poor (associated with dirt, disease, and sexual excess), and from the savage "lower races" who populated the colonial world.[4] Modern history had revealed that supremacy was innately vested in civilized Man, the normative human type, if only at the cost of a Darwinian struggle against his various Others. As Max Weber observed, "in Western civilization, and in Western civilization only, cultural phenomena have appeared which (as we like to think) lie in a line of development having *universal* significance and value."[5] Take away the saving skeptical irony of Weber's parenthesis, and the door is dialectically opened to demonologies like Weininger's.

The core concepts of supremacism were widely entrenched. It was very hard to avoid them, and very easy to find them self-evident, the stuff of common sense. Given the widespread present-day revulsion at the whole idea of cultural supremacy and the many crimes committed in its name, it is important to emphasize how rational and scientific the progression-regression model once seemed and how very explicit it was. One of the founding texts of modern anthropology, Edward B. Tylor's *Primitive Culture* (1871), outlined a typical "order of culture" ascending from black African savagery to northern-European civilization.[6] Scales like this proved to be smoothly interchangeable with divisions of both gender and social class. Mrs. E. Lynn Linton shows just how smoothly in her antifeminist magazine article "The Partisans of the Wild Women" (1892). Too many modern women, Linton claims, resist their naturally secondary status and "desire to assimilate their lives to those of men." The degenerative result is the "translation into the cultural classes of certain qualities and practices hitherto confined to the uncultured and—savages."[7]

In this context Strauss's operas of hysteria, like Weininger's hysterical book, could be received as sensationalist in their rhetoric yet rational and even profound in their misogyny, their primitivism, and (*Elektra* aside) their anti-Semitism. A fully historical understanding of both *Salome* and *Elektra* would accordingly be one that unsparingly grasps the participation of the operas in the cultural logic of supremacism, while at the same time realizing that this participation may be critical, revisionist, and transformative as well as compliant. This is not a matter of glibly balancing oppression against subversion, with a final nod to one or the other, but of absorbing oneself in the multiple, more than ambivalent logics of cultural engagement. Having approached *Salome* along these lines in the previous two chapters, I will try now to extend the approach to *Elektra*, interweaving an account of the music with an account of cultural dynamics—in both cases encountering something like the ne plus ultra of the heavy pendulum swing between supremacy and debasement.

1

Elektra is an especially striking instance of the multiple logics at work. The protagonist that Strauss found in his libretto, the Sophocles-inspired tragedy by Hugo von Hofmannsthal (1903), is a blatantly regressive figure. As if in reversal of the historical sequence traced by Nietzsche in *On the Genealogy of Morals*, Hofmannsthal has Elektra translate moral judgments into elaborate fantasies of abused bodies—bodies hunted down, tortured, penetrated:

[to Klytämnestra:]
Was bluten muss? Dein eigenes Genick,
wenn dich der Jäger abgefangen hat!
... Das Dunkel und die Fackeln werfen
schwarzrote Todesnetze über dich—
Hinab die Treppen durch Gewölbe hin,
Gewölbe und Gewölbe geht die Jagd
und ich! ich! ich! ich! ich! die ihn dir geschickt,
ich bin wie ein Hund an deiner Ferse.

[What must bleed? Your own neck, when the hunter has caught you! ...
The darkness and torches throw black-red death-nets over you—under
the stairs, through the vaults, vault after vault, goes the chase—and I! I!
I! I! I! who set the hunter on you am like a hound on your traces.]

The imaginary death-nets not only ensnare Klytämnestra's body but also
score it with the signs, black and red, of guilt and retribution. A later image
fuses the victim's agony with the avenger's orgasm:

[to Chrysothemis:]
Wie du mich abwehrst,
fühl' ich, was das für Arme sind. Du könntest
erdrücken, was du an dich ziehst. Du könntest
mich, oder ein Mann in deinen Armen
ersticken[!]

[As you ward me off I feel what arms you have. You could squeeze whatever you drew to you to death. Me or a man you could smother in your
arms!]

The pleasure Elektra takes in fantasies like these, culminating in the far
greater pleasure of their coming true, is meant to provoke cathartic revulsion. When Elektra finally collapses from the weight of her gratification,
her own body first stunned, then convulsed by it, the catharsis is complete
and the audience edified.[8]

This scapegoating conception provoked a double reading from Strauss.
The Elektra of the opera is at once repellent and compelling, both a phobic
personification of womanhood as brute bodily energy—pure Weiningerian
Woman in sadistic form—and a tragic personification of moral outrage. Addicted to the higher portions of an enormous tessitura (g to c'''), punctuat-
ing her vocal line with extravagant leaps, musically characterized by a complexly dissonant signature chord, Elektra embodies all the physical and
emotional anarchy that the ancestral order of culture exists to suppress. But
she does so only as a consequence of her absolute devotion to that order,

which she asserts with ferocious cadential authority at crucial moments, most notably at the ends of her opening monologue (Fig. 61), her diatribe against Klytämnestra (Figs. 258–59), and her colloquy with Orest (Fig. 180a), and again at her moment of greatest triumph after the murder of Klytämnestra and Aegisth (Fig. 230a).

Elektra's double nature makes her the object of intense scrutiny, not only by the other characters but also by the orchestra. To a degree extreme even for Strauss, the orchestra of *Elektra* is dependent on the narrative action, obsessed with illustrating every detail, emotional and physical, remembered or imagined. The result, since the action is wholly dominated by Elektra— by her voice, her presence, her desire—is that the orchestra comes to seem as obsessed with her as she is with her family tragedy.

As the action develops, unfolding continuously for some two hours without intermission, the opera becomes a kind of enormous Lied expressing Elektra's subjectivity. The shifting expressive focus basic to opera as a genre is arrested; what we hear is the musical equivalent of obsessional thinking, half by Elektra, half about her. The orchestra's unremitting vehemence, the literal-mindedness it carries to the point of fetishism, the revulsion with which it immerses Klytämnestra in viscous sonorities, the overripeness with which it mocks and yet envies Chrysothemis's longing for marriage and motherhood, the erotic lyricism with which it backs the anticipation of *Schadenfreude* in Elektra's scenes with Orest and Aegisth: all these qualities are also Elektra's own. From her perspective, they are largely indivisible; from the partial perspectives of the other characters, they are baffling (all of Elektra's interlocutors bombard her with questions).

Translated into the medium of the orchestra, Elektra's personal qualities articulate and problematize her doubleness, so much so that "doubleness" itself ceases fairly quickly to be anything like an adequate concept, even though it cannot be dispensed with. The qualities common to Elektra and the orchestra stand as symptoms of both cultural regression and physical and moral suffering, objects of both revulsion and identification. One result is that the orchestra's relationship to Elektra encapsulates the relationship of supremacist man to his larger-than-life mate and antagonist, here a woman, there (also) a savage, elsewhere (also) an outcast (there is no way to give clear priority to any of these terms). He is obsessed by her, both attracted and repelled; he uses his higher faculties of interpretation and representation to position her properly in the order of things without ever quite succeeding; and he risks, in doing so, being absorbed by her and reproducing her regressive character.

Strauss's double-plus reading of Elektra represents a complex negotia-

EXAMPLE 12. Chrysothemis to Elektra.

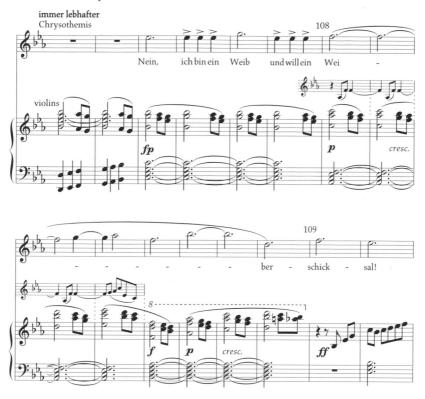

tion with the supremacist imperative. By privileging its heroine's subjectivity, *Elektra* goes against the supremacist grain that denies women legitimacy, and in Weininger's case even existence, as individual subjects. The whole opera is awash, or else befouled, with Elektra's subjectivity, precisely in proportion to her indifference to the usual aims and pleasures of subjectivity as embodied by her sister. Yet the musical characterization of Elektra reproduces all the atavistic traits—animalism, uncleanness, sensual cruelty, erotic perversity, amorality, automatism—routinely ascribed to fin-de-siècle women in justifying their relegation to a presubjective nullity.

Thus when Chrysothemis, the supremacist cover girl, clamors for a properly general feminine destiny—"Ich bin ein Weib und will ein Weiberschicksal" (I am a woman and want a woman's fate)—the orchestra recoils at her mindlessness by reproducing it in a bloated, mechanical sequence on the upper strings over pedal basses (example 12). Even in the bygone days when Elektra still defined herself within the circuit of masculine desires that defines "woman's fate," a differing subjectivity of her own would intervene in the form of narcissistic pleasure. Speaking to Orest, she recalls that she was beautiful: "wenn ich die Lampe ausblies vor meinem Spiegel, fühlt' ich es mit keuschem Schauer" (when I blew out the lamp before my mirror, I felt it with a chaste shiver). The lamp ceremonial lets Elektra take possession of her own beauty; in blacking out the mirror, she turns the visual pleasure her body can give into a sensuous pleasure her body can feel. The orchestra transcribes this process by resolving from dominant to tonic at "fühlt'" (felt) amid "shivering" string tremolos and the "mirroring" of a lyrical motive among several solo instruments. With the tonic arrival, the shivering intensifies and the mirroring stops (Fig. 159a). Yet this is hardly an unequivocal affirmation. The texture is too nervous, too agitated; the fury of the maenad is palpably latent in the young girl's narcissistic shiver. (Note the associative play between *Schauer*, thrill or shiver, and *schauerlich*, dreadful or horrible.) As an individuated subject, Elektra is always already monstrous.

In the famous episode following the murders of Klytämnestra and Aegisth, the opera's double reading of Elektra finds its crowning moment. Rejoicing voices sound from within the palace where the bloodshed has occurred, and Elektra, standing outside as if entranced, is asked by Chrysothemis, "Don't you hear it?" (So hörst du denn nicht?) "Don't I hear it?" Elektra replies, "Don't I hear the music? It comes right out of me" (Ob ich nicht höre? ob ich die Musik nicht höre? sie kommt doch aus mir) (Figs. 229a–239a). The orchestra agrees: it makes this ecstatic statement (a statement about ec-stasis, a going out of the self) audibly true. The music that Elektra claims here as her own is recapitulated from her opening monologue, which had set the terms of retributive desire that have now been fulfilled. An extended expression of rage, grief, and longing, the monologue establishes Elektra as a subject. Before she sings it she has been both a source of quotation (by the chorus of women) and the object of spectacle, running from the palace and "spring[ing] back like a beast" (spring[end] zurück wie ein Tier), but she has not yet been heard. In the monologue she claims her voice. And by allowing her, in the wake of the murders, to appropriate the orchestra's monologue-derived music, its retrospective reading of her subjectivity, Strauss upholds Elektra's claim to be the music's source. From the moment she speaks up to the moment she collapses, the roles of (male) composer and (female) protagonist fuse, at least as a symbolic fiction.

This act of empowerment is remarkable, but like everything else in this opera it is also equivocal. One might well wonder, with Carolyn Abbate, "that

Strauss, cynical, paternalistic, and hardly a feminist advocate, would so efface himself, cede so much of his narrating voice."[9] Yet though Strauss cedes power to Elektra, he does not concede narrative authority to her. (Moral authority, yes; narrative authority, no. Which one trumps the other remains impossible to say.) As we will see in following the course of this episode, what Strauss gives with his right hand he takes away with his left.

Elektra's monologue had ended with intimations of a dance, a solitary waltz, of triumph. The music that Elektra now recognizes as coming out of her is leading, impelling her, toward that dance, though a strange heaviness, "the enormous, the twentyfold ocean" (der ungeheure, der zwanzigfache Ozean), engulfs her limbs. Nonetheless she soon begins what the stage directions call her "nameless dance" (ein namenloser Tanz), her knees and arms flailing, "her head thrown back like a maenad" (zurückgeworfen wie eine Mänade). The dance is at once the consummating expression of Elektra's subjectivity and a willing transition—in terms of supremacist culture a willing regression—from voice to body, spirit to matter, subject to object. Strauss's music projects this contradiction with merciless clarity. As a climatic elaboration of the close of Elektra's monologue, the dance forcefully articulates the large-scale structure of the opera. It establishes Elektra as both choreographer and composer of her own story, her own destiny. Yet as a dance the music is grotesque, its movement a heavy-footed lurching, its orchestral texture a suffocating mass. The music on which Elektra stakes her identity is a projection of her mysteriously heavy body: the repellent, engulfing, degenerative body prescribed by the fin-de-siècle culture of supremacism.

For Strauss and his audience, the music of *Elektra* may have offered a vicarious means to release the atavistic bodily energies supposedly embedded in women, and that the social and cultural subordination of women existed to constrain. The problem thus raised is the old one of getting the genie back in the bottle. At the close of the opera, Elektra collapses to—is felled by— the *fortissimo* sound of a dark, sustained, brutally orchestrated E♭-minor chord (Fig. 261a; see example 17). The orchestra spits out the same chord, similarly orchestrated, in place of the dominant in the concluding (C-major) cadence. Strauss, who as we know thought of tonalities symbolically, chose this one carefully. Chrysothemis uses E♭ major to celebrate the natural destiny of women as sexual beings and childbearers; Elektra appropriates the key seductively in order to win Chrysothemis as an accomplice in the murder of Klytämnestra and Aegisth, and then, the seduction failing, curses her sister in E♭ minor. The curse, in a standard tragic irony, finally redounds upon her; the natural order of gender has its revenge. To what extent, however, does Elektra's scourging in E♭ minor objectify and distance her, so that the restoration of the social order coalesces with the assertion of musical structure? To what extent does the scourging come to grief, intentionally or not, against the force of Elektra's haggard charisma and the braying C-major fanfares that actually end the opera?

2

Clearly, these questions do not pose genuine alternatives, but specify the terms of a dynamic relationship. The best means to describe that relationship will prove to be a further character trait of Strauss's Elektra grounded in supremacist thinking. The operative trait, to which Weininger's *Sex and Character* again serves as a shop-of-horrors guidebook, is a polymorphic energy that effaces boundaries, collapses distinctions, and confuses identities.

Like her spiritual ancestor, Donna Anna in Mozart's *Don Giovanni*, Strauss's Elektra is fanatically, masochistically devoted to the Father's law, "passionately in love with the death of her father" and the retribution it mandates.[10] Donna Anna, however, is also a *musical* fanatic, restricted to a vehement opera seria fury that Mozart edges toward shrillness, tediousness, and self-parody. At the end of the Enlightened eighteenth century, as Julia Kristeva notes, "[the Father's] political and moral law are crumbling enough . . . to allow Mozart not to treat [their collapse] as a tragedy" (152). But Strauss's Elektra, offshoot of an age in which the lightest infractions of the Father's law can be treated as tragedy, is musically as compelling as Donna Anna is bemusing. A virtuoso of styles and voices, she croons, howls, exults, mourns, teases, muses, admonishes, and scourges, shifting her voice and her character to suit each new occasion with a volatility that matches the orchestra's obsessional tone-painting and onomatopoeia. Her emotional range, like her vocal range, is enormous: utter self-absorption in her opening monologue, prophetic rage in her denunciation of Klytämnestra, sadistic irony in her baiting of Klytämnestra and Aegisth, erotic pathos in her dialogue with Orest, predatory eroticism conflating wishes and lies in her attempted seduction of Chrysothemis. Although no less a monomaniac than Donna Anna, Elektra is also a polymorph: or, more exactly, she becomes a polymorph in order to service her monomania. That is why neither Aegisth nor Orest can recognize her at first, and why she can so easily mingle same-sex and cross-sex desire, fantasies of exogamy and incest, in her relations with Orest and Chrysothemis.

In supremacist terms, what this amounts to is *così fan tutte:* Elektra acts

FIGURE 5. Gustav Klimt, *Moving Waters* (1898). Oil on canvas. Private collection. Courtesy Galerie St. Etienne, New York.

just like a woman. According to Weininger, the materiality of women endows them with unlimited plasticity. Both their bodies and their characters are indeterminate, threatening the determinacy of men. "Woman," Weininger writes, "is always living in a condition of fusion with all the human beings she knows, even when she is alone. . . . Women have no definite individual limits" (198; note the characteristic elision of "woman" and "women").

The dangerous fascination of polymorphism is arguably the leading theme of fin-de-siècle supremacism; the presentation of this theme in sexual terms is arguably its leading form. One measure of its importance is the popular consumption of paintings that show women in groups, typically in wooded or watery settings, their bodies rhyming or overlapping with each other and blending into the material medium that envelops them. Gustav Klimt's series of underwater scenes—*Watersnakes* I and II, *Moving Waters*, the drawing *Fish Blood*—are among the best-known treatments of this subject; *Moving Waters* (figure 5) alerts the male spectator to his danger with a perhaps ironic candor. A bearded head, decapitated by the edge of the picture plane, stares at floating female bodies from the lower right-hand corner just above Klimt's signature. The center of the visual field, to which his stare is drawn, is the pelvis of one of the floaters, slightly thrust forward and crowned with red pubic hair—an icon of feminine sexuality as a self-reproducing, other-obliterating power.[11]

Broadly speaking, the fin-de-siècle construction of a primary gender antagonism on the axis of fixed versus fluctuating boundaries can be taken as a social projection of the reigning epistemic paradigm of positive science. The positivist subject of knowledge represents the acme of what might be called applied Cartesianism; it is normatively masculine, inflexibly clear and distinct, and capable of doubting everything but itself.[12] This epistemic perspective, however, does not account for the specific salience of fin-de-siècle misogyny; it does not clarify the sharp, panicky quality of the antagonism, or the obsessiveness with which the virile subject stages, paints, theorizes, or otherwise represents the feminine or feminized matrix that endangers him.

A more local understanding might begin with the supremacist principle that savages, the uncultured, and wild women are interchangeable terms, each of which both defines and threatens a cultural boundary: concentrically arrayed, the boundaries of civilization (colonial empire), social hierarchy, and private (domestic) life. Given, for example, the popular idea that "up from the lowest savagery, civilization has . . . caused an increasing exemption of women from bread-winning labor" (Herbert Spencer), the legitimation of nondomestic work for women would be "complexly ruinous . . . a step backwards toward savagery" (Joseph Leconte) taken in defiance of the evolutionary law that "the pre-eminence of the male over the female . . . [is characteristic] of superior races and species, the adult age, and the higher classes" (G. Delauney). Supremacist ideology represents boundaries like these as sites of conflict between civilization and an atavistic, promiscuously transgressive energy that is constantly shifting its point of attack from one boundary to another. "Complexly ruinous," this energy can break through the system of boundaries at any point and overrun the whole with degeneration or *"anti-differentiation"* (Leconte).[13] The ironic result is that supremacist culture is a culture of panic, the ideological mandate of which is to police its boundaries at all times and at all costs.

By the fin-de-siècle this mandate had brought forth, again ironically, a close correlation between the preoccupations of "advanced" European civilization and what René Girard calls the "sacrificial crisis" of primitive societies.[14] Girard argues that social order traditionally depends on a system of differences governing role and status, and that when these differences break down the community is threatened by an eruption of indiscriminate violence. This threat is countered by a dose of preventive medicine: the community unites to sacrifice a scapegoat, a "surrogate victim" in whose "monstrous" person the breakdown of differences is epitomized. The sacrifice concentrates and discharges the force of violence, symbolically expunges the source of the crisis, and rallies the community to restore the all-important system of differences. This historical event—if it is that—is later commemorated (or constructed in retrospect) by the ritual sacrifice, literal or figurative, of a "substitute victim."[15]

In civil society sacrificial ritual migrates primarily to tragic drama,[16] and nowhere more fully than to the series of tragic operas produced between *Rigoletto* and *Lulu*. Most of these operas participate, though more ambivalently than she recognizes, in the ideological project that Catherine Clément assigns to opera in general: the lamination of the Father's laws, of narratives bound to the "undoing" of women, with so much musical beauty that critical resistance is lulled to sleep.[17] These "sacrificial" operas, however, do more specialized and explicit cultural work than this, though many of them do it no less ambivalently. They are operas that culminate when a woman's sexuality leads to her murder (Carmen, Gilda, Desdemona, Nedda, Salome, Marie, Lulu) or when brutality drives her to suicide (Butterfly, Tosca, Liù, but not Brünnhilde). Within the operatic fiction, these characters are surrogate victims; as elements in an operatic fiction, substitute victims. All of them are polymorphs, Weiningerian dissolvers of boundaries, Girardian embodiments of the collapse of differences, vessels for the ritual reenactment of sacrificial crisis.

But not just any crisis: these victims are also historically specific. The identification of their polymorphism with their femininity, often supplemented by low racial or social status, marks them as the privileged victims of supremacist culture, figures of degenerative allure. As Girard notes, sacrificial victims are almost never women (12). The most salient feature of fin-de-siècle supremacism is its reversal of this principle. A trio of theater works premiered within a few years of each other can be said to epitomize both this reversal itself and the impulse to put it, ritualistically, on stage: a play, Oskar Kokoschka's *Murderer, Hope of Women* (1907), made into an opera by Paul Hindemith in 1921; a ballet, Stravinsky's *The Rite of Spring* (1913), revered for its score as one of the breakthrough works of modernism, but with the sacrifice at its center commonly disregarded in the abstraction of concert performance or musical analysis; and an opera, *Elektra*, scornful of abstraction and set athwart the razor-thin border between civilization and atavism to make the logic of sacrifice as explicit as possible.

The operatic revival and revision of sacrificial crisis was fed by yet another contextual stream that can help localize the phenomenon. The first great support of the supremacist imperative was evolutionary theory, or more often its many popularizations. This backing allowed the imperative to authorize itself on the basis of advanced intellectual principle combined with the prestige of scientific rationality. But as things turned out, there was much more to come. As the nineteenth century waned, a second layer of support developed with the rise to both intellectual and popular preeminence of evolutionary anthropology. The new discipline gave the culture of supremacism a surprising new material resource, a fictitious but highly potent substance, the dissemination of which helps explain the depth of irrationality that imbued the drive to establish supremacy and also kept it so closely tied to the theater of debasement.

The most famous text of this tradition was Sir James George Frazer's *The Golden Bough* (1890), but even more pivotal in its own era (certainly for Frazer himself) was W. Robertson Smith's *The Religion of the Semites* (1889), which established a set of tropes that would become almost second nature for several generations of thinkers. Robertson Smith argued that in primitive religion the sacred and the unclean were one and the same thing. And "thing" is the operative term here, as the sacred-unclean amalgam, once released by religious ritual or the violation of taboo, acted like a contaminating, contagious substance capable of spreading everywhere. Primitive matter became dangerous force. The mark of the civilized religions, preeminently Christianity, was to separate the unclean from the sacred and to identify the latter with a higher ethical consciousness. But this cultural achievement was very precarious. The modern world was filled with "survivals" from its primitive heritage—survivals that, as befits contagious matter, constantly posed the immanent (and imminent) threat of outbreak.[18]

The sheer tangibility ascribed to this dangerous Ur-stuff folded all too easily into the imagery of contagion operating elsewhere in the cultural field and enveloping—as we've seen—the racialized bodies of lower cultures, the venereally dangerous bodies of women, and the unwashed bodies of the poor. Hence the phantasmatic power of a figure like the Elektra of Hofmannsthal and Strauss, who embodies all these modes of contamination. Hence too the nightmarish power of the figure designating the origins of this terrible daughter, the even more terrible mother, Klytämnestra, whose status as the source of pollution is memorably embodied in the music Strauss devised to connect her with the filthy crowd of animals led to the sacrifice. And hence, too, the need for the countervailing figure of the good sister, Chrysothemis—

who, however, is never more than a hair's breadth away from contamination herself.

The power of Strauss's opera, including its power to survive the cultural myths on which it rests, lies in its location of intellectual and ethical power in the same Elektra who is the locus of contamination. It is as if Elektra were at one and the same time a figure of atavistic regression and a figure of the ethical consciousness that separates the civilized and the primitive in fin-de-siècle thought. This is the nub of what I call Strauss's double (or double-plus) reading of her. Like Salome, Elektra resists what she embodies and embodies what she resists. But unlike Salome, she does not do this in a way that leaves her alluring as well as repellent. Elektra is repellent to everyone. Her saving grace is that she is also strangely authoritative, the more so, perhaps, the more repellent she becomes. She is a Cassandra whom one is forced to believe; she is the Freudian superego in person, incarnated as a woman a few years *avant la lettre*. This harridan can harry you. Elektra's difference from Salome is a result of transposing the ambivalence of the prototypical woman from the erotic to the moral sphere, a shift that paradoxically enhances the sheerly material, bodily force of Elektra's presence. In a sense, it is because her presence represents what Strauss's era might have recognized as a "survival" of the primitive fusion of sanctity and uncleanness that she must be made the object, not of a backdoor murder like Salome's, but of a spectacular sacrifice.

3

Elektra is surely the most extreme of sacrificial operas, not just because Elektra is the most polymorphic of heroines but because the ultimate murder weapon in this opera is its music. Like Salome, Elektra is crushed to death: not by a mass of shields, musically illustrated with clanging dissonance, but by the Straussian orchestral machine churning out its elephantine waltz, the very waltz that "comes right out of" its victim. Elektra, however, is not the only victim, and there is something strange in the fact that she is sacrificed at all. As commentators often point out, the Electra of the classical tragedies is not the victim of a sacrificial crisis but the author of one; the victim is Clytemnestra, supplemented by Aegisthus. But although the opera overtly concerns this primary crisis, and resolves it into communal solidarity with choral acclamations of Orest following the murders, the staging of a single sacrificial crisis turns out to be ritually inadequate in the face of supremacist panic. To be sure, Klytämnestra is a monstrous polymorph whose presence sends the orchestra into giddy spasms of deformity. But in order to expunge her, Elektra must become even more monstrous, more polymorphic, altogether more dangerous. The opera requires a doubling, a surplus of ritual: once Klytämnestra has been sacrificed to Elektra, Elektra must be sacrificed to the audience.

Strauss articulates these relationships by multiple, overlapping means, all of them typically simple in conception despite the technical complexity involved in their execution. These include the stylistic and harmonic characterization of Elektra and Klytämnestra, some of which has already been remarked on; the encapsulation of the drama in a broad tonal allegory; and the enclosure of the action within a clear-cut double frame structure.

The tonal allegory is grounded in the association of consonant triads with the paternal law of culture and high levels of dissonance with deviance, abjection, and transgression.[19] The name "Agamemnon" is famously associated with a triadic motive (example 13), the most prominent in the opera, and often sounding in truncated form, as if to suggest both violence suffered and violence pursued. In maximal contrast, Klytämnestra is characterized by a six-note collection bitonally combining two minor chords a tritone apart, usually on the roots B and F, and (as Tethys Carpenter observes) more often paired than superimposed. The big scene between Elektra and Klytämnestra, where the Klytämnestra collection figures most prominently, is further marked by a "total lack of definite dominants" and by suffocating whole-tone configurations, notably static clusters and parallel French sixths.[20] Klytämnestra thus represents something incommensurate with the tonal and cultural order, a contaminated residue of otherness that can be neither contained nor banished.

Julia Kristeva suggests one way to name that something in her remarks on the classical Electra:

> Electra wants Clytemnestra dead not because she is a mother who kills the father but because she is a mistress (of Aegisthus). Let *jouissance* [a sexual pleasure unrepresentable within the symbolic order of culture] be forbidden to the mother: this is the demand of the father's daughter, fascinated by the mother's *jouissance*. (152)

Both vocally and orchestrally, Klytämnestra's music suggests the horror of the mother's *jouissance*, a pleasure so transgressive that once released it can appear only as rancid and destructive, even to the mother herself. Centered on a low tessitura from which it rises in flights of desperation, Klytämnestra's vocal line is positively glutinous, distinguished by broken phrasing and bouts of heavy, dragged-out syllabification that retard the flow of her ut-

EXAMPLE 13. The Agamemnon motive.

terance. Glutinous, too, is Klytämnestra's reading by the orchestra. She is introduced by a crude oriental march expressive of animal sacrifice, famous for its brutal insistence, its slaps with the rute and thuds on the bass drum, its chromatic slitherings. And her account of herself is punctuated by bursts of frenzied orchestral activity alternating or combining with static or slow-moving masses of sound, the latter dominated by trombones, Wagner tubas, and the like. In sum, Klytämnestra embodies feminine fluidity in its most horrifying form: in her this fluidity congeals.

Between Agamemnon and Klytämnestra in the tonal allegory stands the figure of Elektra, who moves in both her father's tonal and her mother's bitonal orbit without belonging to either. Elektra is characterized by a five-note collection that can be taken as a conjunction of D♭ major and E major. In its bitonal aspect, this sonority links the daughter and the mother; they are the only characters in the opera with bitonal profiles. The link has obvious psychological overtones suggesting Elektra's obsession with Klytämnestra, and vice versa, but its real work is cultural. Bitonal depiction identifies as pariahs the two women who violate hallowed boundaries and marks them off as sacrificial victims. Bitonal dissonance ascribes a dense, repellent materiality to the women and locates the source of pollution in their polymorphism. (Compare the tonal creampuffs lavished on the unsacrificable good girl, Chrysothemis.)

Unlike Klytämnestra, however, Elektra is not merely an enemy alien in the tonal and cultural order of the Father. Her harmonic signature is presented in a form that betrays both tonal and bitonal leanings: an "Elektra chord" consisting of a dominant $\frac{4}{2}$ over a nonharmonic bass (example 14). Like Elektra herself, this chord is both monomaniacal and polymorphic. Endowed with a "very specific sonority," it is treated by turns as a color chord, a voice-leading chord, and (with varying degrees of fictitiousness) as a functional chord. The Elektra chord is also sometimes associated with higher dominants derived from its seven-note complement, which can be arranged to form a dominant-thirteenth chord.[21] By this means Elektra becomes the vehicle of contrary harmonic impulses, or rather of a single impulse doubly read: the very procedure that yields chromatic saturation also recuperates it through

EXAMPLE 14. The Elektra chord (A) and its motivic elaboration (B).

constellations of dominants—precisely what Klytämnestra's music lacks. Elektra's harmonic character positions her well within the tonal and cultural order and qualifies her to expunge Klytämnestra from it. But her position also guarantees the instability of the very order she so serves and adores. Elektra is more dangerous than Klytämnestra because she pollutes that order from within, or—worse yet—because she reveals and embodies that order's intrinsic susceptibility to pollution.

Elektra's transition from sacrificial agent to surrogate victim is inscribed in her changing relationship to the tonal triad as the retributive bearer of the Father's law. As in Sophocles' *Elektra*, Klytämnestra and Aegisth die at Orest's hands but at Elektra's will. In dramatic terms, Orest's arrival at Mycenae allows the deed to follow the word; Elektra's voice, which has hitherto only invoked the act of sacrifice, now figuratively inflicts it. In musical terms, the weapon Elektra wields is the triad.

When Elektra, alone onstage, hears Klytämnestra scream at Orest's first blow, she herself screams ("wie ein Dämon"): "Triff noch einmal!" ([like a demon] Strike once more!) (Fig. 192a). With her first word she silences the orchestra, halting a wave of agitated chromatic scales on the dominant of B minor. Then, recasting the first degree of the dominant as a leading tone, she flings her voice shrilly on a descending G-minor six-four chord into the silence she has cleared. Without skipping a beat, trumpets and strings deliver the death blow for her with violent triadic figuration in G minor over the root-position triad on horns and trombones, then round back to B minor with a chromatic shudder for a second blow and the second, final, scream from Klytämnestra (example 15).

Elektra's triadic voice precipitates Aegisth's death in similar terms. When Aegisth, frantic for rescue, cries out "Hört mich niemand?" (Does no one hear me?), Elektra condemns him with her with her memorable and terrible answer, "Agamemnon hört dich!" (Agamemnon hears you!) (Fig. 216a).

EXAMPLE 15. Death of Klytämnestra.

The phrase is backed, not by silence, but by a shrill E♭ octave high in the violins, doubled by flutes and piccolo, that pierces the silence and coils the spring of Elektra's rage. The spring uncoils in her voice on a C-minor triad, again followed by two orchestral death blows: one in C minor while she is still speaking Agamemnon's name, the other in A♭ minor following Aegisth's death cry in that key ("Weh mir!) (example 16). Here as before, the music's victim seems to reel from one harmonic space to another while the music follows implacably. The third-relation between C minor and A♭ minor at the death of Aegisth parallels the relation between B minor and G minor at the death of Klytämnestra. The parallel helps bring out an allegorical "cadence" connecting the two deaths: Klytämnestra to Aegisth, G to C.

It may seem surprising that the death of Aegisth bears so much dramatic weight when the object of Elektra's obsession is Klytämnestra. But in allegorical importance Aegisth is second to none. Elektra twice identifies him as a woman, and his vocal line makes the identification a third time: a decidedly high-pitched tenor, punctuated by irrational upward leaps, that rises to squeals of hysteria during his death colloquy with Elektra. A publicity still from the first performance of the opera (Dresden, 1909; figure 6) de-

EXAMPLE 16. Death of Aegisth.

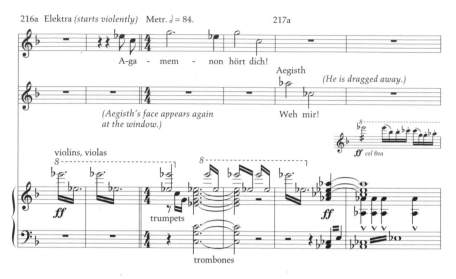

velops the point further. It shows an epicene Aegisth (Johannes Sembach) with long curly locks and rouged lips; half cringing, half posturing seductively, he stands in the palace doorway, upstaged by a savage Elektra (Annie Krull) who glares out of kohl-rimmed eyes and brandishes a phallic torch. In the wax museum of supremacism, Aegisth is the most degraded exhibit, the degenerate effeminate male who, abject in life, must be made even more abject in death. If Klytämnestra is the cause of sacrificial crisis, Aegisth is the effect. In order to restore the Father's name and law, it is not enough to sacrifice his Nemesis; one must also sacrifice her handiwork.

But once the double sacrifice is made, the mantle of Nemesis passes from Klytämnestra to Elektra. The law of the talion strikes home: she who kills by the triad dies by the triad. As we saw earlier, the orchestra's E♭-minor death blow to Elektra stands allegorically for her alienation from the *Weiberschicksal* on which the law she enforces, the law of the Father, depends. The blow is transformed into a judicial act by the new tonal articulation that follows. For its reading of the fallen Elektra, the orchestra shifts from the E♭-minor to the C-minor triad, on which the truncated form of the Agamemnon motive blares out *fortissimo*. Then the E♭-minor chord returns softly, a cold fact, then the blaring C-minor fanfares; and again (example 17). The juxtaposition of third-related minor triads recalls the death-blow chords visited on both Klytämnestra and Aegisth. Elektra is felled by the

FIGURE 6. Annie Krull as Elektra, Johannes Sembach as Aegisth, publicity photo for Dresden premiere, 1909.

EXAMPLE 17. Elektra's collapse and close of the opera.

261a *(Elektra stürzt zusammen.)*   *(Chrysothemis zu ihr.)*

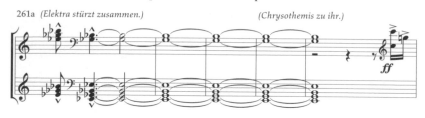

(Elektra liegt starr.)

(Chrysothemis läuft an die Tür des Hauses, schlägt daran.)

262a Chrysothemis **allmählich breiter**   **ritard. molto** *(Stille)*

O - rest!   O - rest!

langsam Metr. ♩ = 80   *(Vorhang)*

musical recoil of her own retributive speech acts, the ultimate form of which condemns her in—and symbolically with—her father's name.

The alternation of E♭-minor and C-minor chords also forms a warped realization of Elektra's bitonal identity. The bitonal pairing of triads has been Klytämnestra's signature; the Elektra chord has been bitonal only by implication, and that implication has never been realized. More exactly, it has never been realized before. The E♭ minor–C minor pairing extracts the essence of the E major–D♭ major pairing implied by the chord. The mode changes, and the paired triads are a half-tone "off," but the all-important third relation remains.[22] Given the action on stage, the differences seem to rectify Elektra's bitonal image in the act of realizing it. Her alienation is overcome by the act of judgment that consummates it by killing her. In her collapse, Elektra is not dispossessed, not degraded from her "own" position to her mother's: the surrogate victim's position to which she falls is already her own as well as her mother's. Her signature chord has deferred, even repressed, her need to take this position, but has also guaranteed it. Elektra's place has been appointed for her from the beginning.

4

The architecture of the opera supports a similar understanding. On the largest scale, the double reading of Elektra as agent and victim is articulated by a double framing of the musical and narrative action. There is an outer frame affirming, however delusively, the law and the name of the Father, and an inner frame affirming, however grudgingly, the polymorphism of the feminine. The outer frame subdues the feminine energies it encloses, a role that, as Susan McClary has shown, frame structures characteristically play in operatic mad scenes.[23] But *Elektra* takes feminine excess not only as a force to be framed but also as a form that frames. The result is to collapse the distinction between "excess" and "frame" (McClary's terms) and in so doing to call forth an outer frame of exceptional violence: violence enough—or is it?—to recapture the usurped boundary.

The outer frame is memorably efficient, as businesslike in the work of justice as an executioner. It begins the opera with a brutal *fortissimo* statement of the Agamemnon motive and ends it with the Agamemnon fanfares resounding over Elektra's fallen body. The long tradition of reading Agamemnon as the "true hero" of *Elektra* rests on the combination of simplicity and grandiloquence in this frame, the "true author" of which is not Richard Strauss but Johann Joachim Winckelmann.[24] Although *Elektra* is obviously not Winckelmannian in its esthetic, its outer frame does invoke

the association of simplicity and grandeur with cultural supremacy and idealized virility by which Winckelmann invented the moral idyll of ancient
Greece for modern Europe.[25] The frame's stentorian minor triads supposedly ground the extravagance of Elektra's ravings in an abstract moral calculus and the gross materiality of her harmonic color in an austere intel-
lectuality. The spirit of the martyred Agamemnon sanctifies what would
otherwise be merely lurid.

It should not be surprising that a male character who never appears should
be said to preside over an opera in which the male voice, rarely heard, does
little more than wheedle and bully. The claim follows entrenched cultural
routines that automatically enshrine any term of authority as masculine.
Besides, Strauss clearly wanted to be understood along these lines. Making
an important alteration in Hofmannsthal's text, he gave Elektra's monologue a tight, clear frame structure based on repetitions of the name, sung
to the motive, of Agamemnon. The structure is emphatically ritualistic, its
fulcrum an internal chiasmus between the phrases "Agamemnon! Vater!"
and "Vater! Agamemnon!" (Figs. 44.3–8, 46.1–3]).[26] As a macrocosmic version of this structure, the opera as a whole does no more than reinscribe
Elektra's slavish dedication to her father's mystique. The possibility of hearing that reinscription as ennobling is largely responsible for the entry of
Elektra into the operatic canon.

Nonetheless, the Agamemnon motive is not as commanding as its partisans would like to believe. The motive is too closely associated with Elektra to be heard or read apart from her tormented relationship to it. The
Agamemnon it invokes is not a man but a fantasy. Carolyn Abbate has even
argued that the motive really refers to Elektra herself, or rather to a special
split-off part of herself: "The thing for which the motive stands, in the classic semiotic sense, is not Agamemnon at all, but rather Elektra's *voice;* more
specifically, the mourning lament that so strongly marks her existence"
(111). This counter-reading is compelling, but only if it engages rather than
replaces the reading it counters. It must be teased apart from the desire to
fix the motive as a univocal sign, to identify *the* thing for which the motive
stands.

As the mantra of Elektra's subjectivity, the Agamemnon motive is necessarily protean in its meanings, which include the obnoxious significations
of Agamemnon as *éminence grise* and "true hero." The only fixed meaning of the motive is its magical, superstitious, or obsessive-compulsive link
to Agamemnon's name, which Elektra confirms by never singing the motive except to utter the name. But this provides no fixity at all. As Kristeva
observes of Sophocles' Electra, "that the father is made a symbolic power—

that is, that he is dead, and thus elevated to the rank of a Name—is what gives meaning to her life" (151). But the price of this meaning is a permanent alienation from the cultural order that confers it. This cruel truth is audible as early as the "Agamemnon! Vater! Vater! Agamemnon!" chiasmus. Elektra seeks to hew to her idealizing triads to pronounce these magic words, and to sing each word the same way, so as to gain both authority and certainty from her ritual utterance. She does not quite succeed. The second "Agamemnon!" slips chromatically out of focus, eroding the chiasmus at its edge and marking Elektra's always implicit expulsion from the closed moral and mental order to which she is so compellingly devoted.

There is no alternative to this potent but compromised position. Elektra's tortured dependence on the return of Orest tells the story: in the end, this is an order for sons, not for daughters. Orest, who inherits Agamemnon's cultural position, sings his father's name with no reference to the famous motive, and with a casualness inconceivable to Elektra. His homecoming fulfills her desires but degrades her fantasies. Asked by the still unrecognized stranger about her blood relations, Elektra plays on the double meaning of the German *Blut* (kinship and blood) and with great ferocity couples her own name with her father's for the first and only time. But she does so without invoking the father's motive; even unrecognized, her brother's presence seems to deplete the motive of its performative magic (example 18). When Orest subsequently addresses her, a distorted version of the motive in violin-cello octaves even seems to swipe abrasively at Elektra's name (example 19). It is telling in this context that when Elektra later employs the motive to call down retribution on Aegisth ("Agamemnon hört dich!"), his execution occurs offstage, as if—but only as if—it had been performed by Elektra's word rather than Orest's hand.

The desires that Elektra voices through the Agamemnon motive, whether for justice or for love, are unappeasable in principle, as she reveals most clearly when she sings the motive longingly, bringing out the *Tristan*-esque rising minor sixth that ends on the stressed syllable of the name. Desperate to ground her identity in the symbolic power of the motive, and so to signify her fusion with the psychic and cultural Father, she repeatedly finds that the motive can ground no identity at all because it is not self-identical. Although the outer frame originally pitches it in D minor, Elektra picks up the motive in B minor at the start of her monologue and carries it through C minor to C major. The death sentence she later metes out to Aegisth presses for a definitive C minor, which returns in the outer frame with the motive's truncated form; but the close of the frame splinters the motive further in—with?—an abrupt blast of C major. Similarly, Elektra is unable to

EXAMPLE 18. Orest and Elektra. ("You must be related by blood to those who died, Agamemnon and Orestes." "Related! I am this blood! I am the shamefully poured out blood of King Agamemnon! Elektra is my name.")

appropriate the motive in any of the several "voices"—lyrical, exultant, doom-laden—in which she sings it. Except at the start of her monologue (in the askew B minor) the orchestra never voices the motive in unison with her, but only anticipates, echoes, or cuts across her utterance. The disparity is particularly marked at her "Agamemnon hört dich!" where Elektra varies the triadic contour so that the longing sixth becomes a judicial fifth while the trumpets overlapping her pronouncement keep to the original form. In sum, Elektra's dealings with the Agamemnon motive provide a literal illustration of Jacques Lacan's principle that the name of the Father is what guarantees the symbolic order of culture.[27] But for Elektra, as Lacan would predict, the true name of the father is literally unspeakable.

5

The daughter's inner exile takes on a different valuation in the inner frame of the opera. This consists of the opening scene, in which a group of five serving maids gossip about Elektra, and the opera's only duet, shared by the

EXAMPLE 19. Orest to Elektra.

ecstatic Chrysothemis and Elektra just before the latter's dance unto death. Constituted by the intricate interweaving of female voices, the substance of this frame is a matrix of undifferentiated femininity, a matrix in which, to recall Otto Weininger's dictum, "woman is always living in a condition of fusion with all the human beings she knows." In supremacist fantasy, which is the only place it exists, this matrix figures as both degraded and seductive. The opera agrees: the maids' scene is dominated by unpleasant dither, both vocal and orchestral, and the duet is rejected as seductive by Chrysothemis, who breaks away from it to seek Orest. Yet the musical treatment of these scenes chafes at the boundaries of supremacist values, and even presses for a reversal of them, a supremacism of the (supremacist) feminine. The maids' scene discloses an impulse toward "higher" development within the matrix of femininity, and the duet carries this impulse into the region most discomfiting to the cultural order: feminine *jouissance*.

The first three maids who speak of Elektra are completely hostile to her, the fourth largely so; their hostility is countered by the fierce, hero(ine)-worshipping partisanship of a fifth maid, still "quite young," not yet subjugated by her *Weiberschicksal*. The fifth maid is an obvious prefiguration of Elektra. In dramatic terms, the moral gravity of her passion differentiates her from the general feminine mass, which is merely spiteful, but the hysteria of her devotion blurs the lines of demarcation. In musical terms this ambiguity becomes a form of empowerment as the fifth maid rehearses what Elektra will assume, a highly discriminate identity still brimming with the indiscriminate polymorphic energy of the feminine matrix.

The vocal lines of the first four maids are not melodically individual and show a strong tendency to run together in a continuous stream. Much of the time the maids complete each other's sentences or make interjections. Pauses for articulation are well marked within each maid's statements, but rare between statements and perfunctory when present; most of the movement between voices goes by overlap or relay, one voice beginning just before or immediately after the other ends. Two passages even heighten the continuity among voices by common-tone links, which seem to act as crystallizations of a common tessitura. In their successive entries, the four maids—an alto, two mezzos, and a soprano—fill out the ordinary spectrum of the female voice, from the low A of the first maid's entry to the high A♭ (quickly reprised as A-natural) of the fourth's. Instead of specializing, however, the voices tend to gravitate toward the common ground of the middle register, where their qualities merge to produce a generalized female voice.

The fifth maid cuts across this web of similitude with a piercing, strongly profiled melodic line, but she is too overwrought to make a difference. The web closes again as the other maids, backed by their overseer, cast the fifth maid out and resume their discourse. It remains for Elektra to claim and hold the position of individuated identity. She does so, however, only in the context set up by the maids' scene, and in that context the formidable dynamism of Elektra's identity does not constitute a denial of her similitude with the maids—all of them, not just the fifth—but an extension and transformation of it.

In their colloquy, the first four maids quote Elektra continually. Her voice is dispersed among them, split off from the frighteningly agitated and feral body that the audience glimpses at the start of the scene. In this form, Elektra's voice is woven tightly into the feminine matrix. The maids make no melodic distinction between their own voices and Elektra's, and for the most part they do not set Elektra's speech off from their own by using rests as quotation marks. In general, it is impossible to draw musical boundaries between Elektra's utterance and the maids'; everything is mixed into the generalized feminine voice. The fifth maid finally breaks this continuity, but only by adding new fragments of Elektra's dispersed subjectivity to the scene. In presenting what must count as Elektra's own self-image, the fifth maid also anticipates her idol's expressive style and elevated tessitura; to the other maids' representation of Elektra's textual voice, the fifth maid joins a representation of her musical voice.

In this context Elektra's subsequent entry for her monologue is above all a rhetorical event, an act of personification in which her body, her textual and musical voices, and her sense of mission are totalized into a single form. (The closed, highly structured character of the monologue supports the effect of totalization on a larger scale.) The Elektra that we see is the temporarily stabilized figure—that is, the trope—in which a loose collection of citational effects crystallizes. And the Elektra we will shortly come to see is a figure, too, one that redisperses this "original" Elektra into the multiplicity of persons who traverse the opera in her name. Given her polymorphism, we should be wary of endowing Elektra with a unified selfhood that the maids' scene presents only in fragments. The fragmentation, in the language of deconstruction, is *originary,* and as such it sponsors the irrepressible feminine dynamism that is (this) opera's obsession.

Elektra's duet with Chrysothemis crowns her affirmative transformation of the feminine matrix. Like the scene with the maids, it is organized as a movement from similitude to contrast and back again. Its point of departure is the strange heaviness, "the twentyfold ocean," that overcomes Elektra in her moment of triumph and prevents her from dancing. The duet is her rite of passage to the dance; it reanimates her by immersing her vocally in an ebb and flow of feminine energy fully as "oceanic" as her heaviness. For some thirty-five measures (Figs. 237a–243a) the two voices, sister-voices indeed in tessitura and expressive style, intertwine closely and sensuously, continually exchanging the upper and lower positions in their counterpoint. As my language suggests, the passage seems to gratify the erotic fantasies voiced by Elektra during her attempted "seduction" of Chrysothemis. In the process, the vocal continuity of the maids' scene is transformed from a vehicle of hysteria to the vehicle of rapture, a rapture so compelling that even Chrysothemis, the good girl, is swept away by it. Eventually, the two voices intertwine more loosely in overlapping solo statements. At the last, though, they reunite again even as Chrysothemis cruelly abandons Elektra for Orest—fleeing from the *jouissance* that her voice cannot help but express.

Chrysothemis, we might say, flees the inner for the outer frame, and in so doing she raises the question of the relationship between the two. No doubt we are supposed to follow her, but if so are we also supposed to be left knocking at a closed door? A possible answer, at least for the audience Strauss expected in 1909, may lodge in the curious manner of Elektra's death. In dramatic terms, it is clear that when Elektra collapses she is, like the Wicked Witch of the East, most sincerely dead. Yet her death is emphatically non-naturalistic. Hofmannsthal's stage direction, faithfully followed by Strauss, says "Elektra liegt starr" (Elektra lies rigid): Elektra passes from maenadic frenzy to rigor mortis in an instant. What is the meaning of this strangely rigid body?

6

One answer is that Elektra, as sacrificial victim, at last becomes the emblem of the order she serves: lying rigid, extinguished as a subject, she becomes the phallus. This suggestion tallies well with another, even more sinister one, that we can fetch back from one final excursion into the badlands of supremacism.

In his monumental study of the *Freikorps*, the proto-fascist private armies that were active in Germany in the years following World War I, Klaus Theweleit describes what I would call a basic supremacist personality type.[28] This "soldier male," in Theweleit's phrase, lacks a normal ego. He cannot draw imaginary boundaries between himself as a subject and either the outside world or the stream of his own sensations and desires. Hence he lives in dread of being absorbed into an indiscriminate mass that can be represented, indiscriminately, by rabble (communists, Jews, the urban poor) and women. In response, the soldier-male trains himself to identify his own body as a kind of armor, a protective barrier that is also a weapon. This steel-hard body is usually secure within the larger machinery of what Theweleit calls the White Terror. In the tumult of battle, however, the soldier-male risks being sucked into the very mass that he is busy exterminating. So, after every encounter with that mass, his body must be rehardened, his armor recast.

Perhaps the fallen Elektra anticipates this rearmoring of the male body. As a sacrificial victim, Elektra restores by her death the cultural boundaries that her life has both defended and dissolved. Her rigid form, materially present in the body of the performer and musically present in Strauss's granitic E♭-minor chords, might be needed as a symbol of that restoration: almost, indeed, as a talisman. Elektra's own sex would do nothing to inhibit this transformation of her into a phallic charm: quite the contrary. Her femaleness would itself be a kind of armor for the supremacist male spectator: something to immunize him against a contaminating identification with the polymorphic mass or matrix that Elektra has scourged in Klytämnestra and the outer frame of the opera has scourged in her.

Some foretaste of the White Terror may help to explain, though it cannot condone, Strauss's unparalleled degree of sadism toward Elektra. The sadism is a cultural, not a personal, pathology. In her remarks on Sophocles, Kristeva observes that "the Electras . . . militants in the cause of the father, frigid with exaltation . . . [may be] the dramatic figures emerging at the point where the social consensus corners any woman who wants to escape her condition" (152). Strauss's Elektra does not corner so easily. With its inner frame, his opera releases energies and pleasures thought to be feminine against the grain of its own discourse. The outer frame cannot revoke these things, but it can, and does, refuse to enfranchise them, all the while sublimating that refusal with music of stark simplicity, the sign of the tragic ethos. Here, too, we meet again the final image of Chrysothemis beating on the closed door, crying for Orest, which is shrewdly chosen to convey the impression of tragedy. Yet it would not be hard to imagine a latter-day staging in which the rigid Elektra held center stage even at the end: a staging that distanced the consolations of the tragic ethos and acknowledged that the opera's true protagonist is not Elektra at all but the condition of being obsessed with her.

Epilogue

Voice and Its Beyonds

This book has sought as often to embody the concept of Opera as to propound it. The writing has drawn no firm line between evocation and explanation, metaphor and theory. On the contrary: the lines have been crossed or effaced time and again. (Disgruntled parties take note: I know about this breakdown. I do it on purpose. I will do it again here.) The reason why is not simply that any such line is ultimately illusory, a law masquerading as a logic, but also that sustaining the illusion—often a useful thing to do— is directly contrary to the spirit of Opera. The world that Opera makes is one that freely, as a matter of principle, breaks this law and defies this logic. There is no way out of the labyrinth that Opera follows through the regime of the norm, the turns of symbolic investiture, and the impasses of supremacy and debasement with their concrete realizations via anti-Semitism in Wagner and the Woman question in Strauss. Opera even offers a model for all this winding, wandering motion, a vocal image that represents both the sine qua non and ne plus ultra of Opera itself. It is to this image, the image of wandering voice, that I propose to turn briefly by way of conclusion.[1]

Begin with an image in the more literal sense. Figure 7 shows Edgar Degas's painting *Café Singer* (1878): not, then, a portrait of operatic voice, but operatic enough to be one, and then some. I will pretend that Degas's chanteuse is also an opera singer, an aspiring diva with a second job, or a model for Puccini's Musetta singing her waltz at the Café Momus, or a real-life fin-de-siècle Salome in her normal *Tingeltangel* setting rather than its mythic mockup as Herod's palace. (In Flaubert's "Herodias" the likeness between Herod's palace and a decadent nightspot in Paris, Casablanca, or Cairo is implicit but unmistakable.) Degas's singer (we know who she was, in fact, Alice Desgranges by name) shows us the effect of voice at its outer limit, a voice we can never truly hear even if it is physically audible, even piercing: hence the truth of the image, which requires the muteness of the pictorial.

Voice in extremis, a voice-more-than-voice—it's fitting that one can't quite find the words to vocalize it—this unconditional voice presents itself as a mighty accumulation of emotional-libidinal capital expended (in a double sense, both depleted and lavished, incurred as expense and proffered as expenditure) in acts of surplus expression. The *Café Singer* offers a paradigm of these relationships. It fully exploits the paradox of representing voice par excellence in a silent medium. This silence, the picture suggests—shows— is not the absence of such voice but one of its registers. Degas's image identifies high voice, particularly the female voice, as the preferred medium of voice-in-extremis and of the prospect of subjective self-immolation in a shriek or paroxysm such as we find (with renewed apologies to Verdi and Puccini for their absence in this book) in the great consumptives Violetta and Mimi ("Che tosse!").

The vocal outpouring both defers and assures this outcome. The image shows the singer, qua subject, on the threshold of annihilation or metamorphosis under the power of her own voice. The event is poised to occur in the second or two beyond the moment captured by the painting, the coming instant when the dramatically upthrust right arm will break through the picture plane that the body partly usurps, already pressing toward immediate contact with the viewer/listener. That powerful arm summons up the shade of Siegfried's corpse, he of the raised arm who, so to speak, has become this sublime figure before the fact by wedding Brünnhilde's voice over his, their, pyre. The impending gesture, the final thrust or great throw, will, we can surmise, sweep away the distance between ourselves and the singer's voice at the instant when the voice reaches the peak it is so clearly approaching.

This impending release of voice-in-extremis, unconditional voice, coincides with the truncation and distortion of the body, and especially of the face—face and voice being the primary means by which the subject presents itself to the world, normally in harmony, but here at the point of being torn apart. The singer's wide open operatic O of a mouth admits the eye into a bottomless, mysterious void or depth. Admits, but also repels, expels the prying eye as it does the voice anxious to burst free. The back-tilted head is bisected as the upper half falls sideways out of the light; voice thus takes full priority over vision even though the one is silent and the other the active means of perception. The bisection also rhymes with that of the upthrust

FIGURE 7. Edgar Degas, *Café Singer* (1878). Courtesy of the Fogg Art Museum, Harvard University Art Museums, Bequest from the Collection of Maurice Wertheim, Class of 1906. Photo: Photographic Services. © 2003 President and Fellows of Harvard College.

arm between the singer's bare flesh and her long black glove—except that the glove is no glove, really, but an extension of the black mysterious eruption of the terrible voice-substance housed in and identical with the void of the mouth.

Above all, the effect of unconditional voice is shown by the relationship between the mouth and head. The head is tilted as if on a bent stalk, pulled to the viewer's right as by a funhouse mirror. But the mouth remains perfectly upright, its elongated o the unperturbed center of the sensorial vortex around it. This is a classic instance of the "anamorphotic" distortion by which, in Lacanian and Žižekian theory, the Real, the substance of the unsymbolizable kernel of human desire, manifests itself as a stain or torsion on what we recognize as reality.[2] And at the same time—an exceptional knot of power, since these two things do not by any means always go together—the image is a classic instance of the inner dynamics of symbolic investiture, with emphasis on the peculiar operatic form of this investiture, whereby what endows the object with a sublime status in excess of any possible justification is the rapt and enrapturing voice. Whatever the Café Singer is singing about will in just one moment rise, as she does herself, to this condition, borne on the performative magic of the voice that is about to escape from her and take on, even more than it has already, a life of its own. This is certainly an extreme, though one we revisit often; it may be a paradigm as well, a best example. Either way, symbolic investiture here is the work of a wandering voice in proximity—the closest proximity—to the Real.

The term "wandering Voice" refers to the voice as an object detached from the subject for whom it speaks, or who wishes to speak through it. The best examples in Opera are all Wagnerian: in *Lohengrin* a cry that detaches itself from the lamenting Elsa during her dream and persists on the woodwinds while her normative voice keeps on singing;[3] in *Götterdämmerung* the voice of the immolated Brünnhilde, the instrument of culmination, as it passes into the orchestra; and in *Tristan und Isolde,* at the height of sheer wandering, the tracery of the *cor anglais* melody heard during the wounded Tristan's delirium as he waits in vain for Isolde to come and heal him.

With regard to the last, Thomas Mann's remark on certain passages in *Siegfried* also applies: "all that is Freud, that is analysis, nothing else."[4] This point, it's important to stress, is not topical but structural; its concern is not with the content of a character's putative unconscious, but with the conception of subjectivity associated with analytical technique. Tristan has heard this melody in the time before the opera when his mother and father died; it returns to awaken him at the start of the opera's last act. And as he works through his memories and links them with his desires, the melody returns and persists as the separated yet intimate voice of both. At that point, too, the wandering of Wagner's *cor anglais*–voice unmistakably echoes that of the oboe-voice heard in Beethoven's *Fidelio* when the imprisoned Florestan has a vision of the "angel Leonora" coming to his rescue. Tristan's rescue, like Siegfried's, occurs only in the mind and voice of his beloved, but in its own way it is no less actual than Florestan's. When Isolde sings during the scene of her transfiguration that concludes the opera, she incarnates the wandering instrumental voice for her beloved no less than Leonora does. Only she does so with the crucial difference that, in relation to "namenlose Freude" (nameless joy, as Beethoven's couple call it), the fact that *her* Florestan is dead matters hardly at all.

Wandering voice achieves what may be its own outer limit in *Parsifal*, the opera Wagner knew would be his last. Early in the third act, Kundry's voice famously deserts her. But it does so, perhaps, or so we might speculate, only to become the voice of the entire act. The figure on stage remains mute, but the whole span between the Good Friday music and the redemption of the Grail becomes, in effect, Kundry's song. And with certain other operatic heroines in mind, Donizetti's Lucia di Lammermoor, with the flute that darts through her mad scene, and Verdi's Violetta, for whom Alfredo's receding offstage voice at the end of act 1 is the true "strayed one" *(traviata)*, the trope of wandering voice might well be understood as the link between Wagner's instantiation of Opera and the broader phenomenon, in which Wagner is a crucial—and for some a catastrophic—intervention.

In other words, wandering voice is the trope for opera, that is, for Opera, itself. If operatic plot often turns on a symbolic excess (symbolic investiture, the formation of the sublime object as a touchstone of identity and/or desire)—and it does; if this preoccupation initiates Opera's seesaw relationship to the regime of the norm—and it does; then operatic voice is the instrument/medium of this relationship, achieving through song the investiture called for by plot but unrealizable by plot alone.

This achievement, though, does not happen uniformly, and not all at once. We cannot speak, except as shorthand, of a single operatic voice. That voice has at least three modalities through which it performs the enunciation, liquidation, and dissemination of self: a conditional mode, or operatic voice proper; the unconditional mode of voice-in-extremis, which in multiple senses is never quite proper and is heard only rarely; and the absolute mode, the beyond of voice, which is utterly improper and heard more rarely still.

1. Operatic voice—effective voice, the voice to which one conditionally gives heed—is a heightened form of the normal vehicle of symbolic investiture. This is the voice that elevates unprepossessing things into sublime objects: a candle, a ring, a name, or, taken to extremes, a severed head.

2. Unconditional voice claims to enact a further investiture, an investiture of the Real, both in the general sense of the true or noumenal, and the Lacanian sense of the unsymbolizable substance of enjoyment, half magnificent, half monstrous. This is the voice of Brünnhilde at the pyre.

3. Absolute voice marks the beyond of even this seemingly ultimate voice, the voice-beyond-voice that in rare instances perfects, yet also negates, the effect of both conditional and unconditional voice. Here stand Isolde's transfiguration and the climactic chord of Salome, which can be regarded as concentrating the transfiguration into a single sound.

In *Tristan*, the essential irrelevance of Isolde's voice at the last—shown both by the voiceless career of the transfiguration in the concert hall and by the overbalancing of voice by orchestra in the opera house—makes the point: whereas in the *Ring* the orchestra echoes and perpetuates Brünnhilde's voice, here the orchestra subsumes and partly obliterates Isolde's. As I suggested in *Music as Cultural Practice*, what Isolde does on stage is to reproduce as a speech act the transfiguration that the orchestra enacts musically.[5] The force of the act, that is, both its performative magic and its effective meaning, are all in the music around her, the music she alone hears, in part, as Tristan's voice, or rather as the voice she has shared with him in the duet that this music revives. What Isolde does is to ratify the performative magic that transfigures her, to embrace it by giving herself up to the music. Her transfiguration—the term, which is Wagner's, should be taken literally— both consummates and demystifies what might be thought of, speculatively, figuratively, as the core fantasy of Opera, the fantasy of moving from symbolic investiture to investiture by the Real.

Regardless of the immortal longings to which many operas are prone, this is a radically secular fantasy, and even appears as such at certain cardinal moments. Isolde's world in the end really contains only Tristan, who fuses and replaces both the sacred and the profane, but Brünnhilde can illustrate the point as the proto-Isolde, the figure in whom unconditional voice most fully prefigures the beyond of voice. In Brünnhilde's transfiguration (or *Liebestod*, to borrow the familiarly misapplied term), the completion of her own path from godhead to mortality and mortal love closes the books on the gods, all the gods. Her action opens up the possibility of a fully de-idealized Operatic world, something that Wagner shunned (act 2 of *Parsifal* shows it as a kind of sugared hell), but that Strauss would seize on in *Salome* and even more in *Elektra*. Wagner's affinities are still with the revolutionary energies of pre-1848 Europe; Strauss's are with the imperial sphere of late-nineteenth-century comparative religion, the world of Robertson Smith and Frazer. That world might be said to enter Opera decisively when Salome rises to the beyond of voice as the culmination of vocalizing her purely profane desire. Nothing short of that gratingly sensuous climactic chord could express her impossibly literal understanding of how to acquire the charisma of prophetic voice and body by kissing the prophet's mouth in the absence of either. Brünnhilde, like Wagner, is an idealist; Salome, like Strauss, is a pragmatist.

Voice seeks the unconditional at the extremes of torment or bliss or on the verge of death. Voice tends to the unconditional when it is near the vanishing point, whether into cry or silence. And if voice tends that way, and if it succeeds, it converts whatever debases it to the stuff of its supremacy. The Café Singer's mouth has swallowed the O of the world and gives it back as voice; Brünnhilde in extremis endows the world she is about to destroy with the meaning that justifies its existence and that survives along with her voice itself in the sphere of orchestral sound. The radiance of the voice replaces the opacity of bodily stuff, the material source (which, though, stays lodged in the eye like a cinder; no transcendence effect without a remainder): supremacy is debasement spiritualized, which is here to say: vocalized. The ambivalence of the Real momentarily stabilizes, becomes luminous, enriches the authority of the symbolic without quite submitting to it.

But in the beyond of voice, as with Isolde and Salome, the ambivalence of the Real is redoubled. In terms of the themes of this book, the condition that results is not just that supremacy and debasement are intertwined, each needing the other to thrive on, but that here the two are indistinguishable: not even one and the same: they are not even different concepts that are equatable. They are a single nameless thing at the farthest extreme of Opera and its world.

The third act of *Tristan und Isolde* gives this indistinction a dynamic temporal form, making good on the lovers' speculation in act 2 that their love should mean the loss of distinction in names, identities, even pronouns: no more Tristan, no more Isolde. And so there are two deaths, two endings, to this opera, each in the beyond of voice; and both are based on acts of musical recapitulation that identify transfiguration with indistinction.

In saying so, we close, like *Tristan* itself, on the return of an earlier instance, drawn full circle by the symbolic power of the Wagnerian enchantment's own best example.

First, then, Tristan dies to the music of the Prelude, the opening that Wagner described as voicing the insatiability of desire "just once" in "music's most unrestricted element":[6] music never sung (not here, and not when quoted in *Die Meistersinger* as Sachs renounces Eva) except to utter Tristan's last word, "Isolde": music with its fatal sweetness long drawn out, identifying debasement and failure with consummation, marking the identity of pleasure and desire embodied in the key term *Lust* (Isolde's last word), and situated at the historical nub of the concept and effect of liquescent libido. Then Isolde dies to the transfiguration music, still longer, still sweeter, the presentation of supreme ecstasy as delusional but not false, of abjection as bliss.

Between these deaths, and linking them, is Isolde's solo recapitulation of an earlier part of the act 2 love duet—a passage sung twice in act 2, first by Tristan alone, immediately afterwards by Tristan and Isolde together. In act 3 Isolde sings this passage through once only, thus acting out the transgressive, impossible mixture of persons, identities, and voices. It is not enough to say here, as I did in *Music as Cultural Practice*, that Isolde recapitulates Tristan's music but not her own.[7] Rather, it's impossible to identify whose music she is singing. Isolde's recapitulatory speech act makes the whole question nonsensical. Both subjects sing; neither sings. The detached, white-hot subjective nucleus around which the figures of Tristan and Isolde form emerges from its cocoon and prepares to be dissolved into the beyond of voice in that transfiguration which is not even rightly described as Isolde's or anyone else's.

The Real has no sound, but if it had one, the closing pages tell us, this would be it. That's why the transfiguration was the most adored and detested passage of music that the nineteenth century produced. It's pure Opera.

Notes

PROLOGUE

1. See, for example, Philip Brett, "Eros and Orientalism in Britten's Operas," in Philip Brett, Elizabeth Wood, and Gary C. Thomas, eds., *Queering the Pitch: The New Gay and Lesbian Musicology* (New York: Routledge, 1994), 235–56; Brett, "Britten's Dream," in *Musicology and Difference*, ed. Ruth Solie (Berkeley: University of California Press, 1993), 259–80; Brett, "Britten's Bad Boys: Male Relations in *The Turn of the Screw*," *Repercussions* 1, no. 2 (1992), 5–25; Richard Dellamora and Daniel Fischlin, eds., *The Work of Opera: Genre, Nationhood, and Sexual Difference* (New York: Columbia University Press, 1997); Lydia Goehr, *The Quest for Voice: Music, Politics, and the Limits of Philosophy* (Berkeley: University of California Press, 1998); Linda Hutcheon and Michael Hutcheon, *Bodily Charm: Living Opera* (Lincoln: University of Nebraska Press, 2000); Wayne Koestenbaum, *The Queen's Throat: Opera, Homosexuality, and the Mystery of Desire* (New York: Random House, 1993); David J. Levin, ed., *Opera through Other Eyes* (Stanford: Stanford University Press, 1994); Susan McClary, *Georges Bizet: Carmen* (Cambridge: Cambridge University Press, 1992); Michel Poizat, *The Angel's Cry: Beyond the Pleasure Principle in Opera* (1986), trans. Arthur Denner (Ithaca: Cornell University Press, 1992); Mary Ann Smart, ed., *Siren Songs: Gender and Sexuality in Opera* (Princeton: Princeton University Press, 2000); Jeremy Tambling, "Toward a Psychopathology of Opera," *Cambridge Opera Journal* 9 (1997), 263–79; Gary Tomlinson, *Metaphysical Song: An Essay on Opera* (Chicago: University of Chicago Press, 1999). This is by no means an exhaustive list.

2. Ian Hacking, *Rewriting the Soul: Multiple Personality and the Sciences of Memory* (Princeton: Princeton University Press, 1995), 23.

3. For more on Auerbach's method, and its relation to the heuristic use of anecdotes in the later New Historicism, see Stephen Greenblatt and Catherine Gallagher, *Practicing New Historicism* (Chicago: University of Chicago Press, 2000), 49–74.

4. Eric L. Santer, *My Own Private Germany: Daniel Paul Schreber's Secret History of Modernity* (Princeton: Princeton University Press, 1996), ix–xiii, 9–18.

5. Pierre Bourdieu, *Language and Symbolic Power*, trans. Gino Raymond and Matthew Adamson (Cambridge, Mass.: Harvard University Press, 1991), 122; quoted by Santer, *My Own Private Germany*, 12. The idea of becoming what one is and its association with "fate" derives from Nietzsche; see, e.g, his *Ecce Homo: How One Becomes What One Is* and "Sanctus Januarius," Book IV of *The Gay Science*. The concept of symbolic investiture has much in common with Louis Althusser's concept of ideological interpellation; see his "Ideology and Ideological State Apparatuses (Towards an Investigation)" (1970), in *Mapping Ideology*, ed. Slavoj Žižek (London: Verso, 1994), 100–140; for the pertinence of this idea to music, see my *Classical Music and Postmodern Knowledge* (Berkeley: University of California Press, 1995), 21–25, and "Recognizing Schubert: Musical Subjectivity and Cultural Change in Jane Campion's Film *The Portrait of a Lady*," *Critical Inquiry* 28 (2002), 25–52.

6. For more on music and the sublime object, see my *Musical Meaning: Toward a Critical History* (Berkeley: University of California Press, 2002), 163–66.

7. Michel Foucault, *Discipline and Punish: The Birth of the Prison*, trans. Alan Sheridan (New York, 1979), 170–228.

8. Søren Kierkegaard, *Either/Or: A Fragment of Life*, trans. Alastair Hannay (London: Penguin Books, 1992), 134–35.

9. Kramer, *Musical Meaning*, 163–93.

10. Foucault, *Discipline and Punish*, 193: "when one wishes to individualize the healthy, normal, and law-abiding adult, it is always by asking him how much of the child he has in him, what secret madness lies within him, what fundamental crime he has dreamt of committing." Kramer, *Classical Music and Postmodern Knowledge*, 37–38.

11. From Kramer, *Musical Meaning*, 26; see also 1–28, 145–72. The "other venues" mentioned in the text include "Musicology and Meaning," *Musical Times* 144 (summer 2003), 6–12; "Subjectivity Rampant! Music, Hermeneutics, and History," in *The Cultural Study of Music*, ed. Martin Clayton, Trevor Herbert, and Richard Middleton (New York: Routledge, 2002), 124–35; and "Signs Taken for Wonders: Words, Music, and the Performative," in *Word and Music Studies 4*, ed. Suzanne Lodato et al. (Amsterdam: Rodopi, 2002), 35–47.

12. "I cannot dance upon my Toes –" (1862), from *The Poems of Emily Dickinson*, ed. R. W. Franklin (Cambridge, Mass.: Belknap Press, 1999), 175.

CHAPTER ONE

1. For a best-case account of opera's association with extravagance, see Herbert Lindenberger, *Opera: The Extravagant Art* (Ithaca: Cornell University Press, 1984). For suggestive readings of operatic extravagance in relation to social and sexual resistance, see Sam Abel, *Opera in the Flesh* (Boulder: Westview Press, 1996), and the essays collected in *En Travesti: Women, Gender Subversion,*

Opera, ed. Corinne E. Blackmer and Patricia Juliana Smith (New York: Columbia University Press, 1995).

2. Michel Foucault, *Discipline and Punish: The Birth of the Prison*, trans. Alan Sheridan (New York: Random House, 1979), 170–94.

3. Jürgen Habermas, "Modernity—An Incomplete Project," trans. Seyla Ben-Habib, in *The Anti-aesthetic: Essays on Postmodern Culture*, ed. Hal Foster (New York: New Press, 1983), 3–15.

4. Michel Foucault, *The History of Sexuality, Volume 1: An Introduction*, trans. Robert Hurley (New York: Random House, 1978), 45.

5. Jacques Derrida, *Positions*, trans. Alan Bass (Chicago: University of Chicago Press, 1981), 41–42. Subsequent citations in text.

6. Jacques Derrida, "Différance," in his *Margins of Philosophy*, trans. Alan Bass (Chicago: University of Chicago Press, 1972), 17.

7. Avital Ronell, "Finitude's Score," in *Thinking Bodies*, ed. Juliet Flower McCannell and Laura Zakarin (Stanford: Stanford University Press, 1994), 87–108; quotation from 90–91.

8. Joseph Kerman, *Opera as Drama* (1956; rpt., Westport, Conn.: Greenwood Press, 1981), 267.

9. Catherine Clément, *Opera, or the Undoing of Women*, trans. Betsy Wing (Minneapolis: University of Minnesota Press, 1988); Susan McClary, *Feminine Endings: Music, Gender, and Sexuality* (Minneapolis: University of Minnesota Press, 1991), 80–111.

10. See note 1 of the prologue for a representative (but not exhaustive) list of titles.

11. Walt Whitman, *Leaves of Grass*, ed. Sculley Bradley and Harold W. Blodgett (New York: W. W. Norton, 1973).

12. For more on the interrelations of opera and sexuality in Whitman, including further exploration of some of the themes and passages addressed in the present essay, see the sheaf of discussions in my *After the Lovedeath: Sexual Violence and the Making of Culture* (Berkeley: University of California Press, 1997).

13. Peter Rabinowitz, "With Our Own Dominant Passions': Gottschalk, Gender, and the Power of Listening," *19th-Century Music* 16 (1993): 242–52.

14. On masochism and coldness, see Gilles Deleuze, *Coldness and Cruelty* (New York: Zone Books, 1989), 47–55, 69–80.

15. Jacques Lacan, *Four Fundamental Concepts of Psychoanalysis*, trans. Alan Sheridan (New York: W. W. Norton, 1978), 174–81, 263–76.

16. It is worth noting that, in the first edition of *Leaves of Grass* (1855), this passage lacked many of its most suggestive features: the blurred boundary between the soprano voice and the orchestra, the "breath"-"death" rhyme, and the key word "throttled." Although Whitman did sacrifice an image of being made to "gulp" by the throbbing of the music, his changes tend to expose rather than evade the oral impetus. For the original version, see *Walt Whitman's Leaves of Grass: His Original Edition*, ed. Malcolm Cowley (New York: Viking Press, 1959), 52.

17. Slavoj Žižek, *Looking Awry: An Introduction to Jacques Lacan through Popular Culture* (Cambridge, Mass.: MIT Press, 1993), 88–96.

18. On magnetism and mesmerism in Whitman, see David S. Reynolds, *Walt Whitman's America: A Cultural Biography* (New York: Alfred A. Knopf, 1995), 259–62.

19. Sigmund Freud, *The Interpretation of Dreams*, trans. James Strachey (New York: Avon Books, 1965), 421.

20. Lacan, *Four Fundamental Concepts*, 197–99.

21. From Jacques Lacan, "Position de l'inconscient,"in his *Ecrits* (Paris: Seuil, 1966), 845; translation here from John Brenkman, "The Other and the One: Psychoanalysis, Reading, *The Symposium*," *Yale French Studies* 55–56 (1977), 420.

22. Ernst Kurth, *Selected Writings*, trans. Lee Rothfarb (Cambridge: Cambridge University Press, 1991), 104.

23. "Sigismund" was a generic derogatory term for a male Jew; it was, incidentally, Freud's original first name. On Wagner's anti-Semitism, see Marc A. Weiner, *Richard Wagner and the Anti-Semitic Imagination* (Lincoln: University of Nebraska Press, 1995); Paul Lawrence Rose, *Wagner: Race, Revolution and Redemption* (New Haven: Yale University Press, 1993); Jean-Jacques Nattiez, *Wagner Androgyne: A Study in Interpretation*, trans. Stewart Spencer (Princeton: Princeton University Press, 1993).

24. Gutrune, however, is by no means the only object of desire that Siegfried addresses through the sexualized abuse of Brünnhilde; for more on the subject, see chapter 3, which also delves further into several of the topics touched on here.

25. Sigmund Freud, "The Relation of the Poet to Day-Dreaming," trans. I. F. Grant Duff, in *Character and Culture*, ed. Philip Rieff (New York: Macmillan, 1963), 43.

26. Philippe Lacoue-Labarthe, *Musica Ficta: Figures of Wagner*, trans. Felicia McCarren (Stanford: Stanford University Press, 1994), xv–xxii; Slavoj Žižek, "'The Wound Is Healed Only by the Spear That Smote You . . . ,'" in his *Tarrying with the Negative: Kant, Hegel, and the Critique of Ideology* (Durham: Duke University Press, 1993), 165–99; Ronell, "Finitude's Score."

CHAPTER TWO

1. The catalysts here were W. E. B. Du Bois and Charlie Chaplin, both discussed below; see my *Musical Meaning: Toward a Critical History* (Berkeley: University of California Press, 2001), 255–56.

2. *"Lohengrin" et "Tannhäuser" de Richard Wagner* (1851), in Franz Liszt, *Artiste et Société*, ed. Remy Stricker (Paris: Harmoniques, Flammarion, 1995), 290, my translation; hereafter AS.

3. This idea presumably stems from the third-act narrative "In fernem Land" in which Lohengrin reveals his name and origins.

4. Undated letter of mid-June, from *Correspondence of Wagner and Liszt*,

trans. Francis Hueffer, 2 vols. (London: H. Grevel, 1888), 35; hereafter CWL. All citations are from volume 1.

5. The pseudonym "K. Freigedank" (K. Freethought), unlike, say, "George Eliot," is not a genuine disguise but an announcement of someone *in* disguise, and hence an invitation to speculate on the very identity it purports to conceal.

6. From "On the Jewish Question," trans. unattributed, in Robert C. Tucker, *The Marx-Engels Reader*, 2nd ed. (New York: W. W. Norton, 1978), 48, 50. On the relation of Wagner's anti-Semitism to its political-revolutionary context, see Paul Lawrence Rose, *Wagner: Race, Revolution and Redemption* (New Haven: Yale University Press, 1993), and Dieter Borchmeyer, "The Question of Anti-Semitism," in Ulrich Müller and Peter Wapnewski, *Wagner Handbook*, trans. ed. John Deathridge (Cambridge: Harvard University Press, 1992), 166–85.

7. "Judaism in Music," hereafter JM, from Richard Wagner, *Judaism in Music and Other Essays*, trans. W. Ashton Ellis (1894; rpt., Lincoln: University of Nebraska Press, 1995), 81, translation slightly modified. Subsequent translations are mine, from Richard Wagner, *Gesammelte Schriften und Dichtungen*, vol. 5 (Leipzig: G. W. Fritsch, 1888), 66–85; hereafter GS. My concern throughout this essay is strictly with the article published in 1850, not with the slightly altered version and supplementary remarks that Wagner published as a pamphlet in 1869. The footnotes to the translation in JM indicates the differences between the two texts.

8. *"Lohengrin" et "Tannhäuser,"* AS, 285, 292.

9. Charles Baudelaire, "Richard Wagner et *Tannhaüser* à Paris" (1861), as cited in Margaret Miner, *Resonant Gaps: Between Baudelaire and Wagner* (Athens: University of Georgia Press, 1995), 55.

10. Max Nordau, *Degeneration* (1892), trans. unattributed (1905; rpt., Lincoln: University of Nebraska Press, 1993), 183–88.

11. "This miracle-working descent of the Grail . . . the tone-poet of 'Lohengrin'—of a Grail knight—chose as the object of a representation in tones as the introduction to his drama, as here may be granted him, by way of explanation, the scenic power to introduce it as an object for the eye" (GS, 179–80).

12. John Deathridge, "A Brief History of Wagner Research," in Müller and Wapnewski, *Wagner Handbook*, 222.

13. Slavoj Žižek, *The Plague of Fantasies* (London: Verso, 1997), 76.

14. On the "obscene superego supplement," see ibid., 75–76, which develops these ideas from a reading of Daniel Jonah Goldhagen's *Hitler's Willing Executioners: Ordinary Germans and the Holocaust* (New York: Alfred A. Knopf, 1996). Here, as in the next paragraph, I have quietly pruned Žižek's account of its psychoanalytic features—not because I am averse to them in principle, but because they are not strictly necessary to the model. For brief discussion of the issue, see my *Musical Meaning*, 208.

15. Slavoj Žižek, *Tarrying with the Negative: Kant, Hegel, and the Critique of Ideology* (Durham: Duke University Press, 1993), 203, 207.

16. On the relation of Wagner's anti-Semitism to the representation of Jew-

ish bodies see Marc A. Weiner, *Richard Wagner and the Anti-Semitic Imagination* (Lincoln: University of Nebraska Press, 1995).

17. The standard reference is Mikhail Bakhtin, *Rabelais and His World* (1964), trans. Hélène Iswolsky (Bloomington: Indiana University Press, 1984); for belligerent versions of the carnivalesque, see Michael André Bernstein, "'These Children That Come at You with Knives': *Ressentiment*, Mass Culture, and the Saturnalia," *Critical Inquiry* 17 (1991): 358–85.

18. "Als durchaus fremdartig und unangenehm fällt unserem Ohre zunächst ein zischender, schrillender, summsender und murksender Lautausdruck der jüdischen Sprachweise auf" (GS, 71).

19. "Dann löst sich wohl das Fleisch dieses Körpers in wimmelnde Viellebigkeit von Würmern auf" (GS, 84).

20. Julia Kristeva, "The Politics of Interpretation," *Critical Inquiry* 9 (1982): 82.

21. I am obviously giving too short shrift to Baudelaire's essay, which has been the object of several critical discussions in recent years. See Philippe Lacoue-Labarthe, *Musica Ficta: Figures of Wagner*, trans. Felicia McCarren (Stanford: Stanford University Press, 1994), 9–31; Susan Bernstein, *Virtuosity of the Nineteenth Century* (Stanford: Stanford University Press, 1998),154–60; and especially Miner, *Resonant Gaps*, 25–98. Miner also provides Baudelaire's French text in full and numbers its paragraphs; the passage quoted here (in my translation) is from para. 13, p. 172.

22. Section 839 of Friedrich Nietzsche, *The Will to Power*, trans. Walter Kaufmann (New York: Random House, 1967), 442; section 7 of *The Case of Wagner* (1888), in Nietzsche, *The Birth of Tragedy and the Case of Wagner*, trans. Walter Kaufmann (New York: Random House, 1967), 171.

23. Thomas Mann, "Sufferings and Greatness of Richard Wagner" (1933), in *Essays of Three Decades*, trans. H. T. Lowe-Porter (New York: Random House, 1957), 235–36; translations of the phrases from Baudelaire modified.

24. W. E. B. Du Bois, *The Souls of Black Folk* (1903; rpt., New York: Dover, 1994), 146.

25. The travesty, I should add, is not limited to the tour of the body. Hynkel also appears as a puppet of the cultural citation machine, itself symbolized by the faux-Nazi banner on the wall, its swastika a cartoonish double X—the knockout sign. In the course of the scene Hynkel's persona morphs from Hitler to a Darwinian throwback who scurries up the drapery, a silver-screen diva (he mimics Greta Garbo's "I want to be alone"), a Roman emperor ("aut Caesar aut nullus," perhaps with a sideswipe at Mussolini), a Nijinsky-like dancer, and a pint-sized Atlas who leaps on his desk to become a giant.

26. "At first [there is] a wide, still sheet of melody, a vaporous ether that speaks out, so that the sacred picture may be drawn on it for our profane eyes; [this is] an effect confided solely to the violins, which, after several measures of harmonics, continue on the highest notes of their registers. The motif [i.e., the theme] is then taken up by the softest wind instruments; the horns and bassoons, in joining them, prepare the entrance of the trumpets and trombones,

which repeat the melody for the fourth time, with a dazzling burst of color, as if in this unique instant the holy edifice had blazed before our blinded gaze in all its luminous and radiant magnificence. But the vivid sparkle, brought by degrees to this intensity of solar radiance, is rapidly extinguished, like a celestial glimmer. The transparent vapor of the clouds closes in, the vision disappears little by little into the same variegated incense from the midst of which it appeared, and the piece ends with the first six measures, [which have] become still more ethereal. Its character of ideal mysticity is above all made perceptible by the pianissimo that is constantly maintained in the orchestra, and that is barely interrupted during the brief moment when the brass instruments make the marvelous lines of this Prelude's sole motif glisten. Such is the image that, upon our hearing this sublime adagio, first presents itself to our excited senses" (my translation from Liszt, AS, 290–91).

27. Ian Hacking, *Rewriting the Soul: Multiple Personality and the Sciences of Memory* (Princeton: Princeton University Press, 1995), 144–50, here 143–44.

28. Ibid., 146; Mary Douglas, "The Person in an Enterprise Culture," in *Understanding the Enterprise Culture: Themes in the Work of Mary Douglas,* ed. Shaun H. Heap and Angus Ross (New York: W. W. Norton, 1992), 41–62.

29. Catherine Clément, *Syncope: The Philosophy of Rapture,* trans. Sally O'Driscoll and Deirdre M. Mahoney (Minneapolis: University of Minnesota Press, 1994), 256.

30. Liszt, AS, 292; Michael Tanner, *Wagner* (Princeton: Princeton University Press, 1996), 85.

31. This division recurs as a motif in the extended paraphrase of *Lohengrin* that takes up about half of Liszt's article. For example: "The farewell that [Lohengrin] addresses to [the swan] is so filled with the sorrows of a separation that there is no need to know who this mysterious hero is to understand that in arriving on this earth of relentless struggle, of persecuted innocence, of crime triumphant, he is quitting a sphere of radiant quietude and tranquil glory" (AS 295).

32. For further discussion see my "The Strange Case of Beethoven's *Coriolan:* Romantic Aesthetics, Modern Subjectivity, and the Cult of Shakespeare," *Musical Quarterly* 79 (1995), 256–80; and chapter 2 of my *Musical Meaning* (on Beethoven's "Moonlight" Sonata), 29–50.

33. Ludwig Wittgenstein, *Philosophical Investigations,* trans. G. E. M. Anscombe (1953; 2nd ed., New York: Macmillan, 1958), 206 (in German; my translation). The alliterative form of Wittgenstein's phrase "Aufleuchten des Aspekts" seems meant to convey the quasi-magical phenomenon the phrase describes. The standard translation, "dawning of an aspect," intrudes a misleading note of gradualness into a sudden perceptual change.

34. Dieter Borchmeyer, "The Question of Anti-Semitism," in Müller and Wapnewski, *Wagner Handbook,* 183. See also John Deathridge's comments on Borchmeyer's argument, and also on Jakob Katz's prosecutorial *The Darker Side of Genius: Richard Wagner's Anti-Semitism* (Hanover, N.H.: University of New England Press, 1986), in the same volume, 220–23. For discussion of the prob-

lem of "keeping silent" in Wagner, with special reference to *Die Meistersinger*, see Lydia Goehr, *The Quest for Voice: Music, Politics, and the Limits of Philosophy* (Berkeley: University of California Press, 1998), 1–87.

35. Theodor W. Adorno, *In Search of Wagner* (1952), trans. Rodney Livingstone (London: Verso, 1981), 20–25; Wagner to Hans von Bülow, 26 October 1864, in *Selected Letters of Richard Wagner*, trans. and ed. Stewart Spencer and Barry Millington (New York: W. W. Norton, 1988), 323.

CHAPTER THREE

1. Friedrich Nietzsche, *The Case of Wagner*, bound with *The Birth of Tragedy*, trans. Walter Kaufman (New York: Random House, 1967), 166; hereafter CW; Thomas Mann, "Sufferings and Greatness of Richard Wagner," in *Essays*, trans. H. T. Lowe-Porter (New York: Random House, 1957), 197.

2. Edward Said, *Musical Elaborations* (New York: Columbia University Press, 1993), 61.

3. Marc A. Weiner, *Richard Wagner and the Anti-Semitic Imagination* (Lincoln: University of Nebraska Press, 1995). See also Paul Lawrence Rose, *Wagner: Race, Revolution and Redemption* (New Haven: Yale University Press, 1993); Arthur Groos, "Constructing Nuremberg: Typological and Proleptic Communities in *Die Meistersinger*," *19th-Century Music* 16 (1992): 18–34; Barry Millington, "Nuremberg Trial: Is There Anti-Semitism in *Die Meistersinger*?" *Cambridge Opera Journal* 3, no. 3 (1991): 247–60.

4. Friedrich Nietzsche, *Beyond Good and Evil*, trans. Marianne Cowan (Chicago: Henry Regner, 1955), sec. 240.

5. Cosima Wagner, *Cosima Wagner's Diaries*, ed. Martin Gregor-Dellin and Dietrich Mack, trans. Geoffrey Skelton (New York: Harcourt, Brace, Jovanovich, 1978–80), 17 October 1882.

6. See Jacques Derrida, *Spurs: Nietzsche's Styles*, trans. Barbara Harlow (Chicago: University of Chicago Press, 1979).

7. Friedrich Nietzsche, *Ecce Homo*, bound with *On the Genealogy of Morals*, trans. Walter Kaufman (New York: Random House, 1967), 248; hereafter EH.

8. It is important to stress the exact terms by which I link Hagen to anti-Semitism here. Simply to identify Nibelungs like Alberich and Mime as "Jews," and Hagen as "at least a half-Jew," as does Jean-Jacques Nattiez in his *Wagner Androgyne: A Study in Interpretation*, trans. Stewart Spencer (Princeton: Princeton University Press, 1993), 60, 70, 87, too bluntly overrides the obliquity of Wagner's practice and its deeply ambivalent motives. Similarly, Theodor Adorno's statement that "all the rejects of Wagner's works are caricatures of Jews" is only a half-truth, if a powerful one (Adorno, *In Search of Wagner*, trans. Rodney Livingstone [London: Verso, 1981], 23). Although the only appropriate response to Wagner's anti-Semitism is merciless critique, the critique loses its edge when it becomes too easy.

9. Aeschylus, *Prometheus Bound*, trans. David Grene, ll. 6–7, 111, 449–50,

500–502, from *The Complete Greek Tragedies: Aeschylus II*, ed. David Grene and Richmond Lattimore (Chicago: University of Chicago Press, 1956).

10. Byron, "Promethus," ll. 36, 38, from *Poetical Works*, ed. John Jump (Oxford: Oxford University Press, 1970); Shelley, *Prometheus Unbound*, II.iv.72–73, from *Shelley's Poetry and Prose*, ed. Donald B. Reiman and Sharon B. Powers (New York: W. W. Norton, 1977); Goethe, "Prometheus," ll. 54–56, from *Gedichte. Versepen* (Frankfurt am Main: Insel Verlag, 1970).

11. Sigmund Freud, "The Acquisition of Power over Fire," *The Collected Papers of Sigmund Freud: Character and Culture*, ed. Philip Rieff (New York: Macmillan, 1963), 294–300; *Civilization and Its Discontents* (New York: W. W. Norton, 1961), 37n.

12. Mikhail Bakhtin, *Rabelais and His World*, trans. Hélène Iswolsky (Bloomington: Indiana University Press, 1984), 303–67.

13. Walt Whitman, "I Sing the Body Electric," from *Leaves of Grass*, ed. Sculley Bradley and Harold W. Blodgett (New York: W. W. Norton, 1973), l. 28.

14. William Carlos Williams, *Selected Poems*, ed. Charles Tomlinson (New York: New Directions, 1985).

15. François Rabelais, *Gargantua and Pantagruel*, trans. J. M. Cohen (Baltimore: Penguin, 1955), bk. 1, ch. 17.

16. James Joyce, *Ulysses* (New York: Random House, 1961), 702 (subsequently cited in text).

17. Beat Wys, "Ragnarok of Illusion: Richard Wagner's 'Mystical Abyss' at Bayreuth," trans. Denise Bratton, *October* 54 (1990): 72.

18. My choice of "rapture" to translate *Entzückung* is part of the thematics of this chapter, a point the text will eventually make explicit. The concept is similar but not identical to (historically, I would suggest, a precursor of) both the familiar Lacanian *jouissance* and Catherine Clément's *syncope* or *ravissement;* see the latter's *Syncope: The Philosophy of Rapture* (1990), trans. Sally O'Driscoll and Deirdre Mahoney (Minneapolis: University of Minnesota Press, 1994).

19. Nattiez, *Wagner Androgyne*, 123–25; Feuerbach quoted (by Nattiez) from *Das Wesen des Christenthums* (1841), in *Sämtliche Werke*, ed. Wilhelm Bolin and Friedrich Jodl (Stuttgart: F. Fromann, 1903), 2:137.

20. Richard Wagner, "Ausführungen zu 'Religion und Kunst.' 1. 'Erkenne dich Selbst.'" [Continuations of Religion and Art. 1. Know Thyself], 1881. Quoted in Nattiez, *Wagner Androgyne*, 167.

21. Richard Wagner, *Das Braune Buch: Tagebuchaufzeichnungen 1865 bis 1882* [The Brown Book: Diary Entries, 1865–1882], 23 October 1881; quoted in Nattiez, *Wagner Androgyne*, 170.

22. Both quotations from Karl Marx, "On the Jewish Question" (1843), in *The Marx-Engels Reader*, 2nd ed., ed. Robert C. Tucker (New York: W. W. Norton, 1978): Bauer, 27; Marx, 48.

23. Richard Wagner, "Das Judenthum in der Musik," in *Gesammelte Schriften und Dichtungen*, 10 vols., 2nd ed. (Leipzig: G. W. Fritsch, 1887–88), 5:69.

24. The idea rose to prominence in the 1980s and quickly became conventional wisdom in certain quarters—which is not to say that it is false because overfamiliar. Key texts here include Luce Irigaray, "Women on the Market," *This Sex Which Is Not One*, trans. Gillian C. Gill (Ithaca: Cornell University Press, 1985), 170–91, and especially Eve Kosofsky Sedwick, *Between Men: Homosocial Desire and English Fiction* (New York: Columbia University Press, 1985).

25. For the nose, with other bodily markers of Jewish difference, see Kristin M. Knittel, "'Ein hypermoderner Dirigent': Mahler and Anti-Semitism in *Fin-de-Siècle* Vienna," *19th-Century Music* 18 (1995), 259–65, and Sander Gilman, *The Jew's Body* (New York: Routledge, 1991). For Wagner on the Jewish voice, see "Das Judenthum," in *Gesammelte Schriften* 5: 71.

26. See Friedrich A. Kittler, *Discourse Networks, 1800\1900*, trans. Michael Metteer with Chris Cullens (Stanford: Stanford University Press, 1990), 26–69.

27. According to David Levin, *Richard Wagner, Fritz Lang, and the Niebelungen: The Dramaturgy of Disavowal* (Princeton: Princeton University Press, 1998), 30–95, Wagner regarded narrative as suspect, overly susceptible to manipulation, especially by the Jews. The treatment of Siegfried in *Götterdämmerung* would seem to be a case in point—until the whole process backfires on Hagen at the moment of its culmination, and Siegfried's rectification of his own narrative sets the stage for Brünnhilde's sweeping redaction of the whole story.

28. T. S. Eliot, "Little Gidding," IV, ll. 5–7, from *Collected Poems 1909–1962* (New York: Harcourt, Brace, and World, 1963).

29. The resemblance to *Tristan* is more than fortuitous. Isolde's transfiguration and Brünnhilde's immolation enact the same cultural trope, one in which the death of the beloved man releases a kind of libidinal flood that washes away, even falsifies, the distressing truths of the dramatic action. For a discussion of this process in *Tristan*, see my *Music as Cultural Practice: 1800–1900* (Berkeley: University of California Press, 1990), 135–66. The most important difference between Isolde and Brünnhilde in this connection is that the latter must overcome a far greater weight of resistance in order to reach her goal. Isolde is visionary, Brünnhilde heroic. On the wider implications of the Isolde-Brünnhilde pairing, see the epilogue to this book.

30. See Jacques Derrida, *Positions*, trans. Alan Bass (Chicago: University of Chicago Press, 1981), 26–27; and "Différance," *Margins of Philosophy*, trans. Alan Bass (Chicago: University of Chicago Press, 1982), 1–27.

31. From Arthur Rimbaud, *Illuminations*, trans. Louise Varese (New York: New Directions, 1957).

32. Michel Foucault, *The History of Sexuality, Volume I: An Introduction*, trans. Robert Hurley (New York: Random House, 1980), 44.

CHAPTER FOUR

A shorter version of this chapter was presented at the conference *The Case of Wagner: A Reconsideration*, sponsored by the Center for Modern and Contemporary Studies at UCLA in May 2003, and organized by Raymond Knapp,

Mitchell Morris, and Vincent Pecora. My thanks go to all the participants in this conference, many of whose observations are tacitly reflected in my text.

1. For a fuller account of Sitte's Wagnerian program, see Carl Schorske, *Fin-de-Siècle Vienna: Politics and Culture* (New York: Alfred A. Knopf, 1980), 68–72.

2. Stéphane Mallarmé, "Hommage (à Richard Wagner)," from *The Poems: A Bilingual Edition*, trans. Keith Bosley (Harmondsworth: Penguin Books, 1977), 178; my translations of ll. 13 ("Le dieu Richard Wagner irradiant un sacre") and 6–7 ("Hiéroglyphes dont s'exalte le millier / A propager de l'aile un frisson familier!"). The verb I paraphrase by "bursting forth," *jaillir*, can mean to gush, shoot forth, spring forth, spurt, or flash; all of these meanings contribute to the invocation of an absolute novelty, and also impart an erotic connotation to the Wagnerian epiphany that is also supported by the poem's imagery.

3. Thomas Mann, "Sufferings and Greatness of Richard Wagner," from *Essays*, trans. H. T. Lowe Porter (New York: Random House, 1957), 206.

4. Ibid.; from Friedrich Nietzsche, *The Case of Wagner*, in *The Birth of Tragedy and The Case of Wagner*, trans. Walter Kaufmann (New York: Random House, 1967), 186.

5. Willa Cather, Stories, Poems, and Other Writings (New York: Library of America, 1992), 235 ("Uncle Valentine"), 494 ("A Wagner Matinée").

6. Marcel Proust, *À la recherche du temps perdu*, trans. as *Remembrance of Things Past* by C. K. Scott Moncrieff and Terence Kilmartin, with Andreas Mayor, 3 vols. (New York: Random House, 1981), 3:156.

7. Eric Santner, *My Own Private Germany: Daniel Paul Schreber's Secret History of Modernity* (Princeton: Princeton University Press, 1996).

8. Sigmund Freud, *Psychoanalytic Notes upon an Autobiographical Account of a Case of Paranoia*, from *Three Case Histories* (1911), trans. James Strachey et al., ed. Philip Reiff (New York: Macmillan, 1963), 173n.

9. Santner, *Private Germany*, 159n.

10. See section 8 of "Analytic of the Beautiful," Book One of Immanuel Kant, *Critique of Judgment* (1790).

11. Walter Benjamin, *The Arcades Project*, trans. Howard Eiland and Kevin McLaughlin, prepared on the basis of the German volume ed. Rolf Tiedemann (Cambridge, Mass.: Belknap Press, 1999), 365, 336.

12. On Debussy's complex relationship to these and other forces of national identity, see Jane Fulcher, *French Cultural Politics and Music: From the Dreyfus Affair to the First World War* (New York: Oxford University Press, 1999), 170–94.

13. The phrase, "avec une grande émotion," is itself ambiguous; the "grande" can mean "great," "noble," "majestic," or "fashionable," and probably means a little of each.

14. On French Wagnerism, see Steven Huebner, *French Opera at the Fin de Siècle: Wagnerism, Nationalism, and Style* (Oxford: Oxford University Press, 1999); Anya Suschitzky, "*Fervaal, Parsifal,* and French National Identity," *19th-Century Music* 25 (2001–2): 237–65; and George Turbow, "Art and Politics: Wagnerism in France," in *Wagnerism in European Culture and Poli-*

tics, ed. David Large and William Weber (Ithaca: Cornell University Press, 1984), 134–66.

15. Philip Brett, "Queer Musical Orientalism," joint meeting of the American Musicological Society and the Society for Music Theory, Columbus, Ohio, 31 October–3 November 2002.

16. On this topic see Mitchell Morris, "Tristan's Wounds: On Homosexual Wagnerians at the Fin de Siècle," in *Queer Episodes in Music and Modern Identity,* ed. Sophie Fuller and Lloyd Whitesell (Urbana: University of Illinois Press, 2002), 271–92.

17. From T. S. Eliot, *Collected Poems, 1909–1962* (New York: Harcourt, Brace, and World, 1963), 64.

18. The relationship of this symphony to Stalin and the Soviet state is an inevitable question, and a vexed one, but not one specifically relevant to my topic. The symphony, in a typical act of equivocation, neither indicts Stalinism nor exempts it. If there is an element of specific political critique here, it perhaps lies in the music's invocation of a symbolic void as its expressive foundation. For those with an ear for implication, the failure of the symbolic is precisely a failure, perhaps the most abject failure, of the state.

19. W. B. Yeats, "The Circus Animals' Desertion," in *Collected Poems* (London: Macmillan, 1967), 392.

20. Two further points about the symphony deserve mention here. During the epilogue, there is a brief allusion to the symphony's opening melody. It is just a flicker, quickly gone: a bleak parody of the standard romantic sign of large-scale unity. A similar parody seems to link the finale as a whole to the slow movement, which not only begins with solemn brass but also centers on its funeral march in the same way that the finale centers on its passacaglia, and with the same movement toward a single climactic outburst. In their obsolescence, the finale's forms expose the hollowness or exhaustion of their counterparts in the slow movement.

21. G. B. Shaw, *The Perfect Wagnerite: A Commentary on the Niblung's Ring* (1883), quoted from the online edition of Project Gutenberg (1998; Etext 1487).

22. Thomas Mann, *Doctor Faustus* (1948), trans. John E. Woods (New York: Random House, 1997), 185.

23. Hans Werner Henze, *Music and Politics: Collected Writings, 1953–81,* trans. Peter Labanyi (Ithaca: Cornell University Press, 1982), 144; from the essay *"The Bassarids: (1) Music and Cultural Heritage."* Subsequent citations in text.

24. Proust, *Remembrance of Things Past,* 3:155.

25. On this resemblance and its implications, see Robert Fink, "Desire, Repression, and Brahms's First Symphony," *Repercussions* 2 (1993): 75–103, at 83–86.

26. Henze, *Music and Politics,* 228. Henze's original text misattributes the quotation to Gottfried von Strassburg, Wagner's primary source; the translation quoted here incorporates the correction silently.

27. Ibid.; translation modified by reference to the German text, reprinted in

the program book to the Deutsche Grammophon recording of *Tristan* and the Second Piano Concerto (Hamburg, 1996), no. 449866–2. *Im Treibhaus* is one of the songs to poems by Mathilde Wesendonk, a married woman with whom Wagner had an intense emotional and possibly sexual relationship during the composition of *Tristan*.

28. *Music and Politics*, 228; translation modified by reference to the German text.

29. Max Nordau, *Degeneration* (1892), trans. unattributed (1905; rpt., Lincoln: University of Nebraska Press, 1993), 1–44; Georg Simmel, "The Metropolis and Mental Life," trans. Edward Shils, in *Modernism: An Anthology of Sources and Documents*, ed. Vassiliki Kolocotroni et al. (Chicago: University of Chicago Press, 1998), 51–60.

30. On the early phonograph and its reception, see John Picker, *Victorian Soundscapes* (New York: Oxford University Press, 2003), 110–45.

31. Rosalind Williams, "The Dream World of Mass Consumption," in *Rethinking Popular Culture: Contemporary Perspectives in Cultural Studies*, ed. Chandra Mukerji and Michael Schudson (Berkeley: University of California Press, 1991), 219, 220.

32. In this context, the concealment of the orchestra at Bayreuth seems more allied with the general imperative of modernity to dematerialize the modern than with the more narrow aim of concealing the economic machinery of production, as famously suggested by Theodor Adorno in *In Search of Wagner*, trans. Rodney Livingstone (London: Verso, 1981), 82–84. The dematerializing effect is, by definition, always virtual. Slavoj Žižek has suggested that the antagonism between magical, idealized virtuality and debased reality is intrinsic to the phenomenon of virtuality; to this it might be added that the phenomenon acquires this antagonism in tandem with the progressive transformation of the material world by the forces of modernity. The results of adding digital technology to the mix remain to be seen. For Žižek's remarks, see his *The Abyss of Freedom/Ages of the World* (Ann Arbor: University of Michigan Press, 1997), 56–66.

33. Proust, *Remembrance of Things Past*, 3:781.

34. Theodore Thomas, "Music at the World's Fair" (official circular), *Music* 2 (1892), 323. Cited in Kiri Miller, "Americanism Musically: Nation, Race, and Public Education at the Columbian Exposition, 1893," joint meeting of the American Musicological Society and the Society for Music Theory, Columbus, Ohio, 31 October–3 November 2002. Given the passionate American Wagnerism embodied by figures like Theodore Thomas and Willa Cather, it is puzzling that American musical modernism offers few parallels to the Wagnerian encounters we have been tracing in European works—French, German, Russian. One reason for this may be the historical imperative to derive an American concert style from native vernacular materials; American listeners could be enchanted by Wagner, but the composers among them could not make much use of the enchantment—which would mean, among other things, that the highest prestige of European accomplishment, the largest symbolic capital, would tend

to elude them. My informal impression is that allusions to Wagner in American music tend to be found mostly in the postwar avant-garde and to be mostly moved by the technical mystique of *Tristan* and its thrice-renowned chord. The chief exception dates from 1985: John Adams's *Harmonielehre* for orchestra, the second movement of which, entitled "The Amfortas Wound," is an effort to work through—and out of—the Romantic "questioning and longing" that stems from Wagner.

35. Proust, *Remembrance of Things Past*, 3:117.

36. Georg Lukács, "The Ideology of Modernism" (1956), trans. John and Necke Mander, in *The Critical Tradition: Classic Texts and Contemporary Trends*, ed. David Richter (Boston: Bedford, 1998), 1137; Lukács quotes Benjamin's remark on 1139.

CHAPTER FIVE

1. For a thorough and copiously illustrated inventory, see Bram Dijkstra, *Idols of Perversity: Fantasies of Feminine Evil in Fin-de-Siècle Culture* (New York: Oxford University Press, 1986).

2. This is the topic of Freud's famous paper "The Most Prevalent Form of Degradation in Erotic Life" (1912), reprinted in Sigmund Freud, *Sexuality and the Psychology of Love*, ed. Philip Rieff (New York: Macmillan, 1963), 58–70.

3. Peter Conrad, *Romantic Opera and Literary Form* (Berkeley: University of California Press, 1981), 171.

4. Emily Apter, "*Figura Serpentina*: Visual Seduction and the Colonial Gaze," in *Spectacles of Realism: Gender, Body, Genre*, ed. Margaret Cohen and Christopher Prendergast (Minneapolis: University of Minnesota Press, 1995), 163–78. Françoise Meltzer, *Salome and the Dance of Writing* (Chicago: University of Chicago Press, 1987), 1–46. Sander L. Gilman, *Disease and Representation: Images of Illness from Madness to AIDS* (Ithaca: Cornell University Press, 1988), 155–81.

5. Gustave Flaubert, *Three Tales*, trans. Robert Baldick (Baltimore: Penguin Books, 1961), 97. Subsequent citations in text.

6. My treatment of this topic is indebted at large to Jacques Lacan, *Four Fundamental Concepts of Psychoanalysis*, trans. Alan Sheridan (New York: W. W. Norton, 1981), 67–119; Norman Bryson, *Vision and Painting: The Logic of Gaze* (New Haven: Yale University Press, 1983); and various studies of the gaze in the visual arts and film, now too numerous to list, but most descended (pro or contra) from Laura Mulvey's familiar "Visual Pleasure and Narrative Cinema" (1975), reprinted in her *Visual and Other Pleasures* (Bloomington: Indiana University Press, 1989), 14–28.

7. Michel Foucault, *The History of Sexuality, Volume I: An Introduction*, trans. Robert Hurley (New York: Random House, 1980). On the continuities between visualizing sexuality and high culture, see Susan Gubar, "Representing Pornography: Feminism, Criticism, and Depictions of Female Violation," *Critical Inquiry* 13 (1987): 712–41, and Gerald Needham, "Manet, *Olympia*, and

Pornographic Photography," in *Woman as Sex Object,* ed. Thomas Hess and Linda Nochlin (New York: Newsweek, 1972), 48–53.

8. Bryson, *Vision and Painting,* 93. For a fuller account of the gaze in relation to nineteenth-century music, my *Music as Cultural Practice: 1800–1900* (Berkeley: University of California Press, 1990), 102–34.

9. Perhaps the most striking critiques of the gaze came from a Lacanian perspective highlighting the way that the gazing subject's illusion of a Cartesian centeredness (the social locus of the "male gaze") is disrupted by a countergaze from the (symbolic) Other that refuses to see him as he wishes to be seen. See Kaja Silverman, *Masculine Subjectivity at the Margins* (New York: Routledge, 1992), 125–56, and Slavoj Žižek, *Looking Awry: An Introduction to Jacques Lacan through Popular Culture* (Cambridge, Mass.: MIT Press, 1993), 125–26. It might be argued that the gaze that works best is, to borrow from Lacan's account of the phallus, the gaze that is veiled. As Charles Bernheimer has argued of the phallus, the more that the gaze is overtly invested with symbolic meaning, the more vulnerable it is to deflation ("Penile Reference in Phallic Theory," *Differences* 4 [1992]: 121). A little indirection can restore much of its power.

A dismissal of the gaze in Strauss's *Salome* can be found in Carolyn Abbate's "Opera; or, The Envoicing of Women," in *Musicology and Difference,* ed. Ruth Solie (Berkeley: University of California Press, 1993), 225–58. Abbate presents Strauss as a kind of feminist champion who invokes the possibility of visual pleasure only to reject it flatly. This argument seems to me to give much too short shift to the pressures of *fin-de-siècle* culture, which might at least be expected to produce some ambivalence in the matter. The argument also depends in part on grossly inaccurate claims that my reading of *Salome* in the first version of the present essay is an account (at some level even a celebration) of unqualified "paternal shutdown" in which the music becomes merely "Herod's accomplice."

Caveat lector. Abbate falsifies my argument in order to set it up as the foil to her own, which she then asserts categorically: "Strauss *rejects* the notion of operatic music as an objectifying gaze" (247, italics in original; this insistence on the simple truth, however complex its argumentative setting, is not what one would expect from a writer who claims to have "extensively used literary theory and postmodern philosophical and critical orientations in her work" [345]). What Abbate takes to be her primary point, the shift of authorial agency from Strauss to Salome, is made just as repeatedly in the original version of my essay as it is here.

10. Text from Charles Baudelaire, *Flowers of Evil* (bilingual edition), ed. Jackson and Marthiel Matthews (New York: New Directions, 1955).

11. Carl E. Schorske, *Fin-de-Siècle Vienna: Politics and Culture* (New York: Alfred A. Knopf, 1979), 224.

12. A further aspect of Judith's visual subjugation is that her own head is imagistically severed from her body by her jeweled neck-collar. Alessandra Comini observes this "decapitation" in her *Gustav Klimt* (New York: Braziller, 1975), 22. For a full discussion of Judith and the problematic of castration see Mary Jacobus, "Judith, Holofernes, and the Phallic Woman," in her *Reading*

Woman: Essays in Feminist Criticism (New York: Columbia University Press, 1986), 110–36. The effect of Klimt's Judith was anticipated by Wilhelm Trübner's "Salome" of 1898, a painting exhibited at the Guggenheim show "1900: Art at the Crossroads" during June–September 2000. Trübner's image proves the phallic value of John the Baptist's head by forming its reductio ad absurdum. His Salome stands alfresco, alone and stark naked, with the head on its charger thrusting forth from her genital region. The Baptist's abundant hair is positioned in front of her pubis; her own head looks away from the spectator, exposing both her body and her phallic fantasy to the curious eye.

13. J.-K. Huysmans, *Against Nature (À Rebours)*, trans. Robert Baldick (New York: Penguin Books, 1959), 64. Subsequent citations in text.

14. For a discussion of this association in nineteenth-century art and literature, see Elizabeth Gitter, "The Power of Women's Hair in the Victorian Imagination," *PMLA* 99 (1984): 936–54.

15. Sigmund Freud, "Medusa's Head," in Freud, *Sexuality*, 212–13.

16. Oscar Wilde, *Salome*, trans. Richard Ellmann in *The Picture of Dorian Gray and Other Writings* (New York: Bantam Books, 1982), 294. Subsequent citations in text.

17. Frank Kermode, *Romantic Image* (New York: Random House, 1957), 49–91.

18. Marjorie Garber, *Vested Interests: Cross-dressing and Cultural Anxiety* (New York: Routledge, 1992), 344; Garber reads Salome more as a transvestite icon than as a figure of cross-gender identification, but the role—in and out of Wilde—can bear both readings. On sexual inversion, see Peter Gay, *The Bourgeois Experience, Victoria to Freud: Volume II, The Tender Passion* (New York: Oxford University Press, 1986), 219–327; George Chauncey, Jr., "From Sexual Inversion to Homosexuality: Medicine and the Changing Conceptualization of Female Deviance," *Salmagundi* 58–59 (1982): 114–46; and, with specific reference to homosexual desire in *Salome*, Elaine Showalter, *Sexual Anarchy: Gender and Culture at the Fin-de-Siècle* (New York: Viking Press, 1990), 151–56. The trope of inversion is uncommon in Wilde's work; he seems to be using it here as a vehicle of representation that, consistent with nineteenth-century usage, integrates male same-sex desire into a larger context. Perhaps regrettably, the subject of a photograph supposedly showing Wilde himself him in drag as Salome is now known to be a real woman, Alice Guszalewicz.

19. For a discussion of the feminization of the authorial role in the nineteenth century, see Carol Christ, "The Feminine Subject in Victorian Poetry," *ELH* 54 (1987): 385–402.

20. Friedrich Nietzsche, *The Birth of Tragedy and the Case of Wagner*, trans. Walter Kaufmann (New York: Random House, 1967), 184.

21. Cited in Barbara W. Tuchman, *The Proud Tower: A Portrait of the World before the War, 1890–1914* (New York: Bantam Books, 1967), 380.

22. Anthony Tommasini, "A Bevy of Eccentrics in a Dreaming Frenzy," *New York Times*, 1 July 2003, E1, E8. The photo referred to at the end of my paragraph is on E8.

23. Comini, *Klimt*, 25, suggests that the pose for this Salome was inspired by the second, and more feral, of Klimt's two Judith paintings (1909); the sets for the production were designed by Klimt's friend Alfred Roller. The detail of the pendant also suggests a link with Moreau's "The Apparition" and/or Huysmans's description of it; at another level, the pendant, crude enough in its way, is a considerably refined form of the head as pictured in Trübner's "Salome."

24. On the reception of both Wilde's *Salome* and Strauss's, see Showalter, *Sexual Anarchy*, 149–51, 159–68. For lighting in the theater, see Gosta Bergman, *Lighting in the Theatre* (Stockholm: Almqvist and Wicksell, 1977), 269, 298–300. The date is somewhat earlier for England, Italy, and (probably) Scandinavia. German theaters went dark after the first Bayreuth *Ring* (1876) produced the effect by accident; France followed suit shortly afterward.

25. To the degree that it is voyeuristic—in other words, to the degree that it accepts rather than resists the offer of disengaged visual pleasure—the unseen gaze of the audience is gendered masculine in a limited historical sense regardless of who exercises it. This gendering may be problematic for women in the audience; hence the kernel of truth in the righteous opera critic's remarks about Occidental women. But of course it may be problematic for some men, too. For a discussion of this problem, see Naomi Scheman, "Missing Mothers/Desiring Daughters: Framing the Sight of Women," *Critical Inquiry* 15 (1988): 62–89. In one of his dream analyses, Freud makes the interesting suggestion that the theater circa 1900 offers women—more exactly, married women—the chance to satisfy the sexual curiosity that their upbringing has frustrated. Sigmund Freud, *Introductory Lectures on Psychoanalysis*, trans. James Strachey (New York: W. W. Norton, 1966), 122–25, 220–21.

26. W. B. Yeats, *The Collected Plays of W. B. Yeats* (New York: Macmillan, 1953), 396; dialogue format replaced by indentation of alternate lines.

27. Scheman, "Missing Mothers," 84. My discussion of the role of the unseen seer has greatly benefited from Scheman's.

28. From Stanley Cavell, *The World Viewed: Reflections on the Ontology of Film*, (Cambridge, Mass.: Harvard University Press, 1979), italics in original; quoted in Scheman, "Missing Mothers," 83.

29. Catherine Clément, *Opera, or the Undoing of Women* (1979); trans. Betsy Wing, foreword by Susan McClary (Minneapolis: University of Minnesota Press, 1988).

30. In reference to Strauss's score, "Fig." stands for rehearsal figure, a number used to index a given section; "Fig. 91.6" refers to rehearsal figure 91, measure 6. For the Dance of the Seven Veils, the score uses rehearsal letters instead of numbers.

31. This and the subsequent quotation are from Huysmans, *Against Nature*, 66.

32. I am referring to the moment at which the dance enters C♯ major (letter R, m. 9). The significance of this key will soon become evident.

33. Salome has at least two other characteristic motives, one of which deserves mention here. First heard on the clarinets during the opening measures

of the opera, this motive is, like the Desire motive, an embellished triadic figure with a wriggle and a fall. But in this case the melodic motion goes from the fifth scale degree to the first; in other words, the initial Salome motive is the complement of the Desire motive. One reading of this relationship might be that Salome has two selves that can never become fully present together, except, perhaps, at the climax of the monologue where the two motives sound—fleetingly—together. For a discussion of the problematic character of leitmotifs in *Salome*, see Derrick Puffett, "Salome as Music Drama," in *Salome*, ed. Puffett (Cambridge: Cambridge University Press, 1989), 58–87.

34. Otto Weininger, *Sex and Character* (1903), trans. unattributed (London: W. Heinemann, ca. 1906); Josef Breuer and Sigmund Freud, *Studies on Hysteria* (1895), ed. and trans. James Strachey (New York: Basic Books, 1957).

35. For a full account of harmonic patterning in *Salome*, see Tethys Carpenter, "Tonal and Dramatic Structure," in Puffett, *Salome*, 88–108. As Carpenter observes, Strauss centers Salome and Jochanaan on conflicting keys (C and C♯, discussed below) and extends the conflict to the keys a third above and below these, but this tonal grid by no means grounds the full spectrum of tonal happenings in the opera. Carpenter concludes by saying that because the central conflict is irresolvable, Strauss "is unable to create either a self-contained tonal structure—with resolution—or any real sense of dramatic progression" (107). I find the dramatic progression pretty clear, but that is a matter of opinion; more problematical is the suggestion that a self-contained structure is in demand here. What about the suggestion that the partial, uncertain presence of such a structure exactly corresponds to the cultural anxieties addressed by the opera?

36. Huysmans, *Against Nature*, 68.

37. Macdonald's essay, which uses a G♭ key signature and $\frac{9}{8}$ time as its title, appears in *19th-Century Music* 11 (1988): 221–37. The passage cited is on 226.

38. Ibid., 230.

39. See Bryan Gilliam, "Strauss's Preliminary Opera Sketches: Thematic Fragments and Symphonic Continuity," *19th Century Music* 9 (1986): 176–88. An amusing example occurs among the sketches for the *Symphonia Domestica:* "The mother's worries: will the child resemble the father (F major) or the mother (B major)?" (178). Anyone familiar with Strauss's marriage to Pauline de Ahna will understand the joke embedded in the B–F tritone. Puffett, *Salome*, 46, reproduces the first page of Strauss's working libretto for *Salome;* "Cis moll" (C♯ minor) is written in the margin by the first line, "Wie schön ist die Prinzessin Salome heute nacht" (How beautiful Princess Salome is tonight). As intimated above, the long-term shift from C♯ minor to C♯ major forms a harmonic précis of Salome's action in the opera.

40. On the vicissitudes of Jochanaan's singing style see Carpenter, "Tonal and Dramatic Structure," and (with wit rampant) Robin Holloway, "*Salome:* Art or Kitsch," in Puffett, *Salome*, 95–101, 146–48, respectively.

41. Susan McClary, *Feminine Endings: Music, Gender, and Sexuality* (Minneapolis: University of Minnesota Press, 1991), 100, 101.

42. Strauss's remarks are cited in Erich Leinsdorf, *The Composer's Advo-*

cate: A Radical Orthodoxy for Musicians (New Haven: Yale University Press, 1981), 57n. The translation of the second remark is slightly modified.

43. Dijkstra, *Idols,* 392.

CHAPTER SIX

The epigraph is from Walter Benjamin, *Das Passagen-Werk,* vol. 5 of *Gesammelte Schriften,* ed. Rolf Tiedemann (Frankfurt: Suhrkamp, 1991), 697. All quotations in German are from this edition.

1. Because VHS is a low-resolution medium and DVDs are copy-protected, it proved impractical to illustrate this chapter with stills. The chapter was written to stand without illustration; it relies instead on the low-tech but time-honored device of ekphrasis.

2. Walter Benjamin, *The Arcades Project,* trans. Howard Eiland and Kevin McLaughlin (Cambridge, Mass.: Belknap Press, 1999). All quotations in English are from this edition (a translation of Tiedemann's text).

3. "Der Jugendstil ist der zweite Versuch der Kunst, sich mit der Technik auseinanderzusetzen. Der erste war der Realismus. Dort lag das Problem mehr oder minder im Bewußtsein der Künstler vor. Sie waren von den neuen Verfahrungsweisen der Reproduktionstechnik beunruhigt worden. . . . [Der Jugendstil] begriff sich nicht mehr als von der konkurrierenden Technik bedroht. Umso aggressiver fiel die Auseinandersetzung mit der Technik aus, die in ihm verborgen liegt. Sein Rückgriff auf technische Motive geht aus dem Versuch hervor, sie ornamental zu sterilisieren" (692).

4. "Die Pointe der technische Welteinrichtung liegt in der Liquidisierung der Fruchtbarkeit. Das Schönheitsideal des Judgendstils bildet die frigide Frau. (Der Jugendstil sieht nicht Helena sondern Olympia in jedem Weibe.)" (694).

5. "Wie Ibsen die Architektur des Jugendstils im 'Baumeister Solness' das Urteil spricht, so seinem Frauentypus in 'Hedda Gabler.' Sie ist die dramatische Schwester der Diseusen und Tanzerinnen, die im Jugendstil nackt und ohne gegenständlichen Hintergrund in blumenhafter Verdorbenheit oder Unschuld auf den Affichen erscheinen" (684).

6. "Unter dem Stilelementen, die von Eisenbau und der technischen Konstruktion aus in den Jugendstil eingehen, ist eines der wichtigsten das Vorherrschen des vide vor dem plein" (684).

7. "Wie gewisse Darstellungsweisen, typische Szenen etc. im 19ten Jahrhundert beginnen, in die Reklame hinüber zu 'changieren,' so auch in das Obszöne" (234).

8. Covent Garden, Royal Opera, cond. Edward Downes, dir. Derek Bailey with Peter Hall. Kultur #1494 (1992).

9. Slavoj Žižek, *Looking Awry: An Introduction to Jacques Lacan through Popular Culture* (Cambridge, Mass.: MIT Press, 1992), 29–34.

10. Deutsche Oper Berlin, cond. Giuseppi Sinopoli, dir. Peter Weigl, video dir. Brian Large. Teldec Video 73827–3 NTSC (1990).

11. Vienna Philharmonic, cond. Karl Böhm, dir. Götz Friedrich, film ed. Gu-

drun Mockert-Keyser. Polygram Video (Deutsche Grammophon) 072–209–3 (1974, 1988).

12. Quotation from the last line of "Avec ses vêtements ondoyants et nacrés," in Charles Baudelaire, *Selected Poems*, ed. and trans. Joanna Richardson (Harmondsworth: Penguin, 1975), 70.

13. The monologue fully unfolds the paradoxically visual nature of Salome's "envoicing." The envoicing is a material necessity; in this scene, Salome must sing full-throatedly or she cannot be heard. But what, in this case, does singing full-throatedly mean? One answer may be suggested by a passage from Roland Barthes's "Music, Voice, Language" (1977), in his *The Responsibility of Forms: Critical Essays on Music, Art, and Representation*, trans. Richard Howard (Berkeley: University of California Press, 1985), 283–84:

> [F]or music to enter language [and discover there what is "musical"] there must be, of course, a certain *physique* of the voice (by *physique* I mean the way the voice behaves in the body—or in which the body behaves in the voice). What has always struck me in [Charles] Panzéra's voice [i.e., the voice in which Barthes had located the concept of "grain," the vocal realization of the singer's body] is that . . . this voice was always secured, animated by a quasi-metallic strength of desire: it is a "raised" voice—*aufgeregt* (a Schumannian word)— or even better, an erected voice—a voice which gets an erection. Except in the most successful pianissimi, Panzéra always sang with his entire body, *full-throatedly:* like a schoolboy who goes out into the countryside and sings for himself, as we say in French, *à tue-tête* [to kill the head]—to kill everything bad, depressed, anguished in his head. In a sense Panzéra always sang with the *naked voice.*

Barthes, the critic as Salome, executes a symbolic inversion of beheading into an anticastration, a second elevation of the erected voice-phallus. At the same time, he suggests that the corporealization of the voice, although it kills the head (drive, Lacan says somewhere, is "acephalic," headless) turns the connection between the voice and the ear into something visual, pictorial, or voyeuristic rather than auditory in its pleasure. On one hand he projects a landscape in which the mind's eye sees a boy singing "for himself," that is, unheard. On the other he shows us the image of the vocal erection itself, both as edifice and the column of its imaginary twin, the phallus. He thus renders the full-throated voice something at which the ear, so to speak, stares. And that stare is magnified, or rather shown at its actual life size, by the intimacy of the video image as we watch Salome's full-throated voice emerge from her wide-open mouth.

CHAPTER SEVEN

A portion of this essay was published as part of the program book for the Los Angeles Opera's 1991 production of *Elektra,* included in *Performing Arts* 25, no. 2 (1991), pp. P23–P26.

1. Ford Madox Ford, "Women and Men," *The Little Review* 4, no. 11 (1918), pp. 40–41; cited in Bram Dijkstra, *Idols of Perversity: Fantasies of Feminine Evil in Fin-de-Siècle Culture* (New York: Oxford University Press, 1986), 218.

2. Otto Weininger, *Sex and Character*, translation unattributed (London: W. Heinemann, 1906), 260. Subsequent citations in text.

3. On the stage Jews, see Sander Gilman, "Strauss and the Pervert," in *Reading Opera*, ed. Arthur Groos and Roger Parker (Princeton: Princeton University Press, 1988), 306–27.

4. Dijkstra, *Idols*, 3–24, 160–234, documents the coalescence of evolutionist and misogynist thought; see also Sander Gilman, "Black Bodies, White Bodies: Toward an Iconography of Female Sexuality in Late Nineteenth Century Art, Literature, and Medicine," *Critical Inquiry* 12 (1985): 204–42, and Cynthia Eagle Russett, *Sexual Science: The Victorian Construction of Womanhood* (Cambridge, Mass.: Harvard University Press, 1989). A conspectus of nineteenth-century primitivism can be found in Nancy Bentley, "Slaves and Fauns: Hawthorne and the Uses of Primitivism," *ELH (English Literary History)* 57 (1990): 901–38; see also Patrick Brantliger, "Victorians and Africans: The Genealogy of the Myth of the Dark Continent," *Critical Inquiry* 12 (1985): 166–203. On primitivism and modernity, see Marianna Torgovnik, *Gone Primitive: Savage Intellects, Modern Lives* (Chicago: University of Chicago Press, 1990).

5. Max Weber, *The Protestant Ethic and the Spirit of Capitalism*, trans. Talcott Parsons (London: Allen and Unwin, 1930), 13.

6. Edward B. Tylor, *Primitive Culture*, 2 vols. (London: J. Murray, 1871; rpt., New York: G. P. Putnam, 1920), 27; cited in Bentley, "Primitivism," 914–15.

7. E. Lynn Linton, "The Partisans of the Wild Women," *The Nineteenth Century* 31 (1892): 596; cited in Dijkstra, *Idols*, 213.

8. On catharsis in Hofmannsthal see Allan Janik and Stephen Toulmin, *Wittgenstein's Vienna* (New York: Simon and Schuster 1973), 82–84, 112–17.

9. Carolyn Abbate, "Music and Language in *Elektra*," in *Richard Strauss: Elektra* (hereafter RSE), ed. Derrick Puffett (Cambridge: Cambridge University Press, 1989), 127. Subsequent citations in text.

10. The quoted phrase is from Julia Kristeva, "About Chinese Women," in *The Kristeva Reader*, ed. Toril Moi (New York: Columbia University Press, 1988), 152. Subsequent citations in text.

11. Dijkstra, *Icons*, reproduces a large number of these paintings. A good color reproduction of *Moving Waters* appears in *Pre-modern Art of Vienna: 1848–1898*, ed. Leon Botstein and Linda Weintraub (Detroit: Wayne State University Press, 1987). On *Fish Blood* and fin-de-siècle sexuality, see my *Music as Cultural Practice: 1800–1900* (Berkeley: University of California Press, 1990), 142–43.

12. On gender and post-Cartesian epistemology, see Genevieve Lloyd, *The Man of Reason: "Male" and "Female" in Western Philosophy* (Minneapolis: University of Minnesota Press, 1984), 38–50, and Susan Bordo, *The Flight to Objectivity: Essays on Cartesianism and Culture* (Albany: State University of New York Press, 1987).

13. Quotations from Russett, *Sexual Science*, 148, 149, 146, and 149, respectively.

14. The term "primitive" refers nonprejudicially to the absence of a legal system or the investment of custom with the force of law.

15. René Girard, *Violence and the Sacred*, trans. Patrick Gregory (Baltimore: Johns Hopkins University Press, 1977). Subsequent citations in text.

16. Girard observes that Aristotle's *Poetics* "is something of a manual of sacrificial practices, for the qualities that make a 'good' tragic hero are precisely those required of the sacrificial victim" (292).

17. Catherine Clément, *Opera, or the Undoing of Women*, trans. Betsy Wing (Minneapolis: University of Minnesota Press, 1988).

18. W. Robertson Smith. *The Religion of the Semites: The Fundamental Institutions* (1889; rpt., New York: Schocken, 1972). In "Vampire Religion," *Representations* 79 (2002), 100–121, Christopher Herbert draws a suggestive connection between Robertson Smith's concepts and Bram Stoker's *Dracula* on the one hand and the blood-drinking imagery of Wesleyan hymnody on the other.

19. Here as in *Salome*, the models for this allegory are *Parsifal* and, more remotely, *The Magic Flute*, with the proviso that, if Wagner's tonal authority is decentered with respect to Mozart's, Strauss's is decentered with respect to Wagner's, and desacralized to boot. On the tonal allegory in *The Magic Flute*, see Renée Cox, "A History of Music," *Journal of Aesthetics and Art Criticism* 48 (1990): 395–409.

20. Tethys Carpenter, "The Musical Language of *Elektra*," RSE, 82–83, 96–97.

21. Ibid., 78–82, 96–98.

22. The E–D♭ of the chord is, of course, enharmonically a minor third. Carpenter, ibid., 103–6, identifies the C-minor–E♭-minor pairing of the concluding scene as the bitonal complement of the chord's E–D♭.

23. Susan McClary, "Excess and Frame: The Musical Representation of Madwomen," in *Feminine Endings: Music, Gender, and Sexuality* (Minnesota: University of Minnesota Press, 1991), 80–111.

24. On Agamemnon as true hero, see Kurt Overhoff, *Die Elektra-Partitur von Richard Strauss: Ein Lehrbuch für die Technik der dramatischen Komposition* (Salzburg: Pustet, 1978) and Richard Specht, *Richard Strauss und sein Werk*, 2 vols. (Leipzig: E. P. Tal, 1921), vol. 2, pp. 165–214.

25. For a succinct account of Winckelmann's intellectual legacy, see Joan DeJean, "Sex and Philology: Sappho and the Rise of German Nationalism," *Representations* 27 (1989): 148–71.

26. For more on the structure of the monologue and its relation to the opera as a whole, see Derrick Puffett, "The Music of *Elektra*: Some Preliminary Thoughts," RSE, 33–38. Puffett calls attention to the symmetrical arrangement of important scenes around the "keystone" of Elektra's encounter with Klytämnestra; the rigidity of the symmetry might be taken as yet another image for Elektra's moral and psychological position.

27. Jacques Lacan, "The Field and Function of Speech and Language in Psy-

choanalysis," in *Écrits: A Selection*, trans. Alan Sheridan (New York: W. W. Norton, 1977), 65–68.

28. Klaus Theweleit, *Male Fantasies, Volume II: Psychoanalyzing the White Terror*, trans. Erica Carter and Chris Turner (Minneapolis: University of Minnesota Press, 1989).

EPILOGUE

1. The operatic wandering of voice bears a family resemblance to the winding of musical meaning through mixed-media forms. On the latter phenomenon, punningly called "percephony," see chapter 8 of my *Musical Meaning: Toward a Critical History* (Berkeley: University of California Press, 2002), 175–93.

2. See Slavoj Žižek, *Looking Awry: An Introduction to Jacques Lacan through Popular Culture* (Cambridge, Mass.: MIT Press, 1993), 3–47.

3. For a discussion of this moment, see Berthold Hoeckner, *Programming the Absolute: Nineteenth-Century German Music and the Hermeneutics of the Moment* (Princeton: Princeton University Press, 2002), 124–32.

4. Thomas Mann, "Sufferings and Greatness of Richard Wagner," in *Essays of Three Decades*, trans. H. T. Lowe-Porter (New York: Vintage, 1957), 203.

5. *Music as Cultural Practice: 1800–1900* (Berkeley: University of California Press, 1990), 160.

6. Quoted from Wagner's program note in Wagner, *Prelude and Transfiguration from "Tristan and Isolde,"* ed. Robert Bailey (New York: W. W. Norton, 1985), 46.

7. Ibid., 164.

Index

Italics indicate illustrations.

Compositor:	Integrated Composition Systems
Music engraver:	Mansfield Music-Graphics
Text:	10/13 Aldus
Display:	Aldus
Printer/Binder:	Thomson-Shore, Inc.